Winning Grants

A How-To-Do-It Manual for Librarians® with Multimedia Tutorials and Grant Development Tools

Pamela H. MacKellar
and
Stephanie K. Gerding

HOW-TO-DO-IT MANUALS®

NUMBER 173

Neal-Schuman Publishers, Inc.

New York   **London**

Published by Neal-Schuman Publishers, Inc.
100 William St., Suite 2004
New York, NY 10038

Library of Congress Cataloging-in-Publication Data

MacKellar, Pamela H.
  Winning grants : a how-to-do-it manual for librarians with multimedia tutorials and grant development tools / Pamela H. MacKellar and Stephanie K. Gerding.
      p. cm. — (How-to-do-it manuals ; no. 173)
  Updated and expanded ed. of: Grants for libraries / Stephanie K. Gerding, Pamela H. MacKellar. c2006.
  Includes bibliographical references and index.
  ISBN 978-1-55570-700-2 (alk. paper)
  1. Proposal writing in library science—United States—Handbooks, manuals, etc. 2. Proposal writing for grants—United States—Handbooks, manuals, etc. 3. Library fund raising—United States—Handbooks, manuals, etc. I. Gerding, Stephanie K. II. Gerding, Stephanie K. Grants for libraries. III. Title.

Z683.2.U6G47 2010
025.1'1—dc22
                                                                      2010017965

To all librarians who focus on seeing opportunities, this one is for you.

—Pam MacKellar

To my husband and true love, Patrick, and to my sweetie-pie daughter, Madeline.

—Stephanie Gerding

Contents

Contents

List of Figures

Foreword

I have spent over half of my career working in state library agencies, and I have read hundreds—perhaps thousands—of grant applications. Based on that experience, I can confidently say that every person who is responsible for writing a grant would benefit greatly from reading *Winning Grants: A How-To-Do-It Manual for Librarians with Multimedia Tutorials and Grant Development Tools.* Pamela MacKellar and Stephanie Gerding have created a clear, complete, and easily understood guide that will help novice grant writers create their first proposals and help experienced grant writers fine-tune their skills.

Applying for grants can be a challenging process, particularly with library budgets as stretched as they are now. Some managers see grants as a way to fill the gaps left by budget reductions and want to apply for any and all grants that might provide needed resources. However, starting the grant process by focusing on the library's internal needs is often self-defeating. The library's budget needs are rarely a perfect match for the funders' priorities. Funders don't want just to give the library money. They want to support programs and services that make a difference to the people who use the library.

In this, grant funders reflect the values of the broader public, who also want to know what difference the library is making in the lives of the people in the community. Today's successful library programs and services are user-centered, community-based, collaborative, and evaluated based on quantitative data. These same themes run through *Winning Grants* and reinforce the fact that grants are not just free money. Instead, as noted in the book's preface, they provide resources to "establish valuable partnerships, resolve community needs, and increase community support."

Throughout *Winning Grants*, Pamela MacKellar and Stephanie Gerding emphasize the importance of library planning as the critical first step in writing a successful grant. They provide a host of reasons for this and suggest a variety of possible planning processes, including *Strategic Planning for Results* (Public Library Association, 2008), which I wrote. Although I have a natural bias toward *Strategic Planning for Results*, in this instance I agree with Pamela and Stephanie: the process you use to plan is less important than the final product you create. If you have a community-based plan with clearly defined service priorities, then you will have much of the information you need to complete your grant proposal. If your plan includes clearly defined measures of success, then you will be in an even better position when you write your grant, as most funders will expect you to establish targets and gather the data needed to measure your progress toward reaching your targets.

Winning Grants is more than a print publication. It includes multimedia tutorials and interactive grant development tools. Pamela and Stephanie have given you everything you need to create effective grant proposals, successfully implement your grants, and establish a framework to support future grant-writing endeavors. Use these resources wisely and all your grant-writing efforts will succeed.

Sandra Nelson

Sandra Nelson is a consultant, speaker, trainer, and writer specializing in public library planning and management issues. She is a leader in the development of planning and management tools for public librarians and is the Senior Editor of the Public Library Association (PLA) Results series, an integrated library of planning and resource allocation manuals.

Sandra is the author or co-author of six of the books in Results series, including *Strategic Planning for Results*, the foundation of the series, and the recently published *Implementing for Results*. She has used her planning expertise to help library managers, staff, and board members to develop strategic plans in dozens of public libraries of all sizes.

Preface

Because library budgets have been cut across the nation while library use is increasing, more libraries than ever before are seeking grant funding from both governmental stimulus funds and from private funding sources whose coffers have been eroded by the economic downturn.

Where can librarians charged with writing grant proposals under time and economic pressures turn for help? Library schools do not normally offer courses in grantsmanship, and it's rare for a book on grants to take a library-centric approach. We designed *Winning Grants: A How-To-Do-It Manual for Librarians with Multimedia Tutorials and Grant Development Tools* as a one-stop multimedia tool with both how-to advice and successful examples that can help anyone associated with library grant work. This How-To-Do-It Manual includes worksheets, examples, templates, checklists, an easy-to-follow step-by-step grant process cycle, and instructional videos—all intended to help you prepare a winning proposal.

Grant work is not as difficult as you may think. Librarians and information professionals are often surprised to learn that they possess many of the skills necessary to successfully win grants. They already have the ability to research, synthesize, package, and summarize information; a commitment to reach out, assess community needs, and find solutions; and a cooperative, collaborative professional attitude. This manual provides the necessary tools to create a well-written proposal that describes a worthwhile project planned to benefit your community.

Our manual is written in easy-to-understand language with helpful advice that you can apply immediately. Our instructional videos provide a unique method to learn the essentials of library grant work in a self-paced format.

Purpose and Audience

This manual is for anyone interested in learning about grants and writing proposals to fund all types of library programs and projects. Our knowledge stems from experience in every aspect of grant work—as grant writers, grant evaluators, and grant project managers. We have worked for library non-profits, universities, school libraries, public and special libraries, and state library agencies, and have received grant funding from both government and private sources. We present workshops around the country and consult with libraries, and we have found that our process works for all types and sizes of libraries. *Winning Grants* provides a step-by-step grant process cycle you can follow that will not only save you time and energy but also bring you success in getting the grants you and your communities want and need.

Perspective and Organization

Winning Grants is unique because the focus is on library grant work and the use of strategic planning and goal setting as the foundation of grant work. This not only simplifies the work involved but also ensures that your efforts directly support your library's larger mission, vision, and the actual needs of the community.

The material is arranged in three consecutive sections. Part I, "The Grant Process Cycle," features the full grant process cycle, with each chapter encompassing one phase of the cycle. Easy-to-follow examples demonstrate successful implementation. Part II, "Library Grant Success Stories," features real-life success stories that demonstrate the process in practice and provide motivational tips from successful library staff. Part III, "The Winning Grants Multimedia Toolkit and DVD," includes helpful tools, such as checklists, worksheets, and templates, for you to examine and incorporate into your own grant work. The DVD also includes instructional videos that walk you through each step of the grant process cycle, sample RFPs and grant announcements, example winning grant proposals, and a link to the Library Grants Blog (library grants.blogspot.com) with current grant opportunities. The multimedia approach is unique and serves many purposes, such as appealing to different learning styles, serving as tools for workshops and training, and providing consummate insight from grant experts.

Part I, "The Grant Process Cycle," details the process in ten chapters, as follows:

- Chapter 1, "Making the Commitment and Understanding the Grant Process," outlines the steps necessary to successfully obtain grants. This chapter also provides an overview of the commitments that must be made by a library that is seeking grant funds. Grants are not just free money. Acquiring them requires planning, resources, accountability, and sustainability. Grants also bring in more than funds—they establish valuable partnerships, resolve community needs, and increase community support.

- Chapter 2, "Planning for Success," demonstrates why it is essential to have a strategic plan and community involvement in place before beginning grant work. We help your library get started with developing a successful plan and furnish a sample from the Successful Public Library, the fictitious library we use to depict our process throughout the book.

- Chapter 3, "Discovering and Designing the Grant Project," covers one of the most creative and enjoyable parts of the process—developing the grant project. By developing worthwhile projects that implement your strategic plan and solve community needs, you can prove to funders why you should receive a grant. We show you how to develop project ideas and goals, outcomes, objectives, action steps, timelines, budgets, and evaluation plans. The included project templates and worksheets will be invaluable when it is time to begin writing your grant proposal.

- Chapter 4, "Organizing the Grant Team," helps you form a team of key individuals who will share the workload while increasing the likelihood of success. You will learn what qualities are necessary for a successful grant writer. Some libraries are reluctant to apply for grants due to the misconception that they have no staff with the necessary skills. We explain how much of the knowledge needed is developed in everyday library responsibilities. We also include valuable information on the resources needed and the use of volunteers and professional grant writers. To get your team off to a solid start, we provide the basics for your first team meetings.

- Chapter 5, "Understanding the Sources and Resources," pulls together a wealth of information that will help you explore, locate, and select grant opportunities. This chapter explains the basic types of funding sources, including those specifically geared toward libraries. It also looks at online and print resources you can use to research options or keep current on announcements. We show you that with the increase of electronic information, it is easier to find grant announcements and help with researching your options.

- Chapter 6, "Researching and Selecting the Right Grant," guides you in the selection of the right funder for your project. You will learn how to assess and identify those organizations whose purpose most closely matches your library project's goals. A valuable Keyword Selection Worksheet uses your project plan's goals and objectives as a starting point to increase your search results. The Funder Summary Worksheet will keep your research findings organized.

- Chapter 7, "Creating and Submitting the Winning Proposal," integrates all your planning and research into the actual grant proposal writing. Many applications request the same basic structure and elements—cover letter, proposal summary, organizational overview, statement of needs, project description, methodology, budget, evaluation, and appendix. We explain these components and provide planning and proposal templates that allow you to easily adapt, modify, and replicate content for not just one grant, but multiple grants, saving you time and money. We also cover how to tell the story of your target audience and grant concept. We provide checklists to ensure that you have a thorough and clear proposal that could make the difference between a winning proposal and a rejection letter.

- Chapter 8, "Getting Funded and Implementing the Project," explains what happens after you send off your grant proposal. Find out what to do next, whether your proposal was accepted or rejected. We include an explanation of the most common reasons grants are turned down, details on customary grant report requirements, and steps for beginning your project implementation.

- Chapter 9, "Reviewing and Continuing the Process," helps your library evaluate its process and improve its plan for the next grant. Repeating the cycle will be easier as your experience grows and you learn from your previous attempts. We include questions to facilitate a review session and ways to keep your grant skills up-to-date through professional development and other collaborative opportunities.

- Chapter 10, "Top 10 Tips for Grant Success," lists our best tips for grant success. The ten important elements to keep in mind are these: (1) people; (2) planning; (3) priorities; (4) purpose; (5) pursuit; (6) partnerships; (7) passion, positivity, and persuasion; (8) precision; (9) pitch; and (10) perseverance. These tips will help improve your grant project's potential for success.

Part II, "Library Grant Success Stories," includes sixteen real-life examples of grant projects that were funded. If you need a little help with brainstorming creative ideas for your project or want to get advice from other librarians who have completed grant projects, check out these inspiring success stories from libraries around the country. These selections include best practices and offer you a chance to see how successful programs have been developed, funded, and implemented. Photographs of successful grant projects illustrate project implementation and community participation. There is nothing like a "real life story" to give you inspiration, spark some grant project ideas, illustrate successful partnerships, demonstrate innovative programs, provide best practices, and teach you about what pitfalls to avoid.

Part III, "The Winning Grants Multimedia Toolkit and DVD," contains valuable tools, such as checklists, worksheets, and templates, for you to examine and complete. All of these tools are in the book and reproduced as Microsoft Word documents on the companion DVD. This enables you to make the templates your own by completing them on your computer or printing them and filling in the information by hand. You can also share these materials electronically with your grant team. These are resources that will help you stay on track, keep you organized, and take you through the grant process cycle, starting with your library goals and finishing with a successful grant proposal.

- Tools for Chapter 1 include a worksheet for use in creating a Grant Partnership Agreement (Tool 1.1) and also a Making the

Commitment Checklist (Tool 1.2) for helping you make sure your library is ready to embark on the grant process.

- Tools for Chapter 2 include a Library Planning Checklist (Tool 2.1) as well as Links to Example Library Strategic Plans (Tool 2.2).

- Tools for Chapter 3 are six templates and a worksheet that will prove invaluable for discovering and planning your grant project, and that will also be very useful when writing your grant proposal. Included are Strategic Plan Goals, Objectives, and Activities Template (Tool 3.1); Project Planning Worksheet (Tool 3.2); Project Action Steps Template (Tool 3.3); Project Timeline Template (Tool 3.4); Project Budget Templates (Tools 3.5 and 3.6); and an Evaluation Plan Template (Tool 3.7).

- Tools for Chapter 6 include a Keyword Selection Worksheet (Tool 6.1) helpful for researching grants, a Funder Summary Worksheet (Tool 6.2) for keeping track of funder information, and links to funding resources for libraries (Tool 6.3).

- Tools for Chapter 7 are three checklists and a template that will be useful when writing your grant proposal and help ensure you've covered all of the important points. Included are Questions for Funders Checklist (Tool 7.1); Grant Proposal Template (Tool 7.2); Grant Proposal Checklist (Tool 7.3); and Grant Submission Checklist (Tool 7.4).

- The tool for Chapter 9 is a Debrief and Review Checklist (Tool 9.1) that will give you an opportunity to learn from your successes and failures and make the necessary improvements or adjustments for your next attempt at winning a grant.

The DVD also includes ten instructional videos that cover the entire grant process cycle and provide a self-paced grant workshop from library grant experts.

- Video 1: Grant Process Cycle Overview
- Video 2: Planning for Success
- Video 3: Discovering and Designing the Grant Project
- Video 4: Organizing the Grant Team
- Video 5: Understanding the Sources and Resources
- Video 6: Researching and Selecting the Right Grant
- Video 7: Creating and Submitting the Winning Proposal
- Video 8: Getting Funded and Implementing the Project
- Video 9: Reviewing and Continuing the Process
- Video 10: Top 10 Tips for Grant Success

Example RFPs and Grant Announcements as well as successful Example Grant Proposals from libraries across the country are also included on the DVD as well as a link to our Library Grants Blog where you will find current grant opportunities.

At the end of the book you will find two resources:

- A bibliography of resources mentioned in the book and additional resources for further reading and study
- A glossary full of useful library grant terms

Good Luck and Have Fun!

We know that grant work can seem intimidating, and our hope is that *Winning Grants* will help your library as you create successful proposals and generate new sources of grant funding for your initiatives. We also hope the grants process will be less of a mystery and more of an enjoyable adventure. Your journey may include a little fear, but remember that writing a successful grant is achievable. Our Grant Process Cycle is easy to follow and will set you up for success.

Libraries have distinct advantages in the grant process—we know how to research, attract partners and collaborators, and discover our community needs, and we have a wealth of creative ideas for serving our users and furthering the pursuit of knowledge. By showing the passion you have for your work in the context of a grant proposal, you are sure to find success.

When you finish this book, read the success stories from other libraries and use the worksheets, templates, and checklists provided, and you will be well prepared to seek grants for your own library's projects. There will be nothing holding you back, no reason to hesitate. We wish you the very best of luck! Please let us know about your successes at librarygrants@earthlink.net and winninggrants@comcast.net. We would love to hear from you. Visit our companion website at www.winning librarygrants.com for book news and updates.

Acknowledgments

Pam MacKellar:

Thanks to all the success story contributors for your generosity and willingness to share with others so they can learn from your successes. Thanks to the librarians in small rural libraries with tiny budgets and minimal staff who have taught me the real value of proposal writing skills and the power of winning grants. Thanks to those librarians who have a vision, who are determined to meet community needs in spite of overwhelming obstacles, and who choose to see the possibilities. You are my inspiration. Many thanks to my husband, Bruce, who supports me in what I do.

Stephanie Gerding:

Thank you to my ever-supportive husband for cheering me through yet another writing project. Much appreciation goes to all the librarians who submitted their grant success stories for this book. They were a joy to read and will be helpful to many aspiring grant writers. And a final thank-you to all the library staff who work diligently for their communities and support their library's funding through grant work.

The Grant Process Cycle

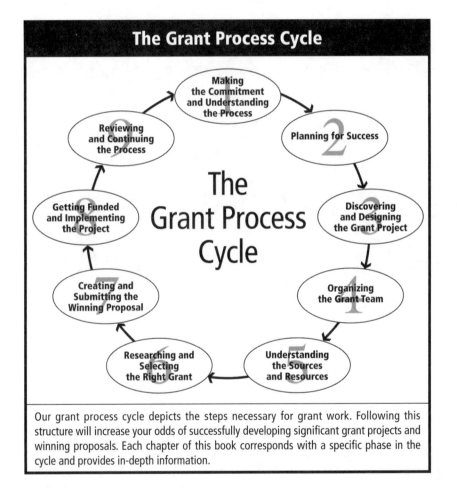

The Grant Process Cycle

- Making the Commitment and Understanding the Process (1)
- Planning for Success (2)
- Discovering and Designing the Grant Project (3)
- Organizing the Grant Team (4)
- Understanding the Sources and Resources (5)
- Researching and Selecting the Right Grant (6)
- Creating and Submitting the Winning Proposal (7)
- Getting Funded and Implementing the Project (8)
- Reviewing and Continuing the Process (9)

The Grant Process Cycle

Our grant process cycle depicts the steps necessary for grant work. Following this structure will increase your odds of successfully developing significant grant projects and winning proposals. Each chapter of this book corresponds with a specific phase in the cycle and provides in-depth information.

Making the Commitment and Understanding the Grant Process

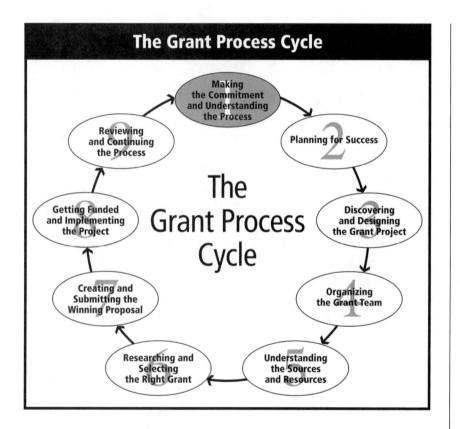

The Grant Process Cycle

Making the Commitment and Understanding the Process

Planning for Success

The Grant Process Cycle

Reviewing and Continuing the Process

Getting Funded and Implementing the Project

Creating and Submitting the Winning Proposal

Researching and Selecting the Right Grant

Understanding the Sources and Resources

Organizing the Grant Team

Discovering and Designing the Grant Project

Overview of the Grant Process Cycle

Successful grant work is the result of planning, organizational capacity, fulfillment of community needs, sustainability, relationship building, and evaluation. Grants are not free money that will magically solve your library's budget problems. This book covers proposal writing and grant research but also focuses on the planning process necessary to have a successful project and a justly awarded grant. It is a holistic process that must include all facets of the library's planning and as much staff and community involvement as possible. It is also a rational process based on project management principles. We will cover the entire grant process and help you develop core grant proposal components, useful for all grant applications.

The accompanying DVD also provides multimedia elements to further demonstrate this process while also appealing to different learning styles, providing tools for workshops and training, and offering consummate peer advice through success stories. Each section of the grant process cycle is explained in a video, which can be used as your own self-paced workshop or used to teach others the grant process.

Phase 1: Making the Commitment and Understanding the Process

Library staff excel at many of the skills necessary for grant work. Librarians who are adept at researching, connecting with the community, creating justifiable, well-planned projects, and effectively writing and communicating, can be successful with the grant process. Grant work is really about four things librarians are great at doing:

> One of your main tasks as an effective grant seeker is to be a master of information. You gather it, synthesize it, and make it available to funders and coworkers in the right format at the right time.
> —Larissa Golden Brown, Martin John Brown, and Judith E. Nichols From *Demystifying Grant Seeking* (2001: 23)
>
> Doesn't this sound exactly like library work?

- conducting research,
- answering questions,
- building relationships, and
- serving the community.

One other important requirement for success with grants demands a strong commitment throughout the entire process from library leadership and grant coordinators. They must be committed to each step of the process: planning, partnering, research, project development, writing, implementation, and follow-up.

This book will give you a firm foundation in understanding the grant process, but your library must be responsible for making the necessary commitments. This book contains inspiring success stories from libraries around the country (see pp. 146–188 and DVD) which help you envision innovative and successful grant projects and provide advice from other librarians who have effectively completed the grant process. This selection of best practices offers you a chance to see how award-winning programs have been developed, funded, and implemented while providing a great view of the big picture of the grant process.

Phase 2: Planning for Success

Throughout the grant process, we encourage you to constantly refer to your library's strategic plan. If your library doesn't have a plan, make it a priority to develop a planning process before applying for grants. If this isn't possible, your library should at least have a written mission statement that can be used as a basis for project development decisions. A strategic plan provides the framework that is needed for the grant process to be effective. Having a library plan in place will help prevent the mistake of mission creep—creating poorly designed or unneeded projects for your library only because grant funding is available. If every grant project is developed from the goals and objectives in your library's plan, it will eliminate the possibility of creating projects or programs that aren't relevant to your library's mission or your community's needs. A plan also answers many of the questions that are found in the Requests for Proposal (RFP) that charitable organizations rely on to determine their grant awards. A library with a strategic plan is a more dependable and organized applicant. A plan demonstrates to a funder that fund money will be used responsibly and not just wasted on a hastily developed new idea.

Your library must also know the compelling issues in your community before applying for grants. Discover the true needs of your community and what will make your library's efforts meaningful and important. This will be very helpful when you begin to develop your project ideas and when you demonstrate need in a grant proposal. Chapter 2 covers planning and methods for needs assessments in more detail, including a sample strategic plan of the Successful Public Library, the fictitious library we use to demonstrate our process throughout the book.

Phase 3: Discovering and Designing the Grant Project

Chapter 3 covers a step-by-step method for developing grant projects. This is often one of the most creative and enjoyable parts of grant work. Every project should be a worthwhile solution to a community need identified in the planning process. Whether you want to build a new library or create a program for teens, your project consists of the actual activities you will perform based on your library's plan. Projects are the implementation arm of your strategic plan and should be designed before beginning to research funders and grant opportunities. The slickness or length of an application is seldom a critical factor in determining who will receive a grant. Rather, it is the project that counts. And when projects are based on community needs, funders can understand the reasons why the project is important and relevant for funding. If a funder can't determine why you are developing a project, they will not be willing to support it. We show you how to plan your project by developing goals, objectives, outcomes, action steps, timelines, budgets, and evaluation plans. The included Project Planning Worksheet in the Toolkit will be invaluable when it is time to begin writing your grant proposal (see p. 198 and DVD).

Phase 4: Organizing the Grant Team

Once you have identified a viable project that fulfills a need in your community, you will be ready to form and organize a grant team. This team should include representatives from library leadership, community advisors and partners, grant researchers, grant writers, staff members who will plan and implement the grant project, and subject matter experts. The size of your grant team will correlate with the size of your library. These key individuals will help minimize the workload while increasing the likelihood of success. If you are working in a small library, you can still have a team, especially with the addition of community volunteers. We explain the qualities necessary for an ideal grant writer. Some libraries are reluctant to apply for grants due to the misconception that they have no employee with the necessary skills. You may be surprised to find that many of the needed abilities are ones that are developed in everyday library work. The responsibilities and skills of all team members are also covered, including the grant coordinator, and how to successfully organize grant team meetings.

Phase 5: Understanding the Sources and Resources

This step of the cycle is often a straightforward one for librarians as it involves research. The two major types of funding sources (government and private) are explained, including how to locate current library funding opportunities in both online and print formats. With the increase of digital information, finding grant resources and researching your options is easier and faster than ever.

Phase 6: Researching and Selecting the Right Grant

This chapter clarifies how to locate applicable and viable grant opportunities for your specific project. Once you know the sources and resources covered in Chapter 5, next you must research and select the right funder and the right grant. Selecting the right grant necessitates knowing what a funder is interested in supporting and knowing how closely their mission matches yours. Learn how to increase your search results with a useful Keyword Selection Worksheet (see p. 204 and DVD) that will use your strategic plan's goals and objectives as a starting point. Keep your research findings organized with the Funder Summary Worksheet (see p. 205 and DVD). Our Library Grants blog (librarygrants.blogspot.com) is a helpful free website to use in your research.

Library Grants
Ⓑ Ⓛ Ⓞ Ⓖ

Phase 7: Creating and Submitting the Winning Proposal

Once you reach this part of the grant cycle, your planning work will be complete and writing the proposal will involve refining your ideas into the stipulations requested by the funders. Most grant proposals have the same basic structure and requirements. The common components include: cover letter, proposal summary, organizational overview, project description, statement of needs, methodology, budget, evaluation, and appendix. Some parts of the proposal are narrative and involve telling the story of the grant project and people it will serve. We provide checklists to ensure you have a thorough and clear proposal that could make the difference between a winning proposal and a rejection letter.

Phase 8: Getting Funded and Implementing the Project

It may be weeks or months before you receive notification that your grant application has been accepted. You may be contacted by the funder with questions or requests for more information. Whether your proposal was accepted or rejected, find out what to do next. Included is an explanation of the most common reasons grant proposals are turned down. If you are funded, the implementation process begins. You will need to revisit your timeline and budget and make any appropriate updates. We include details on customary grant report requirements. Don't forget to celebrate this great accomplishment with the entire grant team and library.

Phase 9: Reviewing and Continuing the Process

Grant work is an ongoing process, so the cycle should be repeated. This is the time to look back and then move forward with the knowledge you've learned from your first completion of the grant process cycle. Facilitate a review session with your grant team with our provided questions and keep your relationships with partners and funders thriving. Remember to thank funders and follow up with any reporting requirements. Keep in contact with them and let them know how your project is progressing. Many professional development opportunities are related to grants for libraries, so keep up-to-date by attending workshops, subscribing to electronic discussion lists, networking, and researching new opportunities.

The Importance of Partnerships and Collaborations

Many funders request or require that partners or collaborators be involved in your grant project. The basic reason for this is that they realize the greater the number of people at the table, the higher the probability of success and the bigger the impact of the funding. Funders want their grant money to be used for successful projects rather than squandered on mistakes or lack of follow-through.

All communities have real needs that the library can help fulfill. The most urgent situations require a concerted team effort that will bring together the contributions of many talented individuals and responsible organizations. As has been said before, "None of us is as smart as all of us." By combining resources of several entities, the library is better positioned to solve community problems.

For a partnership to work there must be common goals, mutual responsibilities, shared rewards, and plenty of communication. You will find that there are many organizations in your community that share the same goals as your library, whether it be eradicating illiteracy, helping teens develop into accomplished individuals, or bridging the digital divide. Sharing the workload and the resources is of course a good thing, but good communication is essential. There should definitely be a project director or someone designated to represent each partner. A partnership agreement or memorandum of understanding (MOU) can be used to specify the details of your partnership in writing. This can help avoid many common difficulties that collaborators often encounter. A sample Grant Partnership Agreement Worksheet is included in the Toolkit section of the book (see p. 191 and DVD).

Making the Commitment

Can your library really commit to the grant application and implementation process? The library leadership (director, board, trustees) and any staff that will have responsibilities tied to the grant or grant project should be involved in the decisions. Most grants will have benefits, but also obligations, and in some cases maybe even specific constraints or drawbacks that need to be considered. If your project does not fulfill the funder's guidelines, you are wasting your library's time and funds by preparing a hopeless grant application. And of course, you are also wasting the funder's valuable time. This is not the best way to build a relationship with a potential funder.

There are both advantages and disadvantages to applying for and receiving grants. Sometimes it may not be worth the effort and requirements necessary to apply. There may be too many hoops to jump through, you may not be able to fulfill the stipulations requested in the RFP, or your library may not have the support necessary for implementation. The funding must be worth the time, effort, and resources needed. These resources include not just the staff time spent planning a project and writing a proposal, but the time to be spent in implementation and evaluation of the project as well.

All grants have costs for the submitting library. Sometimes this is obvious, such as matching funds or staff time, but there is also the impact of assigning key staff members to the duration of the project, the building space and supporting materials needed, time for meetings and communication with everyone involved, or the impact of neglecting existing essential activities while focusing on the new project.

Depending on the type of library you work with, applying for a grant may include working with other departments or meeting requirements set by your local authorities, system, or development office. This is especially true in university settings, so make certain you understand the local stipulations that will affect your library's grant work.

Although there are a lot of considerations to weigh, grant money can also make a huge difference in a library's ability to provide service for your community. Even small grants can be worth the effort as they may be easier to obtain and may fit your project scope and intent better. One grants officer said they would love to give huge grants, but sometimes

[The most difficult part of the grant process is] the paperwork and understanding the process. It's extremely important to have good communication with all involved—from an institution's financial officers to the idea people to the entity giving the grant.
—"A Few Good Women: Advancing the Cause of Women in Government" Pennsylvania State University Libraries, University Park, PA (see Library Grant Success Stories, pp. 146–147)

smaller grants are more appropriate for certain projects and libraries. Numerous small grants are available from local funders, and many have fewer strings attached than those from larger private or government agencies. You could also apply for several small grants that in combination could provide for all the facets of a larger project.

Ask yourself the following questions before you begin a grant proposal:

- Does the funder have restrictions or requirements that would shape or affect our grant project in an unacceptable or undesirable way?
- Can we continue the project if grant funds are discontinued? What would be the effect on our clients or organization if the project were stopped abruptly?
- Should we propose a new project when we really need money for existing programs?
- Would this project take too much time and attention away from core library programs?
- Is this the right grant for this project?

Specific Commitments

The grant process cycle is ongoing, which means the commitments should continue as well. Some of these commitments should be made before the library decides to pursue grant funding. Others cannot be made until you have designed your grant project and researched and selected the appropriate funder's grant. At that time you should revisit these commitments. Your library must be able to commit to: accountability, effective communication, meeting community needs, planning, partnerships, evaluation, sustainability and following the grant guidelines.

The Making the Commitment Checklist will help you determine if you can really make the commitment. The questions are also available as a checklist in the Toolkit section of this manual (see pp. 192–193) and as a downloadable file on the DVD.

Gathering Knowledge

Hopefully this long list of commitments hasn't made grant work seem too daunting. It is a process and once you've gone through it the first time, it really does get easier.

If you are a novice to grant work, here are some tips for finding out more about the process.

- Ask other librarians to share their grant proposals. We've also included sample winning grant proposals on the DVD.
- Become a grant reviewer or talk to grant reviewers. This is a great way to find out how difficult it can be to give money away! You will learn exactly how grant decisions are made, which can help you immensely.

Go for it! Even though it is difficult and time-consuming to fill out a good application, winning a grant can take your library into new territory, and make exciting ventures possible. Winning a grant is definitely a commitment, however, so you do need to make sure that you have some staff time to devote to its implementation.

—"Promoting Easy Access to Online Consumer Health Information for Los Alamos County Senior Citizens" Los Alamos County Public Library System, Los Alamos, NM (see Library Grant Success Stories, pp. 158–160)

MAKING THE COMMITMENT CHECKLIST

Commit to Accountability
☐ Will the grant project definitely support your library's vision and mission?
☐ Will your library leadership support the project?
☐ Will the library director commit the necessary resources to the project/grant?
☐ Will the library staff have the time needed to complete the application process and to implement the grant project?
☐ Will the grant team have all the necessary supplies, equipment, services, and space?
☐ Can the library follow through on the agreements made in the grant proposal?
☐ Will the library spend the funds as specified and keep accurate accounts?
☐ Will you make sure there are not other organizations in your community already doing your project and filling the need?
☐ Can all deadlines be met and grant reports be filed on time?

Commit to Effective Communication
☐ Will your proposal be as clear, concise, and honest as possible?
☐ Will your goals, objectives, and activities be clearly identified and understandable?
☐ Will you be able to convey that your library and the project are important?
☐ Will you ask the funder for what you really need?
☐ Will all the library staff, board members, leadership, partners, and volunteers be continually informed about the grant?
☐ Will you ask the funders if the library's grant project clearly fits their interests?
☐ Will you communicate with all your contacts?

Commit to Meeting Community Needs
☐ Will your library identify the needs of your community?
☐ Will your analysis include enough information to educate and inspire the funder?
☐ Will statistics be used to quantify the problems identified?
☐ Will stories and cases be used regarding specific patrons or programs that illustrate the needs?
☐ Will your grant project focus on solutions to meeting community needs?
☐ Will you identify a target audience for your grant project and involve representatives in the planning process?

Commit to Planning
☐ Does your library have a strategic plan? Will you review it before writing your grant?

☐ Will you have a project plan that includes goals, objectives, and activities and is based on your strategic plan?
☐ Will you set deadlines?
☐ Will you organize your materials (research, grant materials, etc.)?
☐ Will you have a budgetary goal?
☐ Will you have a method to track tasks and contacts?

Commit to Partnerships
☐ Will you cultivate a strong relationship with your grant funder?
☐ Will you develop the appropriate collaborations to leverage resources, share expertise, and support the project?
☐ Will you determine what groups in your community share your library's vision and goals and approach them as partners?
☐ Will you invite community members to focus groups and planning sessions?
☐ Will you complete a partnership agreement outlining goals, responsibilities, and benefits?

Commit to Evaluation
☐ Can your library clearly identify success in respect to the grant project?
☐ Will you have an evaluation plan and/or logic model to determine if your project has met its goals?
☐ Will you be able to identify what impact your project achieves; what difference the project makes?
☐ Will you identify outcomes for the project? Will your project have meaningful results that cause a change in people's behavior, attitudes, skills, condition, or knowledge?
☐ Will you have a benchmark plan designed to measure each outcome?

Commit to Sustainability
☐ Will your project be completed?
☐ Will your project be supported by leadership after grant funds are depleted?
☐ Will you plan a funding strategy to continue your project after grant funds are depleted?
☐ Does your project involve more than just one person?
☐ If your project involves hiring new staff members, will their positions be maintained after the grant period ends?

Commit to Following the Grant Guidelines
☐ Will you check and double-check all instructions?
☐ Will you answer all questions and complete any required narrative sections?
☐ Will you compile all allowable attachments including letters of support?
☐ Will you obtain all the required signatures?
☐ Will you submit the grant on time?

- Contact your state library for help. Some state libraries offer free classes and consultants often know which libraries in the state are expert grant seekers that you could contact for advice. Many state libraries also provide grants to libraries through LSTA funding and state grants-in-aid.

- Find out if potential grant funders will share successful proposals. Not all funders will do this, but it is worth asking. Many funders' websites list the organizations they have funded in the past and may also showcase successful grants.

- Tell everyone about your grant project ideas and get input. You never know who may know of a good lead or what opportunities may develop.

- Talk to the leaders in your community to find out about local grant funding.

- Contact other non-profits and community organizations in your area. Do they know of funders? Are they applying for grants? Are they looking for partners?

- Discover the professional development opportunities available in your area. Often foundations will offer seminars for free or low cost. Many online educational sources are covered in Chapter 9.

Once you complete the grant process cycle, you may find that you have achieved more than you had expected. There are often additional benefits beyond the grant funds. If you follow the guidelines in this book, you will increase community support and find new partners and collaboration opportunities. You may even see an increase in the library's local budget and an increase in library use. Use the checklist on p. 10 to evaluate your readiness to make the commitment to doing grant work. If your library has made these commitments, you are now ready to continue the grant process cycle.

 For reproducible and customizable versions of the Making the Commitment Checklist, see pp. 192–193 in the Toolkit and the companion DVD.

Planning
for Success

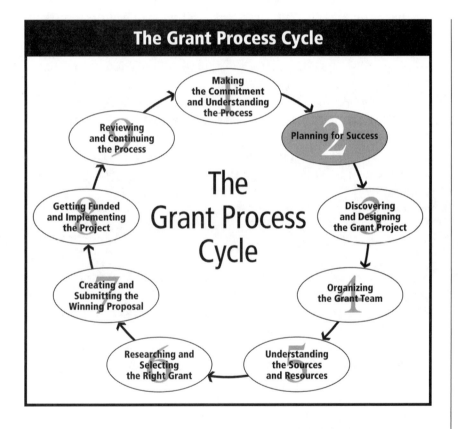

Why Planning Is Essential for Success with Grants

The grant process cycle emphasizes planning because plans are the foundation upon which grant proposals are written and provide the framework for project development. Libraries with plans have much greater prospects for a successful future, and are able to contribute to their community's biggest aspirations, which is what funders are striving

Whatever you can do or dream you can, begin it. Boldness has genius, magic, and power in it.
　　—Johann Wolfgang von Goethe

for as well. Strategic planning is about being proactive, rather than reactive—not responding to the RFPs, but starting with your library's mission and vision to create the desired future.

The next two chapters focus on planning. Chapter 2 focuses on strategic planning as the foundation for your library's grant work. Chapter 3 will take you to the next step of planning your specific grant project(s). The focus of a strategic plan is usually on the entire organization, while the focus of a project plan is typically on a particular service, program, or product. Both types of planning are essential to successful grant proposals. You must know what you do and why you do it. Essentially, this means you need to know your library's mission and vision, its purpose, and the true needs of its community. Then you can establish how you are going to meet those needs.

During this tough economy, grant funds are going to the libraries that are successful and organized. They have a strategic plan, they are creating programs that are needed and efficient, they operate their organizations professionally, and they succeed at their missions. This is what any funder/investor would want (which is what the community wants, as well)—that the needs in the community the library serves are being addressed in the best possible way.

If your library doesn't have a strategic plan, how do you even know that you need grant funds? Only because your budget is slim? You should never create new projects for your library just because a grant is available. The process of obtaining grant funding should directly tie into your strategic plan. You will find that the main components for grant proposals and the inspiration for grant projects are easily found in a well-developed strategic plan. Just by examining your library's mission statement and vision, you can gain essential information that will be helpful when seeking grant funding.

If you ignore your strategic plan, you may soon find that your library suffers from mission creep. This means that your organization's mission changes due to external factors such as money or outside influences. For example, if your library mission is focused on literacy, you should seek funding for literacy projects. If you submit a grant application to fund a project titled *Cake Decorating for Teens* because a local cooking school wants to fund teen cooking classes, your library's mission may "creep" into focusing on teen cooking classes and resources rather than literacy. Teens in your area really have a need for literacy classes, which means the cake decorating grant does not support your community in the best way possible. Your mission has changed to fit the guidelines of the funder rather than the needs of your community. Funding for hiring tutors or purchasing homework resources would be a better match for your mission.

"If you don't know where you're going, it doesn't matter which way you go," said the Cheshire Cat in *Alice in Wonderland*. Your library must have a purpose, indentify an audience, and determine what you are trying to achieve to be successful.

There are many resources you can refer to that will be helpful in implementing a planning process for your library. This chapter and the bibliography section of this book include helpful recommendations. Strategic planning does not happen overnight. It should be a deliberate activity conducted by the library director, staff, board, and community participants. If your library doesn't have a plan yet, it should at least have a mission statement and vision. Your grant committee should be able to extrapolate and outline brief goals and objectives from the mission and vision.

Fundraising Plans

This book focuses exclusively on grants as a source of fundraising; consequently, we do not go into detail on comprehensive fundraising plans. But we do want to make clear that they are a necessary part of library planning if your library is also raising funds through means such as endowments, capital campaigns, a library foundation, and major donor/gift cultivation.

Your fundraising plan will branch from your strategic plan and may include fundraising goals, a budget, polices and procedures, regulations, and guidelines, such as these:

- **Overall Fundraising Strategy**—detailing how fundraising supports the library mission and strategic plan, what types of fundraising methods are acceptable, and designation of the person or group with authority to approve any fundraising approaches or projects.

- **Donor Recognition and Communication**—including appreciation, solicitation, acceptance, or refusal.

- **Fundraising Roles and Responsibilities**—those of library staff, library foundation, and Friends of the Library; it should be clear whether third parties such as outside organizations or community members can fundraise on behalf of the library, and if so, how the projects will be approved and supported by the library.

- **Gifts and Donations**—explaining how your library handles any gifts received (whether they are books, funds, property, or artwork). This should include how gifts are approved, processed, and acknowledged.

- **Sponsorships**—clarifying whether outside organizations can sponsor or partner with the library. You may want to incorporate the signing of a partnership agreement or other type of documentation that will confirm the responsibilities and expectations of each organization involved.

- **Fundraising Ethics**—outlining the appropriate practices that should guide anyone fundraising on the library's behalf. This usually involves specifying that the individuals will not benefit themselves from the fundraising and that there will be no conflict of interest that may result from any acts associated with the fundraising. It may also specify how donors should be treated, and express the library's commitment to the appropriate use of donated funds.

Basics of Strategic Planning

Strategic planning is a powerful tool used to guide a library to improve, to prioritize, to ensure that all staff are working toward the same goals, to assess and adjust the library's course in response to changing situations. Strategic planning is a deliberate effort to determine the appropriate decisions and actions that shape and guide what a library is, what it does, and why it does what it does. Strategic planning helps guide the future, establish new partnerships, form creative and innovative relationships between stakeholders, and ultimately better address the needs of your community.

A strategic plan should be dynamic, constantly updated to reflect changes in the library and community. Once developed, it should not be imprinted with gold leaf and placed in a safe. When a major change or improvement is needed, you should revisit and update the plan. Major changes may include planning for a new or remodeled building or creating a new political arrangement, such as combining city libraries into a county system or dealing with budget cuts. Strategic planning stresses the importance of making decisions that will ensure the library's ability to successfully respond to changes in the environment.

Many governmental and non-profit funders require a plan to be submitted as part of grant applications. For example, if your library wants to be eligible to apply for grants from many state libraries under the federal Library Services and Technology Act (LSTA) program or other federal- or state-funded grants, you may be required to complete a library plan. Also, libraries and schools are required to have an approved technology plan to participate in the federal Universal Service Fund program, commonly known as the E-Rate program.

Involving the Entire Library and Community

Throughout your strategic planning process, it is vitally important that all library staff and community representatives become involved. A communitywide strategic planning process will benefit from the wisdom of a diverse array of participants and ensure greater likelihood of success.

We've talked to librarians all over the United States and are always amazed at the passion they have for their jobs and how they love contributing to their community. Many have a *dream library*—a place they envision as the perfect setting for their library—a place where they and others can do their best work. If staff are involved with the planning process, they can contribute their energies toward reaching that dream. The result will be a staff that feels ownership and joy in their jobs. Likewise, if the community is truly involved in building their dream library, the library will become a true center of the community.

You need a planning committee. At the very least include the library director, library board, staff, and community representatives. If possible invite governing officials, library volunteers, and patrons to public planning meetings. In a small library, strategic planning might take place as part of quarterly or monthly board and staff meetings; with a larger library the planning committee can make progress reports to the board and meet more frequently. The committee should have representatives of all your community's demographic and socioeconomic groups from all parts of your service area. Think about including members of your Chamber of Commerce, local government officials, school districts, churches, and social service agencies.

While it is important to involve the community in the library's planning, it is also very important for the library to be involved in any community planning and to support the community's plans. A great example of this is Denver Public Library (DPL).

Figure 2.1 shows Denver Public Library's Balanced Scorecard (based on Kaplan and Norton, 2001). The balanced scorecard helps transform a strategic plan from an attractive but passive document into the "marching orders" for the library on a daily basis. It provides a framework that not only provides performance measurements, but helps planners identify what should be done and measured to achieve the vision.

> The Library specifically contributes to the City's goal—"Making Denver a Better Place to Live and Create Jobs" by focusing on determining our role in addressing the macro issues facing Denver (job growth, quality education, public health, etc.). The E-Team Balanced Scorecard ensures that the priorities of the City are always in front of us and properly represented. The objectives and their

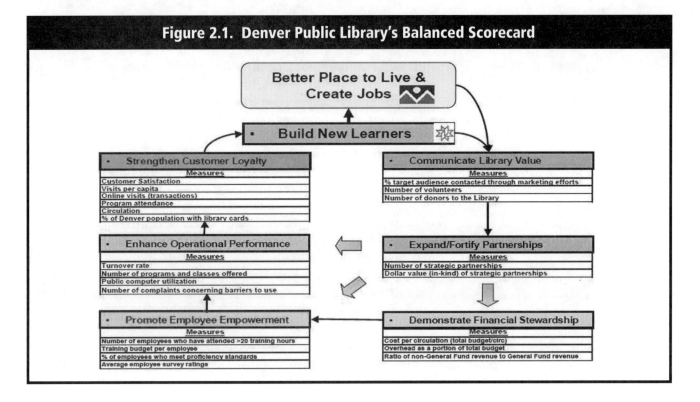

Figure 2.1. Denver Public Library's Balanced Scorecard

placement within the Strategy Cycle compose a compelling story of what DPL must achieve to best serve our customers and the City of Denver. Achievement of our objectives is accomplished by determining key measures that embody our progress toward goals. This figure displays these key measures, which provide a diverse set of "pulse points" indicative of our overall success in achieving our Vision. ("Agenda," 2008)

What a great method for ensuring that the library is truly serving its community.

Creating a Strategic Plan

Planning—formulating a mission, vision, goals, and objectives—is an involved and continual process. As a busy librarian, your first reaction may be that you don't have the time or the resources to accomplish this strategy. In actuality, planning can save a lot of time and resources that will enable your library to accomplish more with less. Good strategic planning involves creating space for what can emerge when we bring all the resources to the table, share freely, reflect . . . and then plan to create the future.

Various perspectives, models, and approaches are used in strategic planning. Development of a strategic plan depends on many factors, such as the library leadership, the culture of the library, the complexity of the library's environment, the size of the library, and the expertise of the planners. Large urban libraries may hire outside consultants to coordinate the planning process, whereas smaller libraries often oversee the process internally. We have included an example strategic plan in Figure 2.2 (see pages 34–36) as well as links to library strategic plans online (see p. 195 in the Toolkit and the companion DVD for live links).

Funders often favor organizations that incorporate community awareness and involvement. Libraries have repeatedly confirmed how important the process of completing this type of plan has been in their local efforts to gain recognition, funding, and staffing for accomplishing the goals and objectives set out in their plans.

Don't be concerned about the "perfect way" to conduct strategic planning. If you do some research, you will find there are many models and thousands of books written on the best methods of planning. Among the variety of strategic planning models, there are those that are based on goals, issues, scenarios, and those that are organic. Planning typically includes several major activities or steps in the process. Although there may be many different ways to identify these steps, many are common to most strategic plans. They might not be conducted in the same order, and they may have different methods for writing goals and objectives, but usually the core elements are similar. Once you start strategic planning, you'll soon find your own particular approach or favorite method to complete the process. You may modify a planning process or combine two or three methods to create one that works for your library. The following are some planning methods to examine.

It was challenging to execute long-term planning while simultaneously focusing on day-to-day issues related to the project and our duties as librarians. The good news is that we were compelled to learn new time management and delegation strategies.

—"A Few Good Women: Advancing the Cause of Women in Government" Pennsylvania State University Libraries, University Park, PA (see Library Grant Success Stories, pp. 146–147)

Strategic Planning for Results

The Public Library Association's latest community-based planning process, *Strategic Planning for Results* (Nelson, 2008), provides a great planning structure for libraries. This type of plan is not at all limited to public libraries, as every library serves a community, whether it is a neighborhood, campus, corporation, or school. It has proven successful with all sizes of libraries, as well as museums, churches, and schools. This book provides precise details on everything you need to do to create a library plan, including aspects of every meeting and how to help staff respond to change. This process is based on involving a community committee and prioritizing the library's services. The example strategic plan used in this book is based on this process.

Scenario Planning

Scenario planning is a strategic planning method used to make flexible long-term plans. It is an adaptation and generalization of classic methods used by military intelligence. The idea is to create possible futures based on current trends and emerging issues of change. Scenarios do not create predictions, but use stories or narratives to explore possible futures.

There are many methods based on considering variables, such as having an increase or a decrease in funding, or investigating important decisions, such as building a new branch, selecting a new vendor, or forming a new partnership. Looking ahead and considering uncertainties can help us recognize and adapt to changing aspects of our environment. They form a method for articulating the different pathways that might exist tomorrow, and finding appropriate actions down each of those possible paths.

The best scenarios do so by describing alternative future outcomes that diverge significantly from the present. Some questions that can be asked when examining library scenarios include these:

- What skills do staff members need to thrive in this scenario?
- What does the organization look like? How many staff? What kind of staff? What are imperative organizational behaviors?
- What services and programs does the library provide?
- How is the library budget allocated? (staffing, collections, technology, etc.)
- What is a collection?
- What is literacy?
- What does research look like? Is reference still a viable part?
- Is there a physical space? If so, what does it need to have?
- What is the role of the library in the community?
- What kind of technology is needed?

If you are interested in exploring this method, many resources are available, listed in the bibliography.

> The end result, however, is not an accurate picture of tomorrow, but better decisions about the future.
> —Peter Schwartz
> From *The Art of the Long View* (1996: 9)

AI is based on a deceptively simple premise: that organizations grow in the direction of what they repeatedly ask questions about and focus their attention on. AI does not focus on changing people. Instead, it invites people to engage in building the kinds of organizations they want to live in. That's hard to resist.

—Gervase Bushe
From *Appreciative Inquiry*
(www.gervasebushe.ca/appinq.htm)

Appreciative Inquiry

Appreciative Inquiry (AI) can be used to discover what the library does well, how it does it, and to design ways to do more of what works best for the community. It offers a model for harnessing the imagination and passion of each individual's dream library in a process that can be applied to a total library or a unit within the library.

AI is an organizational change and planning methodology developed by Professor David Cooperrider and his colleagues at Case Western Reserve University. The approach has been used successfully all over the world to learn from shared experiences, to involve whole communities in change and development, and to build a shared vision for the future that everyone can help put into practice.

AI honors the past. It isn't about what is being done wrong, what isn't working, or what services have to be eliminated; instead, it focuses on the fact that libraries are wonderful places and what we do well needs to be nurtured. It is easier to make changes if we believe that in moving forward, we won't lose what we are most passionate about. By having everyone possible share the answers to the questions "What is it that we want to bring forward into the change effort and the library of the future?" and "What is the ideal library for our community?" and focusing on the positive instead of the negative, we have a truly proactive planning method.

This process often results in staff who are committed and take accountability—often in new ways. Outcomes of the AI process include high productivity, common vision, more effective teamwork, increased employee satisfaction, increased customer satisfaction, improved work relations, energy, enthusiasm, empowerment, sustainability, and an appreciative learning culture.

The following five steps summarize the AI process:

1. Choose the positive as the focus of inquiry.
2. Inquire into stories of what is working best.
3. Locate themes that appear in the stories and select topics for further inquiry; find the root causes of success.
4. Create shared images of a preferred future.
5. Find innovative ways to create that future.

More information and free resources are available in the bibliography.

Common Plan Elements

There are common elements found in most strategic plans. A sample library plan at the end of this chapter (see Figure 2.2) is based primarily on the PLA's *Strategic Planning for Results* (Nelson, 2008) method. This is a two-year, goal-based plan of the Successful Public Library, the fictional library that we use as an example for this book. Most plans range from two to three years. Any further into the future and it becomes increasingly difficult to incorporate imminent changes in the library infrastructure, community, technology, etc. Plans vary in length from the more succinct, which are four to eight pages in length, while others are considerably longer and more detailed.

At minimum, the strategic plan should include the following elements:

1. Vision
2. Mission
3. Community and Library Profiles
4. Needs Assessment
5. Goals
6. Objectives
7. Activities

Start with focusing on the library's vision and mission. Then identify the key background information on your community and library. Next, conduct a needs assessment to determine community needs, how well your library is serving your community, and what improvements can be made in terms of services and programs. Finally, establish goals to work toward the vision, objectives to achieve the goals, and specific activities that will be the implementation part of the plan. The objectives and activities will determine which grant projects you develop.

Vision

The vision depicts an ideal library that is instrumental in creating the future of the community and is the motivating force for your strategic plan. Vision statements are inspiring and easily communicate what drives your library's day-to-day efforts. Before you start developing your plan, your vision will tell you what the successful implementation of your strategic plan will look like.

Your vision should include the following qualities:

• Exciting
• Provocative—should stretch and challenge your library
• Realistic
• Desired
• Representative of legitimate beliefs
• Described in positive terms
• Written in the present tense, as if already achieved

Vision provides "pull" for organizational practices. This is sometimes called the heliotropic principle. Just as plants grow toward their energy source, communities and organizations move toward what gives them life and energy. Using Appreciative Inquiry and other forms of community involvement engages people and organizations in discovering what empowers libraries when they are most effective and using that knowledge to envision and create the preferred future. Vision allows us to imagine beyond the circumstances and reach something truly original, not just reactionary. Real vision is a picture of a desired outcome we want to create, not just a dream.

Visioning must be a participatory process. A vision won't be effective if it's handed down from a single library leader or administrator. To achieve a shared community vision, key stakeholders and interested community members will need to spend time together talking about their ideas and listening to each other. As you incorporate everyone's ideas, the vision is likely to evolve and grow stronger. Indeed, you will increase your community's ownership of the vision and commitment to achieving it.

Try to remain focused on what you want to create, not in terms of problem solving. This will concentrate on situations we don't want, on what isn't working. Of course, most of us, in both professional and private life, spend far more time problem solving and reacting to circumstances

EXAMPLE VISIONS

The Successful Public Library is the true community center. Our library understands and responds to the community's essential needs, informs and inspires its members, and is significant to all.

Denver Public Library, Colorado

Our vision of "Building a Vibrant City, One Learner at a Time," includes:

- Build New Learners
- Strengthen Customer Loyalty
- Communicate Library Value
- Enhance Operational Performance
- Promote Employee Empowerment
- Expand / Fortify Partnerships
- Demonstrate Financial Stewardship

Rio Rancho Public Library, New Mexico

(nm-riorancho.civicplus.com/index.aspx?NID=115)
RRPL balances traditional library services for all age groups with new information technologies in a visible, dynamic, properly housed facility whose staff serves and understands the work- and school-related, recreational, and family-centered concerns and interests of its diverse community.

The University of Texas at Austin Libraries

(www.lib.utexas.edu/vprovost/mission.html)
The University of Texas Libraries is the preeminent public university library in the country, providing

- campus information resources (the raw materials of University research and learning) that sustain the intellectual environment required to be a preeminent research institution;
- an evolving technology environment with effective tools and services for the discovery and delivery of information to campus scholars and the citizenry alike;
- an inviting and comfortable space for individual or group study and learning, equipped with appropriate infrastructure;
- the University community with skills to master information strategies appropriate to the classroom, laboratory, and lifelong learning;
- staff expertise that strengthens state and national collaborations focused on improving the preservation and dissemination of scholarship and creative works; and
- a talented and diverse staff that fully embraces University values.

than focusing our energies on creating what we really value. We can get so caught up in reacting to problems that it is easy to forget what we actually want. Problem solving becomes the busywork of organizations in which people have forgotten their purpose and vision.

Mission

The mission is a broad statement of the role or purpose of the library. It identifies who the library serves and justifies its existence. All the library staff should know the library's mission and be able to connect their specific responsibilities to it. It should inspire their actions and give them an understanding of what the library is working to achieve. The library community should also be able to identify the library's purpose and the services it offers by reading the mission.

EXAMPLE MISSION STATEMENTS

The Successful Public Library
The mission of The Successful Public Library is to provide community members with an unbiased social and intellectual gathering place which includes resources and opportunities to enrich and fulfill their lifelong learning, informational, and leisure needs.

Salt Lake City Public Library
(www.slcpl.lib.ut.us)
The mission of The City Library is to promote free and open access to information, materials and services to all members of the community to advance knowledge, foster creativity, encourage the exchange of ideas, build community and enhance the quality of life.

Nashville Public Library
(www.library.nashville.org/about/abt_mission.asp)
Nashville Public Library is committed to:

- Extending the benefits and joys of reading, lifelong learning, and discovery to all people through collections and services;
- Promoting the value and power of knowledge, essential in an informed democracy, by providing open and equal access to the records and opinions of the world;
- Providing emerging technologies and instruction as a gateway to information resources within and beyond our walls;
- Serving the community with integrity and skill;
- Providing an environment welcoming to all people which serves as a gathering place within the community;
- Preserving and sharing across generations the wisdom, culture, and history of our community.

Fayetteville (NC) Public Library
(www.faylib.org/information/vision_mission.asp)
Our mission is to provide citizens with access to information, kindle the imagination of children and adults, and encourage lifelong learning and achievement for all.

Swansboro Elementary School Library (Richmond, VA)
(richmond.k12.va.us/schools/swansboro/our_media_center.htm)
It is the mission of The Swansboro Elementary School Library to function as the nucleus for creating a foundation for a community of lifelong learners by focusing on the needs of the students. This will be accomplished through a learning environment which promotes information literacy and has as its foundation a creative, energetic library/media program, literature rich resources, and intellectual and physical access to information.

Mission statements should be brief, but powerful and easy to understand. Some mission statements comprise many paragraphs; some contain just one sentence. Mission statements should be broad so that they do not need to be rewritten when new initiatives or directions are undertaken. They should be free of language that may discourage potential funders or partners from participating. Often funders will evaluate a potential grant recipient by how well their mission statement aligns to their own.

The mission should answer the following questions:

1. What are the basic purposes for which we exist?
2. Who do we serve?
3. What basic community needs are we meeting and with what services?
4. What makes our purpose unique and distinguishes us from others?
5. Is our mission in harmony with our community?

If your library is not succeeding at the work of its mission it may be time for training, re-evaluating the needs in the community, re-evaluating the library's work, to fire and hire new talent, or more. Foster a culture of mission-based decision making (not decision making based on insecurities, limits, unwillingness to try new things, ego, personal agendas, entitlement, etc.).

Organizational Values

Although we didn't include Organizational Values or Library Service Responses (see p. 30 for more details) as one of the six common elements in strategic plans, they are helpful and we encourage you to integrate them into your planning process.

Values define the set of beliefs and principles that guide the library. They are the basis of the ethical standards that govern how a library serves the community, works with partners and vendors, appreciates staff members, and is represented to the world. Values can be single words (such as integrity, trust, teamwork) or short phrases. They define what is respected and what is not, and often carry emotional connotations. They should drive the priorities of staff and leadership and how they perform and make decisions. Major and minor decisions alike should always align with the mission.

Values can be identified through a group exercise with the entire library staff, or through surveying of staff by the planning committee.

Community and Library Profiles

We need to look at our environment and truly understand our library and community before we do any planning. A preliminary step to conducting a community needs assessment is developing a community profile.

EXAMPLE VALUES

Arizona State University Libraries' Core Organizational Values

(www.asu.edu/lib/library/ulsp/ul2000/values.htm)

During the strategic planning process, more than 100 staff members participated in sessions in which they identified the core values held by the Libraries. The following draft statement of core values is the product of this critically important activity:

As a service organization, we value:

- the educational process of which we are an integral part,
- friendly, helpful, superior service to our user community,
- generosity: providing open access to all our resources,
- technology in the service of people,
- the diversity of our resources and collections,
- inclusiveness: outreach to all our users.

In the process of getting our work done, we value:

- work of high quality that results in satisfied customers,
- the competence, knowledge, efficiency, expertise, and diversity of skills that foster superior quality,
- the development of our staff and their skills,
- professionalism at all levels,
- innovation, creativity, and risk-taking,
- flexibility and adaptability.

As a community, we value:

- cooperation, teamwork, esprit de corps,
- open communication,
- respect and trust among members,
- idealism and vision,
- the diversity that makes us strong.

Monroe County Public Library in Indiana Values

(www.monroe.lib.in.us/general_info/mission_statement.html)

- Equitable access to information, ideas, and creative works
- Intellectual freedom and diversity of opinion and cultures
- Lifelong learning and the love of reading
- Responsiveness to community demands
- Excellence in service
- The library as a welcoming place for all
- Effective and efficient delivery of library services
- Responsible stewardship of public resources
- Partnerships to advance the library's mission

Shaker Library, Shaker Heights, Ohio

(www.shakerlibrary.org/Library%20Guide/Administration/?Library+Strategic+Plan+2009+-+2011)

We value:

- Community responsiveness
- Continuous improvement
- Diversity and inclusiveness
- Education
- Equal access to information
- Excellent service
- Fair employment
- Fiscal responsibility
- Intellectual freedom
- Lifelong learning
- Organizational collaboration
- Outstanding employees
- Trustworthy information

San Jose Public Library System

(www.sjlibrary.org/about/sjpl/vision.htm)

- Our users are not only our customers, they are the reason the library exists. We provide quality service and treat all users fairly and equally. Services are provided in a non-judgmental manner that is sensitive to and supportive of human differences.
- Our employees and volunteers are valued as individuals and for their important contributions to the organization. An open exchange of ideas is encouraged throughout the system. We nurture our talents and each other.
- We are a learning organization that is not afraid to change and take appropriate risks in pursuit of meeting community needs. We constantly reassess our services and methods and try to see ourselves through the public's eyes.
- We maintain high standards in our work and help instill a sense of pride in all employees, as well as a strong sense of responsibility and integrity.
- Both staff and users are encouraged to enjoy their library experience.

Changes in politics, society, and economics impact our libraries. Libraries are in the business of providing information and must respond to the changes in our communities, keeping up with new and different community needs, and reaching out to new populations. An analysis of the community will reveal important information that the library director, staff, and board should know about, including what people need and expect from their library. The library can then respond by redefining its mission and roles and reallocating the collection, services, and programs to more accurately match the current needs.

Community Profile

A community profile is a brief description about the population and area served by the library. This may already be done by your city, university, or other local organization. If so, it is fine to use that information instead of creating your own profile. This is usually done every three to five years.

If you do need to develop your own community profile, you will need to gather specific information about the library's service area and the people it serves. The profile will document changes and new trends in people's lifestyles, interests, family and business pursuits, recreational activities, and social, civic, and educational concerns and will help the library reallocate its resources to provide what the community needs and expects.

This information can reveal major phases in a community's existence, whether it is growth, stagnation due to economic hard times (loss of businesses, jobs, homes), rebirth because of outside forces (new businesses, new populations), or the need for dramatic change to remain viable and economically strong. The two major influences to be examined are the environment and the population. Include analysis of the following:

- Community setting: environment, geography, climate, and recreational opportunities
- Growth and development
- Local government
- Business and industry
- Communications
- Educational facilities
- Cultural opportunities
- Local organizations and civic groups
- Population characteristics (age groups, race and language, educational levels, occupation and income levels, household size)

Library Profile

The Library Profile will be specific to your institution. It is a component often requested in a grant application and sometimes called an Organizational Overview. The library's history, service population, achievements, primary programs, current budget, leadership, board members, and key staff members should all be included. Answer the questions, "Who are we?" and "What do we do?"

The Library Profile should include basic information, but can also incorporate recent changes and interesting details on these topics:

- History
- Service population
- Achievements
- Primary services, programs, collections, and facilities
- Current budget and resource reallocations
- Leadership and staff
- Cultural diversity initiatives
- Technology infrastructure
- Collaboration and partnerships
- Proof of significance
- New laws and regulations

Needs Assessment

A needs assessment will determine how well the library is serving its community and what other services or resources it can provide in the future. Identifying the needs and issues of your community is an important part of your information-gathering process, in order to determine the preferences and perceptions of those most affected by your work. Focus on finding out how the library can help improve and support your community, whether it is to focus on literacy, job-seeking skills, educational support, reducing school drop-out rates, providing a safe place for teens, or closing the digital divide. Needs assessments can later serve as a benchmark for your progress.

Needs assessments or needs statements are often requested in grant applications and are an excellent way to prove the necessity of your proposed grant projects. You should always determine a need before you create a grant project. It will tell the funder why your project is necessary and who will benefit from the project. The grant project will be part of the solution to the need.

It is important to involve your community and use assessment methods to identify true community needs. This means you should get input from all segments of your community, not just the politicians, leaders, and people who use the library, but from farmers, teens, recent immigrants, and all large groups in your community including people who don't use the library. The Las Vegas Clark County Library District (LVCCLD) did just that. *Library Journal* reported LVCCLD Director Dan Walters as saying, "We hired consultants who conducted both English- and Spanish-language telephone surveys in order to get at non-users. The Latino community indicated that they would use the library much more if our collections were more diverse. This year we will circulate more than

EXAMPLE NEEDS STATEMENT

Successful Public Library includes an underserved population of students whose test scores as well as their general knowledge of library research are below desired levels. These students will benefit from increased exposure to libraries and increased levels of instruction in information literacy and research skills.

200,000 items in Spanish." The system strives for diversity in language and format, including videos, DVDs, and audiobooks (Berry, 2003).

Results of a needs assessment study can be used to determine the following:

- How the collections and technologies can be used to meet community needs
- Who is using the library and how to reach non-users
- What are the most and least desired services and programs
- Whether the facility and parking are acceptable
- How the community is changing
- What staffing and library hours changes are needed to accommodate the community

The first step in performing a needs assessment is to decide who will oversee the project. Needs assessments can be carried out by outside consultants, library volunteers, or library staff. Your available resources, time frame, and comfort level with performing this type of research may influence your decision. It is best to use a combination of these methods. For example, you might hire an outside consultant to help you set up the needs assessment study and design surveys, but then use volunteers to actually complete a telephone survey, and staff to interview community leaders.

- **Outside consultants** will have expertise in how to conduct research studies. They provide objectivity by offering an outsider's view. Since consultants are experienced at performing research, this option makes better use of your limited time. The primary disadvantage to using outside consultants is often the cost.
- **Volunteers** are another possibility. Volunteers are free and save library staff time. However, they may present a biased interpretation of what the community needs. It is important to select volunteers who reflect a broad array of the community and to select volunteers that have experience in performing needs assessments. Volunteers will also need to be trained and managed, so some staff time will also be involved.
- **Library staff** can also perform needs assessments. While library staff are less expensive than hiring outside consultants, they may be inexperienced in needs assessments or not have time to perform a needs assessment on top of their regular library responsibilities. However, basic needs assessments can be done through interviews and research, as outlined in the following section on collecting data.

The second step in performing a needs assessment is to decide what you want to learn about your community and what kind of information you plan to collect. For example, will you perform a broad-based study or one that is focused on a particular area or issue? Some categories of information you might be interested in collecting include historical, demographic, economic, social, cultural, educational, and recreational. Some libraries perform a SWOT (Strengths, Weaknesses, Opportunities, and Threats) analysis or use Appreciative Inquiry or other strategic method to identify the challenges and opportunities facing their community and library. Then they prioritize the issues and use the needs assessment to focus on addressing those specific issues.

Collecting the Data

Now that you have decided on the types of information you want to collect about your community, you need to determine how to collect that information. You can collect data by interviewing key leaders in the community, holding a community forum, researching demographic data from public records and reports, and performing surveys. It is best to use more than one of these data collection methods.

Interviews

By interviewing key members of your community, you can better understand their impressions of the community needs. Interviews may also yield future partners that could support grant projects. However, this method provides subjective data since it is based on opinions that may not reflect the needs of the entire community. If you are interested in a target audience, such as Spanish-speaking members of your community that aren't using the library, you can contact leaders that work with that specific population, such as church officials, health care workers, or teachers. If you have two staff members to assign to this task, they could split up and each conduct five interviews or they could go together so that one could take notes while the other asks the questions. A volunteer could also help with note taking.

Focus Groups

Focus groups can provide very honest and useful information. Members can be selected by age, gender, occupation, or social interests and groups can be organized into manageable numbers. If the participants are comfortable, they may give very helpful feedback. You will need to have a facilitator for each group, and organizing and scheduling focus groups can take a lot of time. This information is also subjective, and it could be time-consuming to compile the data as well.

Community Forum or Town Meeting

A community forum involves holding a group event and inviting your entire community. This can provide a lot of good information, give visibility to your library, and even raise its status within the community. However, these forums require a lot of planning and publicity. The majority of the attendees will probably be active library users, rather than those who do not use the library. This can make it difficult to determine the needs of the entire community. Another disadvantage of this method is that it tends to provide subjective and impressionistic data about the community's needs. Also, the less vocal and participatory segments of your community may not be represented.

Public Records

A more objective method of data collection is to use public records to research secondary data such as the social indicators or demographics of your community. A well-known source that is reliable and available for county- or city-level analyses is the U.S. Census Bureau (www.census.gov). Using these records, you have access to such community information such as ages, genders, languages spoken, education levels, income levels, and marital statuses.

Surveys

Surveys can be distributed by mail, phone, in the library, or online. While mailed surveys are the most expensive option and get low response rates, the mailed survey method requires very little time to implement and is easy to coordinate. Some utility companies will include surveys with their bills for no charge, so this is an option to explore for some types of libraries. Several online surveys are available for free or little cost. These are easy to develop, implement, and compile. Take a look at Survey Monkey (www.surveymonkey.com) or Zoomerang (www.zoomerang.com). Both have free versions for smaller surveys. Some libraries have links to online surveys available on their websites to gather information from online users.

Information gathered from surveys is only as good as the questions asked. If you are performing the needs assessment yourself, you might want to consult an experienced surveyor as you design the questions. The shorter a survey, the easier it will be for a busy customer to complete. Be sure to provide confidentiality to your survey participants. Reassuring your participants that their survey responses will be kept confidential and anonymous might help improve your response rates, especially in a small community.

Using and Sharing Community Feedback

To make use of the information you have collected, the results have to be interpreted and evaluated. When the data analysis is complete, prioritize the responses. At the end of this process, the findings should be compiled and shared with the library leadership, staff, and the community. This can be done through meetings, public displays, or articles on your library webpage or in the local newspapers. Of course, once you have broadcasted these needs, make sure that the library will follow up on the top priorities.

Library Service Responses

Library Service Responses were created by the Public Library Association (PLA) and are used in the community-based planning process outlined in *Strategic Planning for Results* (Nelson, 2008). They are used to prioritize library services and programs that match the community needs identified through a visioning process. By doing this, libraries can choose to do a few things very well instead of spreading energy and resources across too many efforts to be really effective. It is better to

LIBRARY SERVICE RESPONSES

- Be an Informed Citizen: Local, National, and World Affairs
- Build Successful Enterprises: Business and Nonprofit Support
- Celebrate Diversity: Cultural Awareness
- Connect to the Online World: Public Internet Access
- Create Young Readers: Early Literacy
- Discover Your Roots: Genealogy and Local History
- Express Creativity: Create and Share Content
- Get Facts Fast: Ready Reference
- Know Your Community: Community Resources and Services

- Learn to Read and Write: Adult, Teen, and Family Literacy
- Make Career Choices: Job and Career Development
- Make Informed Decisions: Health, Wealth, and Other Life Choices
- Satisfy Curiosity: Lifelong Learning
- Stimulate Imagination: Reading, Viewing, and Listening for Pleasure
- Succeed in School: Homework Help
- Understand How to Find, Evaluate, and Use Information: Information Fluency
- Visit a Comfortable Place: Physical and Virtual Spaces
- Welcome to the United States: Services for New Immigrants

meet a few needs of your community than to miss the mark and not help solve any of the community issues. *Strategic Planning for Results* (Nelson, 2008) includes more detailed information as well as the website: ourlibraryplace.com/elearn/course/view.php?id=5. Log in as a guest and go to Power Tools for Planners, Power Tool 3.

See the Successful Public Library Strategic Plan in Figure 2.2 on pages 34–36 for an example of the Library Service Responses selected by their Community Planning Committee.

Goals

Goals are the actions we will take to achieve our vision. One of the main functions of a strategic plan is to establish clear goals and realistic strategies to achieve those goals. Goals are broad, general statements describing a desired condition or future toward which the library will work. They are the path to achieving the vision of the library and part of the solution toward fulfilling the needs identified in the needs assessment. Set your sights high when it comes to goal setting. Some libraries are really only compiling a checklist of what they know will be achieved, rather than pushing themselves to go beyond the norm. If a goal is never accomplished, it shouldn't be viewed as a failure; rather, it means that a review should occur, changes may be needed for success, or perhaps it should just be viewed as a learning experience.

Some goals may be short term, while others will cover a multiyear period. Achieving a goal may mean changing the services or programs offered by the library. All goals should be written in positive language. Goals often become the services, programs, or projects that may be supported by grant funding. Goals must be framed in the context of the community served. If it can't be stated as a community benefit, the library should think twice about taking this path.

EXAMPLE GOALS

From the Successful Public Library's Strategic Plan:

- The Successful Public Library's resources and services are easily accessed and meet the diverse and changing information needs of our customers.
- Spanish-speaking community members are able to find information, resources, and pursue learning opportunities.
- The library successfully serves the lifelong learning, informational, and leisure needs of the community's mature adult population.

Objectives

Objectives are written for each goal but may also relate to more than one goal. Objectives are short range and more focused than goals. The acronym SMART is often used as a way to remember the important elements in writing objectives. SMART stands for Specific, Measurable, Achievable, Realistic, and Time-Bound. Check each objective you write to make certain it meets these conditions. Objectives are the way the library measures its progress toward reaching a goal. For that reason, it must be very clear what the objective will accomplish and how the objective will be measured.

Statements of objectives should include the following:

1. A specific, realistic, and achievable end result (for example: To increase the number of teens as registered borrowers)
2. The method of measurement (for example: by 40 percent)
3. The time frame (for example: March 2011)

When you combine these elements, your objective is: *The number of teens who have library cards will increase by 40 percent by March 2011.*

Activities

Part of the strategic planning process is to develop a series of activities or strategies you can use to reach the goals and objectives. These activities will form the basis for many of the library's actions and resource allocations for the period covered by your overall plan. At this point in strategic planning, you will need to be very specific about what will be done. This is sometimes called project planning, and involves detailing everything necessary for effective implementation of the project, including identifying action steps, allocating resources, creating timelines, determining the budget, and establishing evaluation methods. And of course, as you plan for these activities, you are also planning possible grant projects. The specifics of grant project planning and evaluation are covered in Chapter 3, "Discovering and Designing the Grant Project."

This can be a creative process done by a committee. Brainstorm the activities necessary for accomplishing individual goals and objectives or combinations of goals and objectives from your library's strategic plan. There should be a direct link between your objectives and your activities. You might find that a single activity addresses more than one goal or objective. Also, some activities might help accomplish more than one objective.

Monitoring and Updating Your Strategic Plan

Regularly revisit your plans and evaluate whether the goals are being met and whether action steps are being implemented. Perhaps the most important indicator of the library's success is positive feedback from the community concerning services, programs, and resources. Having established clearly defined outcomes and outputs will provide a feedback mechanism to evaluate program performance and will influence future planning, resource allocation, and operating decisions. Chapter 3 covers creating and measuring outcomes.

While we may create strategic plans, we need to continue to take into account the trends, emerging issues, and critical events that impact our plans. We need to pay attention to outside forces that may sway our strategic goals toward other directions. This is sometimes called environmental scanning, and involves finding dynamic connections among the trends and patterns to identify opportunities and challenges. You can do this for your library by using these simple techniques:

- Reading/watching/listening/trying—looking outside of your interests

- Keeping a file of interesting technologies or social changes and recording the patterns that you see

- Paying attention to the current issues in society, technology, economy, ecology, and politics

- Discovering opportunities—looking at what is current and the implications it has for the library to serve the community (For example, the iPod—the library could create podcasts of book

LIBRARY PLANNING CHECKLIST

To compete seriously for a grant, review your library's organizational attributes periodically by considering each of the following:

□ Does your library have a clearly defined mission statement that is the foremost consideration in all decision making?

□ Are your goals obtainable and supportive of your library's mission?

□ Are your objectives clear, measurable, and tied to goal achievement?

□ Do you periodically evaluate your objectives to be certain progress is being made?

□ Have you selected a strategy for collecting data on your community and library?

□ Are statistics aggregated to allow easy retrieval of necessary information?

□ Are you recording all participants' attendance in all of your programs and projects, their feedback after their participation, and the participants' demographics?

□ Are all statistics that are collected actually used?

□ Are you involving library staff and community members in the planning process?

□ Did you communicate the final plan to staff, leadership, and community members?

□ Do you have an accurate timetable for implementation of your library's plan and designated specific dates for assessing progress toward goals?

□ Are the library's programs, services, projects, current?

□ Have you reviewed the latest needs among the population or community that your library serves?

□ Are all programs, services, and operations conducted in a lean but sustainable fashion?

□ Are all unnecessary expenses cut, savings implemented, and fundraising for each program and project stepped up?

□ Are you reporting all bookkeeping and accounting thoroughly, honestly, and does your library complete grant reports and donor requests on time and honestly?

□ Does your library use public relations and marketing opportunities to share successes, achievements, and thank the community for its support or does the community only hear about budget cuts and closings?

□ Are your leadership, beneficiaries, staff, and volunteers sharing information about their work with the library with their friends, colleagues, and family, and why they've chosen to become involved with it?

For reproducible and customizable versions of this checklist, see page 194 in the Toolkit and the companion DVD.

reviews, storytimes, "how to" podcast classes, audio tours, digital audiobooks.)

Funders appreciate strategic plans and project plans because they demonstrate that your project ideas are realistic and prove that the library is capable of responsibly handling funds and implementing projects. It also provides evidence that the library monitors, evaluates, and measures progress toward goals.

The professional, polished, and beneficial organizational attributes in the Library Planning Checklist earn confidence in capabilities, raise buy-in, set higher expectations of outcomes and efficiency, and generally engender support. Donors, as with all other community partners in a library's work, support organizations that show potential for excellence. If your library isn't operating professionally, you could lose grant opportunities. When grant donors receive applications from libraries that demonstrate professional best practices AND also articulate in their grant application that this is how they conduct themselves—these are the libraries whose grant applications will be awarded.

Figure 2.2. Successful Public Library Strategic Plan for 2011–2012

VISION

The Successful Public Library is the true community center. Our library understands and responds to the community's essential needs, informs and inspires its members, and is significant to all.

MISSION

The mission of The Successful Public Library is to provide community members with an unbiased social and intellectual gathering place that includes resources and opportunities to enrich and fulfill their lifelong learning, informational, and leisure needs.

LIBRARY SERVICE RESPONSES TO THE COMMUNITY

With the Successful Public Library's Vision and Mission statements as a starting point, the Community Planning Committee, made up of members representing the community, established five service priorities for library services, which they felt will best meet the needs of the community:

1. **Celebrate Diversity: Cultural Awareness**
   Residents will have programs and services that promote appreciation and understanding of their personal heritage and the heritage of others in the community.

2. **Stimulate Imagination: Reading, Viewing, and Listening for Pleasure**
   Residents who want materials to enhance their leisure time will find what they want, when and where they want them, and will have the help they need to make choices from among the options.

3. **Satisfy Curiosity: Lifelong Learning**
   Residents will have the resources they need to explore topics of personal interest and continue to learn throughout their lives.

4. **Make Informed Decisions: Health, Wealth, and Other Life Choices**
   Residents will have the resources they need to identify and analyze risks, benefits, and alternatives before making decisions that affect their lives.

5. **Understand How to Find, Evaluate, and Use Information: Information Fluency**
   Residents will know when they need information to resolve an issue or answer a question and will have the skills to search for, locate, evaluate, and effectively use information to meet their needs.

(Continued)

Figure 2.2. Successful Public Library Strategic Plan for 2011–2012 *(Continued)*

GOALS, OBJECTIVES, AND ACTIVITIES

Based on the five service priorities selected by the Community Planning Committee, the Library Board adopted three goals designed to meet anticipated community needs. Each goal has specific objectives and activities designed to achieve these objectives.

GOALS	OBJECTIVES	ACTIVITIES
Goal 1 The Successful Public Library's resources and services are easily accessed and meet the diverse and changing information needs of our customers.	**Objective 1.1** During 2010 the library will increase programming by 100 percent to help people in tough economic times.	**Activities** 1. Provide programming on finding employment online. 2. Provide training in completing online applications. 3. Provide training in preparing résumés using technology. 4. Reallocate staff time to provide training and plan programming. 5. Partner with Workforce Training Center, Unemployment Office, One Stop Employment Center, and area employers.
	Objective 1.2 By 2012, 20 percent more library customers will indicate that their information needs were met during a library visit.	**Activities** 1. Develop responsive collection development plan. 2. Increase number of public Internet workstations. 3. Develop subject-specific workshops on finding information. 4. Develop standardized research guides on popular topics. 5. Update current information literacy program to include critical inquiry and website evaluation. 6. Provide instruction on the use of online catalog and research databases. 7. Survey library customers when leaving the library/library website as to whether they found something that met their needs.
	Objective 1.3 By 2012, library customers will be able to meet 50 percent more information needs and requests online.	**Activities** 1. Investigate how to serve customers online and implement new web tools. 2. Reallocate staff to better serve online customers. 3. Redesign library website to better serve customer needs. 4. Improve website user interface. 5. Regularly update website. 6. Develop current resource link page. 7. Survey library customers when leaving the library/library website as to whether they found something that met their needs.
Goal 2 Spanish-speaking community members are able to find information, resources, and pursue learning opportunities.	**Objective 2.1** By 2007, evaluate and improve the library's ability to serve Spanish-speaking customers.	**Activities** 1. Allocate funds to support collecting English as a Second Language and Spanish language materials, and provide interpreters. 2. Perform assessment regarding needs of Spanish-speaking community members. 3. Provide staff training on cultural awareness, sensitivity, and service.

(Continued)

Figure 2.2. Successful Public Library Strategic Plan for 2011–2012 *(Continued)*		
GOALS	**OBJECTIVES**	**ACTIVITIES**
Goal 2 *(Continued)*	**Objective 2.1** *(Continued)*	**Activities** *(Continued)* 4. Revise current library policies that impact delivery of services for Spanish speakers. 5. Seek bilingual intern. 6. Make website accessible for Spanish speakers.
	Objective 2.2 Coordinate at least six programming activities per year for members of the Spanish-speaking community.	**Activities** 1. Investigate venues for providing programs outside the library for Spanish-speaking community. 2. Find a library liaison in the Spanish-speaking community. 3. Perform assessment regarding programming needs of Spanish-speaking community members. 4. Coordinate programs. 5. Evaluate effectiveness of programs.
Goal 3 The library successfully serves the lifelong learning, informational, and leisure needs of the community's mature adult population.	**Objective 3.1** By 2011, at least 40 percent of the total older adult population will be registered library borrowers.	**Activities** 1. Conduct promotion with incentives to sign up people over 55. 2. Assess all possible barriers in library for people over 55. 3. Evaluate library's ADA compliance. 4. Develop a plan to spotlight materials in areas of collection heavily used by older adults. 5. Conduct a needs assessment to determine lifelong learning, informational, and leisure needs of the mature adult population. 6. Incorporate results of needs assessment into library programming, services, and material selection.
	Objective 3.2 Participation in programs geared toward the mature adult population will increase by 80 percent by 2012.	**Activities** 1. Organize speakers for seminars on health and wellness, retirement, financial and legal issues, relationships and stress in retirement, working in retirement, leisure and volunteer pursuits, Social Security, and health insurance. 2. Plan programs that will meet the needs identified in older adults' needs assessment. 3. Spotlight library materials relating to programs. 4. Develop relationships with Senior Center, University's Lifelong Learning Department, Meals on Wheels, Senior Bus Tours, and other community organizations serving this population. 5. Collaborate and partner with other organizations to provide programs for older adults.

Discovering and Designing the Grant Project

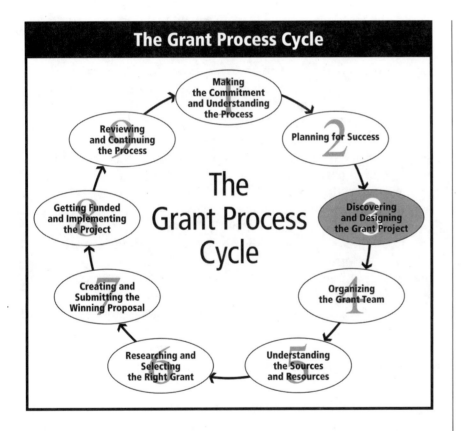

In Chapter 2 we discussed the planning process where you, other library staff, community members, partners, and stakeholders participated in assessing and analyzing the needs of your community and your organization, and you devised a strategic plan to meet those needs. You looked at the gaps between what your library currently offers and the desired results, and you decided which gaps you want to address in the time period covered by your plan. Then you developed and defined goals and specific, measurable, achievable, realistic, and time-bound objectives, and activities designed to close the gaps.

What Does Project Planning Have to Do with Getting Grants?

Discovering and designing your grant project and proposal writing are closely linked. Proposal writing does not stand alone or separately from project planning. As you define your project you will be designing (and sometimes even writing) your proposal. By planning your project before sitting down to write your proposal, you are ensuring that your project comes from your desire to meet real needs in your community, that you are working within the vision and mission of your organization, and that your project is an integral part of your library's strategic plan.

Attempting to write your grant proposal before planning your project puts the primary focus on getting the dollars, not on implementing a project that meets your community's needs. If you approach proposal writing this way, you may end up with a grant that does not address the needs of your community, or which is not tied to your organization's mission or planned path. Project planning based on your library's strategic plan not only orients you within the existing plans and mission of your organization, it will keep you focused on working to better the lives of people in your community. Remember: It's about the people, not the money.

It is essential that your projects emerge from your plan, as this is the groundwork and the foundation you have built to serve your community and its specific needs. Ideally, you have already done this planning, so all you need to do is pull the plan out and start working. This is not the time to begin thinking about organizational goals. If you have not done your strategic planning, consider stopping here and taking the time to do it. Going through the organizational planning process first will save you lots of time and headaches in the end and it will increase your chances of being funded. Planning first will ensure that you are developing projects that are in sync with your mission, projects that will benefit your community, and projects that include potential partners. Creating the plan first will decrease the chances that you will spend your valuable time on a project that has no real benefit to the community, does not include partners, and is not in line with your organizational goals.

The preliminary steps in the grant project design process encompass these elements:

1. The community needs assessment that identifies the areas that need change or improvement, or the problems to be solved in the community

2. The strategic plan that outlines the solutions—or goals, objectives, and activities—that you have identified for the period covered by the plan

3. Community input, the participation of stakeholders, and relationships with potential partners that have been established as a foundation for project planning and implementation

> Should you ask "Did your grant improve quality of life for your community and especially assist handicapped patrons?" we are able to respond with a resounding "YES!"
> —"New Library Signage"
> Columbia County Library, Magnolia, AR
> (see Library Grant Success Stories, pp. 148–149)

What Is a Grant Project?

For the purposes of this book, "grant project" is defined as a project of any kind for which you will be writing a proposal to seek grant funding from an outside source. In other resources you may see a grant project referred to as a "grant program." A grant project can be an equipment project, a capital project, a planning or implementation project, a research project, a model demonstration project, or a project for operating expenses, to name a few. At this point we are concentrating on discovering and designing your potential projects, regardless of what kind they are. In Chapter 5 we identify what kinds of projects you have developed as we look more closely at specific funding sources and what kinds of projects they fund. You will discover your grant projects by beginning to work with the goals, objectives, and activities in your strategic plan.

With your strategic plan in place, you now have what you need to design grant projects that are directly related to the library's plan. Because they come straight from your plan, these grant projects will inherently be mission driven and will be designed to meet specific identified needs in your community.

The Project Planning Process

Step 1: Clarify Your Library's Goals, Objectives, and Activities

Placing your library's goals, objectives, and activities into a chart will help you see them clearly. It will also serve as a starting point for the project planning team to understand them, and it will quickly orient project planning team members who may not be very familiar with the library's strategic plan. Figure 3.1 shows some sample Goals, Objectives, and Activities taken from the Successful Public Library's strategic plan developed in Chapter 2 (see Figure 2.2).

Use the Strategic Plan Goals, Objectives, and Activities Template in the Toolkit on pages 196–197 to chart your organization's goals, objectives, and activities from your plan.

Step 2: Form a Project Planning Team

Next, convene a project planning team of creative thinkers that includes library staff, community members, potential partners, local business-people, and other stakeholders. Include people from potential partner organizations who you think may be participating in implementing a community project in which the library could be a partner. If you are in a large organization, you may want to create more than one project planning team, one for each organizational goal. These teams will include different people with different areas of expertise or community involvement depending on the goal with which they are working. If you are in a small library, a team of two people may be sufficient. Try to

	Figure 3.1. Sample Goals, Objectives, and Activities, Successful Public Library, 2010–2012 Strategic Plan	
Sample Goals	**Sample Objectives**	**Sample Activities**
Goal 1 The Successful Public Library's resources and services are easily accessed and meet the diverse and changing information needs of our customers.	**Objective 1.1** During 2010 the library will increase programming to help people in tough economic times by 100 percent.	1. Provide programming on finding employment online. 2. Provide training in completing online applications. 3. Provide training in preparing résumés using technology. 4. Reallocate staff time to provide training and plan programming. 5. Partner with Workforce Training Center, Unemployment Office, One Stop Employment Center, and area employers.
	Objective 1.2 By 2012, 20 percent more library customers will indicate their information needs were met during a library visit.	1. Develop responsive collection development plan. 2. Increase number of public Internet workstations. 3. Develop subject-specific workshops on finding information. 4. Develop standardized research guides on popular topics. 5. Update current information literacy program to include critical inquiry and website evaluation. 6. Provide instruction on the use of online catalog and research databases. 7. Survey library customers when leaving the library/library website as to whether they found something that met their needs.
	Objective 1.3 By 2012, library customers will be able to meet 50 percent more information needs and requests online.	1. Investigate how to serve customers online and implement new web tools. 2. Reallocate staff to better serve online customers. 3. Redesign library website to better serve customer needs. 4. Improve website user interface. 5. Regularly update website. 6. Develop current resource link page. 7. Survey library customers when leaving the library/library website as to whether they found something that met their needs.
Goal 2 Spanish-speaking community members are able to find information and resources, and pursue learning opportunities.	**Objective 2.1** By 2012, evaluate and improve the library's ability to serve Spanish-speaking customers.	1. Allocate funds to support collecting English as a second language and Spanish-language materials, and provide interpreters. 2. Perform assessment regarding needs of Spanish-speaking community members. 3. Provide staff training on cultural awareness, sensitivity, and service. 4. Revise current library policies that impact delivery of services for Spanish speakers. 5. Seek bilingual intern. 6. Make website accessible for Spanish speakers.

(Continued)

Figure 3.1. Sample Goals, Objectives, and Activities, Successful Public Library, 2010–2012 Strategic Plan *(Continued)*		
Sample Goals	**Sample Objectives**	**Sample Activities**
Goal 2 *(Continued)*	**Objective 2.2** Coordinate at least six programming activities per year from 2010–2012 for members of the Spanish-speaking community.	1. Investigate venues for providing programs outside the library for Spanish-speaking community. 2. Find a library liaison in the Spanish-speaking community. 3. Perform assessment regarding programming needs of Spanish-speaking community members. 4. Coordinate programs. 5. Evaluate effectiveness of programs.
Goal 3 The library successfully serves the lifelong learning, informational, and leisure needs of the community's mature adult population.	**Objective 3.1** By 2011, at least 40 percent of the adult population over 55 will be registered library borrowers.	1. Conduct promotion with incentives to sign up people over 55. 2. Assess all possible barriers in library for people over 55. 3. Evaluate library's ADA compliance. 4. Develop a plan to spotlight materials in areas of collection heavily used by older adults. 5. Conduct a needs assessment to determine lifelong learning, informational, and leisure needs of the mature adult population. 6. Incorporate results of needs assessment into library programming, services, and material selection.
	Objective 3.2 Participation in programs geared toward mature adult population will increase by 80 percent by 2012.	1. Organize speakers for seminars on health and wellness, retirement, financial and legal issues, relationships and stress in retirement, working in retirement, leisure and volunteer pursuits, Social Security and health insurance. 2. Plan programs that will meet the needs identified in older adults' needs assessment. 3. Spotlight library materials relating to programs. 4. Develop relationships with Senior Center, University's Lifelong Learning Department, Meals on Wheels, Senior Bus Tours, and other community organizations serving this population. 5. Collaborate and partner with other organizations to provide programs for older adults.

include one person from outside the library, preferably from another organization or agency in your community, a potential partner or a prominent business leader. It is sometimes difficult to think creatively about new project ideas on a team consisting of all library staff who see each other daily and deal with the same issues continuously.

More about Including Potential Partners

It is very important to include potential partners from the very beginning in the project planning process. Ideas from potential partners are invaluable as you discover new projects. These people tend to look at things from a different angle and they may even tell you about related activities they are already doing in the community that you may not know about. This information can help to shape the project planning process, and is likely to save you time and effort in the long run. By including potential partners from the community in project planning, you will decrease your chances of developing an idea that has already been planned or is already being done by another organization or agency in your community. In addition, partners can build on your ideas during the planning stages, bringing a dimension to your projects that you may never consider without their perspective, knowledge, talents, and resources.

If your partners are participating in planning library projects from the beginning, you will not have to go out into the community later to convince them to join you in an idea that library staff has already planned. Also, if they are in on creating the project from the beginning, they will already have ownership without lots of extra effort on your part. Funders across the board are looking for partnerships and collaborations among community organizations in grant applications. In difficult economic times, this is likely to become increasingly important. This is because funders know their dollars will go much farther if more than one organization is involved in developing and implementing a project. They also know that a project is more likely to make a difference in the lives of people and that it is more likely to be sustainable when more than one organization (and more people) is committed to making it work.

Of course, it is impossible to predict who the ideal partners will be for your projects before you have even planned them. Use your best judgment based on what you know about your organization's goals and objectives, projects already going on in your community, other organizations doing activities in the community that might combine well with potential library projects, and business and organizational leaders who are likely to be good partners and with whom your library already has good relationships. If you discover during the project planning process that you have overlooked potential partners, invite them into the process right away.

Step 3: Start the Project Planning Process

The project planning process must be facilitated. Someone needs to be responsible for leading the team through the process of discovering and designing the project. It could be a member of the library staff who was instrumental in the strategic planning process, or if you have the funds, you could hire an outside consultant to facilitate this process. In general, planning is easier, more efficient and effective when an objective third person is responsible for keeping things on track. It is very difficult to facilitate and participate at the same time; however, if you do not have enough staff or money for a separate facilitator, this can be done. Just be aware of the pitfalls and appoint someone who can play the two roles without confusing them. If you are a one- or two-person library, you can share facilitating. In short, this process cannot be left to the

> Our partners were extraordinarily valuable and brought a unique element of creativity to the project. With many people focused on one objective, outstanding projects, programs, and events were conceived and multiple avenues to reach the intended audience were created.
>
> —"Get Graphic: Building Literacy and Community with Graphic Novels" Buffalo & Erie County Public Library, Buffalo, NY
> (see Library Grant Success Stories, pp. 152–155)

free-flowing organic method and be expected to conclude with a project plan. Project planning is a focused and purposeful activity.

At the first meeting distribute copies of your library's Strategic Plan Goals, Objectives and Activities Chart to all team members. (This is the Strategic Plan Goals, Objectives, and Activities Template in the Toolkit on pp. 196–197 that you completed in Step 1.) The team's first task is to understand the library's vision, mission, service responses to the community, goals, objectives, and activities. It may be necessary to share some background information about the community needs assessment and how the goals were determined, for those team members who were not involved in the strategic planning process.

Make it clear to the team that their purpose is to plan one or more projects from the goals, objectives, and activities in the plan. These are projects that the library may work on over the next few years as ways to accomplish the goals established in the plan. If any of these projects require supplemental funding they may become grant projects. Encourage brainstorming and creativity, but keep the parameters of the projects you plan within the scope of the library's strategic plan.

The team's ultimate goal is to develop specific projects using the goals, objectives, and activities in your library's plan. Your goal is not to tackle all the elements in your plan by thinking up projects for them all. You may want to come up with one or several small projects rather than one large project. As you work with the smaller projects, try combining several into one larger project. It is much easier to grow a project than to shrink it. Also, your project can accomplish more and be a bigger difference in people's lives this way.

Step 4: Discover the Project Idea and Goals

Make this a fun activity for the whole team. Have flip charts, colored index cards, markers, scissors, favors, or prizes for the best ideas, or group activities, for example. Move around. Brainstorm. Try dividing the larger group into smaller groups of three or four. Maybe you could assign each group a goal, and then tell them they can draw from any objective or activity to accomplish the goal. Give team members permission to expand or alter the objectives and create new activities for the purposes of this process, as long as they still address reaching the goals and objectives stated in the plan. Try to remove any barriers that you think may be restricting this process without compromising the library's strategic plan. Remember to record all ideas and compile them into one document for team members to use in future meetings as they work through project ideas. Have fun!

An example project idea developed from Successful Public Library's goals, objectives, and activities that we charted in Step 1 appears in the sidebar.

Developing the "Your Library for Life" Project Idea

Next, let's work on some project goals, objectives, and activities. Every project must have a goal. The goal is the accomplishment you seek. Ask

---

EXAMPLE PROJECT IDEA

From the Successful Public Library's Goals, Objectives, and Activities (charted in Step 1):

Your Library for Life Project Idea
The Successful Public Library in partnership with the Successful Senior Center, the Successful University Lifelong Learning Department and the Successful Computer Users Group will focus on serving mature adult community members. This project will: assess their needs, recruit these community members as library users, develop the collection in topics of interest to them, provide programs and seminars based on their needs, and develop curriculum and offer classes on the availability and use of information technology and databases in the Successful Public Library on the Library's website.

yourself what you are seeking to accomplish. How do you want your services, situation, or community to change as a result of your efforts? It is important not to confuse goals with organizational mission or vision. The goal must be consistent with your mission and vision but at the same time be program specific.

Any or all the goals in the Successful Public Library's strategic plan could be used to develop a goal for the Your Library for Life Project. By addressing the target population—mature adults—within your library's existing goals, you can easily develop potential project goals. Your project can incorporate any or all of the goals from your library plan, and you can also develop other project goals as long as they are within the framework of your library's plan. At this point it is worthwhile to develop some "working" project goals so you can stay focused on developing and designing a manageable project. You can always come back to these goals and rework them if necessary or replace them with new ones you missed the first time around.

For the purposes of illustrating the process, let's choose some "working" project goals:

1. Mature adult community members will easily access the library's resources and services.

2. The library is responsive to the changing information needs of mature adults in the community.

3. The library successfully serves the lifelong learning, informational, and leisure needs of the community's mature adult population.

Step 5: Define the Project Outcomes

The Importance of Outcomes

As you begin to discover your project ideas, it is important to think about outcomes. Outcomes are used to identify a change in behavior, attitude, skill, life condition, or knowledge in the people served by the project, and they reflect the long-term impact a project is making toward solving a community problem or toward improving the lives of the people it serves. Most funders require applicants to state the outcomes of their project in the proposal. The fact that a library proposes to provide assistive technology, Spanish-language materials, after-school programs, information technology training, or any other services is admirable—but the funder wants to know that those services will make a difference in the lives of the people who are served, and how they will make a difference. You want to make sure that the project will not only address or solve a problem in the community by changing the behavior, attitude, or knowledge of the people served by the project but also how your project will accomplish these things and to what degree. This is not only good practice; it also makes good sense.

From the preliminary project planning stage and throughout the planning process, continue to ask yourself these questions:

1. How will the project help to solve a problem or meet a need in the community?

2. How will the project improve the lives of the people we serve?

3. How will people's behavior, attitude, or knowledge change as a result of the project?

Asking these questions of yourself periodically will help you to focus on why this project is needed in your community. Staying grounded in the difference it will make for your community is essential. It is not uncommon for personal wants and desires to sneak in during the planning process, and checking in with these questions is a good way to keep all team members together on the right track.

If you do not clarify your project outcomes from the outset, it will be impossible to build them in later, when you are preparing your grant proposal. So, let's develop some desired outcomes for Your Library for Life.

Remember, outcomes identify a change in behavior, attitude, or knowledge in the people served by the project. As we think about outcomes for this project, we might want to focus on a particular subject or topic of interest to mature adults, address a specific segment of information technology, or work on the library's website usability for mature adults. Some desired outcomes for this project idea might be as follows:

1. The ability of mature adult community members to research their questions using information technology in the library will increase their ability to make informed choices.

2. Mature adult community members will be knowledgeable about the information technology available in the library, and they will know how to use it to improve their quality of life.

3. Mature adults in the community will be able to use the library's website to find information that will improve their quality of life.

4. Mature adult customers will gain knowledge as a result of library programs and seminars that will improve their condition.

More about the Definitions of Outcomes and Objectives

Outcomes and objectives present a unique challenge. Funders do not always use the same definitions when it comes to outcomes and objectives. The definitions for Goals, Outcomes, Objectives, and Activities or Action Steps can vary widely by funder. What one funder considers an outcome another may consider an objective. In some cases your goal may actually be an outcome. Remember that you are trying to identify a desired change and measure that change, regardless of what the funder calls it. Proposal writers who fail to recognize the difference in how funders define terms may be unsuccessful because they present this information incorrectly.

While the definitions of goals, outcomes, and objectives may vary by funder, you can manage these differences by investigating a little further. If a funder uses an example, follow it back to your own goals, outcomes, and objectives. Use the funder's language and definitions for the purposes of submitting your proposal. If you have done all the work to this point it is fairly simple to label proposal elements differently to comply with the funder's guidelines. If you are not sure about a funder's definitions, contact the funder and ask.

Step 6: Plan Your Project

Now it's time to plan your project. Start using the Project Planning Worksheet on page 198 in the Toolkit to help you develop your project ideas. Based on the planning we have done so far, try working on #1–#7. Make sure that these elements tie back to your library's plan, vision, and mission. It is not necessary to complete the worksheet for each project idea at this point. Don't spend too much time on perfecting the worksheet. It is meant to facilitate the planning process, help you work out some of the details, record your ideas, and test their feasibility. Think of it as a project outline tool. Use a new Project Planning Worksheet for each new project idea. Figure 3.2 illustrates a Sample Project Planning Worksheet for Your Library for Life.

Figure 3.2. Sample Project Planning Worksheet

Your Library for Life

1. Project Description: Describe your project in one sentence. Include what you will do, where, why, and with whom.	The Successful Public Library in partnership with the Successful Senior Center, the Successful University Lifelong Learning Department and the Successful Computer Users Group will focus on serving mature adult community members. This project will: assess their needs, recruit these community members as library users, develop the collection in topics of interest to them, provide programs and seminars based on their needs, and develop curriculum and offer classes on the availability and use of information technology and databases in the Successful Public Library on the Library's website.	
2. Keywords: List keywords that describe your project.	Mature adults Seniors Aging Information technology Computers Website Online	Community Library Public awareness Curriculum Classes Training Economy
3. Needs Statement: Describe the need in your community or the problem your project will address.	Lack of awareness of library's information technology services and resources among the mature adult community; lack of library programming for this population; increased need for information among this population in hard economic times.	
4. Target Audience: Identify target audience for the project.	Mature adult community members over 55	
5. Project Goals: What are the goals of the project?	By addressing library services for mature adult community members this project will: 1. Facilitate access to the library's resources and services by mature adult customers. 2. Respond to the lifelong learning, leisure, and changing information needs of the community's mature adult population.	

(Continued)

Figure 3.2. Sample Project Planning Worksheet *(Continued)*	
Your Library for Life	
6. **Project Objectives**: What are the specific changes you expect to make in your community or among the beneficiaries of your project?	1. 20 percent more mature adults will find information that meets their needs during a visit to the library or the library's website. 2. Mature adult library customers will be able to meet 50 percent more of their information needs and requests online. 3. 85 percent of mature adult community members will find library services valuable and applicable to their lives. 4. 25 percent more mature adult community members will determine that library programming designed to help them in tough economic times improved their quality of life. 5. 40 percent of the adult population over 55 will be registered library borrowers.
7. **Project Outcomes**: What are the expected changes in people's behavior, attitude, or knowledge? How will the project improve the lives of people? How will the project impact a community problem?	1. The ability of mature adult community members to research their questions using information technology in the library will increase their ability to make informed choices. 2. Mature adult community members will be knowledgeable about the information technology available in the library, and they will know how to use it to improve their quality of life. 3. Mature adults in the community will be able to use the library's website to find information that will improve their quality of life. 4. Mature adult customers will gain knowledge as a result of library programs and seminars that will improve their condition.
8. **Project Action Steps**: List the steps required to make the changes listed above. Develop activities or strategies required to reach an objective. How are you going to solve this problem?	*See* **SAMPLE PROJECT ACTION STEPS** (Figure 3.3).
9. **Resources Needed**: List the resources you will need to accomplish the steps. What resources do you already have?	Computer lab Telephones Meeting rooms Copier Office supplies Projector Staff Partners
10. **Project Budget**: The cost of the project.	*See* **SAMPLE PROJECT BUDGETS** (Figures 3.5 and 3.6).
11. **Partners and Collaborators**: List your partners on this project. Who else is addressing this problem in our community? Who is likely to partner with us on this project?	Successful Senior Center Successful University Lifelong Learning Department Successful Computer Users Group
12. **Evaluation**: Describe how you will measure your success. How will things be different or what will the improvement be?	*See* **SAMPLE PROJECT EVALUATION PLAN** (Figure 3.8).

Source: Form adapted from Project Profile/Planning Worksheet, JUST GRANTS! Arizona.

Step 7: Develop Project Objectives

You must design specific, measurable, achievable, realistic, and time-bound objectives that specifically address your project outcomes. You may find that you can use objectives already developed in your strategic plan; however, it is more likely that your project objectives will be a subset or adaptation of the objectives in your library's plan.

Going back to the library's strategic plan, your "working" project goals and established outcomes, ask yourself how you will demonstrate that Your Library for Life was a success. For instance, how will you show that as a result (or outcome) of the project more mature adult library customers will be able to find something that meets their information needs during a visit to the library or the library's website? A possible objective that would demonstrate this outcome is this:

- 20 percent more mature adults will find information that meets their needs during a visit to the library or the library's website.

Other possible objectives for this project include these:

- Mature adult library customers will be able to meet 50 percent more of their information needs and requests online.
- 85 percent of mature adult community members will find library services valuable and applicable to their lives.
- 25 percent more mature adult community members will determine that library programming designed to help them in tough economic times improved their quality of life.
- 40 percent of the adult population over 55 will be registered library borrowers.

Look at your project outcomes, develop your project objectives, and record them on your Project Planning Worksheet. Eventually you will use the objectives to design your evaluation methodology.

Step 8: Define Project Action Steps

Now it is time to develop the action steps that will accomplish your project's objectives and produce the desired outcomes. Review the "working" project goals, and sample project objectives and outcomes from the Project Planning Worksheet for Your Library for Life.

Here are a few possible project Action Steps designed to achieve the sample project goals, objectives, and outcomes:

- Conduct a needs assessment and ongoing focus groups with seniors to determine their current and changing information needs.
- Recruit older adults as library customers.
- Assess physical and psychological barriers in the library for mature adults and evaluate the library's ADA compliance.
- Spotlight library materials in areas heavily used by older adults.

- Develop a collection development plan that is responsive to current topics of interest to mature adults and accommodates their needs.
- Organize speakers, workshops, and programs for seniors on topics of interest to them and important to their quality of life.
- Develop curriculum and implement classes to teach mature adult community members about how to use information technology to find what they need in the library and on the library's website.
- Develop standardized research guides on topics of interest to mature adults.
- Incorporate features on the library's website to accommodate mature adult library customers.
- Cooperate actively with other community agencies serving mature adults to share resources and provide services.
- Conduct pre- and post-tests, surveys, and other evaluation methods to measure progress of project.

Note that these action steps are either taken directly from activities in the Successful Public Library's Strategic Plan (see Figure 2.2); adapted from activities in the plan; or enhance activities already in the plan. Figure 3.3 illustrates some possible objectives, action steps that will help to achieve them, and what personnel will be responsible for implementing the action steps for Your Library for Life.

What are some action steps that might accomplish your project goal through your stated objectives and result in the outcomes you have

Figure 3.3. Sample Project Action Steps

Your Library for Life

Project Objectives	Personnel	Action Steps
20 percent more mature adults will find information that meets their needs during a visit to the library or the library's website.	Reference Librarian Librarian	Develop curriculum. Teach classes. Design pre- and post-surveys. Develop standardized research guides.
	Library Assistant	Update and enhance links on website. Advertise classes.
	Library Technician	Schedule classes. Reserve computer classroom. Register people for classes. Implement pre- and post-surveys.
	Circulation Clerk	Track statistics.

(Continued)

Figure 3.3. Sample Project Action Steps *(Continued)*		
Your Library for Life		
Project Objectives	**Personnel**	**Action Steps**
Mature adult library customers will be able to meet 50 percent more of their information needs and requests online.	Reference Librarian	Develop curriculum. Teach classes. Design pre- and post-tests/surveys. Incorporate web features.
	Library Assistant	Advertise classes. Advertise information technology resources and services.
	Library Technician	Schedule classes. Reserve computer classroom. Register people for classes.
	Circulation Clerk	Track computer usage. Track statistics.
85 percent of mature adult community members will find library services valuable and applicable to their lives.	Reference Librarian	Develop a plan to spotlight library materials in areas heavily used by older adults. Conduct a needs assessment. Conduct focus groups.
	Library Director	Develop a collection development plan.
	Library Assistant	Hold focus groups.
25 percent more mature adult community members will determine that library programming designed to help them in tough economic times improved their quality of life.	Library Director	Collaborate and partner.
	Reference Librarian	Plan programs. Design pre- and post-tests/surveys.
	Library Technician	Schedule programs. Reserve meeting rooms. Register participants. Advertise programs.
40 percent of the adult population over 55 will be registered library borrowers.	Library Director	Develop a public awareness plan and marketing strategy.
	Library Assistant	Recruit older adults. Hold public awareness activities.
	Reference Librarian	Assess barriers. Evaluate ADA compliance.
	Library Technician	Create a brochure. Create advertisement. Offer incentives or prizes.

identified? Use the Project Action Steps Template on page 199 in the Toolkit to define your project's action steps. As you complete this form, think about who will be doing the action steps, and enter the position name in the Personnel column. Feel free to come up with new ideas that are specific to your project. It's okay to brainstorm here; however, make sure any new ideas relate back to the goals and objectives in your strategic plan. In your grant proposal, the action steps and who will do them will become your methodology, strategy, or approach. This information also becomes the basis for your timeline.

Step 9: Do the Research

As you are planning your project, read about other projects like yours that have already been done. Take notes and collect this research. Based on the experiences or products of others, you may want to alter your project. It makes sense to build on what others have done. If there are curricula already in place that will meet your project's needs, use them. If another community like yours had success reaching a similar target population, learn from their successes—and failures. Build this experience and research into your project plan. It will be more viable, be more likely to succeed, and have a better chance of being sustainable. Call or e-mail the manager of a project like the one you are considering and ask him or her to share experiences. Conversely, know the pitfalls of projects like yours and build in preventative measures.

Include this information in your grant proposal. It shows the funder that you are well informed about what has already been done in the field and that you are knowledgeable about best practices. Extrapolate your outcomes to the outcomes documented in the literature. For instance, "Based on the results of XYZ Library, we have chosen to take ABC approach in our community." The funder wants to know that you will not be doing something that has already been tried without success. Let the funder know that you have educated yourself and you are in familiar territory.

Step 10: Make a Project Timeline

Timelines are project-planning tools that are used to represent the timing of tasks required to complete a project. They are easy to understand and construct, and most project managers use them to track the progress of a project.

There are many ways to construct timelines. For our purposes each action step takes up one row in a simple table. Dates run along the top row, heading columns representing days, weeks, or months, depending on the total length of the project. The expected time for each task is represented by checkmarks or horizontal bars marking the expected beginning and end of the task. Tasks may run sequentially, at the same time, or overlap each other. Include the personnel responsible for each action step. Use the Project Timeline Template on page 200 in the Toolkit to create a timeline for your project.

In constructing a timeline, keep the tasks to a manageable number (no more than 15 or 20) so that the chart fits on a single page. If your project is complex it may require subcharts and subtasks. This timeline can go directly into your grant proposal for this project. Figure 3.4 illustrates a timeline using the action steps we developed for Your Library for Life.

Figure 3.4. Sample Project Timeline

Your Library for Life

Action Steps	Personnel	Jan	Feb	Mar	Apr	May	June	July	Aug	Sept	Oct	Nov	Dec
Conduct needs assessment.	Library Director (LD)	➤											
Hold focus groups.	Library Assistant (LA)	➤											
Create brochures/advertisements.	LA		➤	➤	➤								
Develop standardized research guides.	Reference Librarian (RL)			➤	➤								
Hold public awareness activities.	LA			➤	➤	➤	➤	➤	➤	➤			
Design pre- and post-surveys/tests.	RL	➤	➤										
Plan programs.	RL				➤	➤	➤						
Coordinate programs.	Library Technician (LT)						➤	➤	➤	➤	➤	➤	
Implement pre/post-surveys.	LA			➤	➤	➤	➤				➤	➤	
Assess barriers/ADA.	RL	➤											
Track statistics/computer usage.	Circulation Clerk (CC)		➤	➤	➤	➤	➤	➤	➤	➤	➤	➤	➤
Develop curriculum.	RL	➤	➤					➤	➤				
Teach classes.	RL			➤	➤	➤	➤			➤	➤		
Schedule classes./Reserve computer classroom.	LA		➤	➤	➤	➤	➤			➤	➤	➤	
Advertise classes.	CC		➤	➤	➤	➤	➤	➤	➤	➤	➤	➤	
Register people for classes.	LA		➤	➤	➤	➤	➤	➤	➤	➤	➤		
Update website.	LA	➤	➤										
Project management.	RL	➤	➤	➤	➤	➤	➤	➤	➤	➤	➤	➤	➤

Step 11: Develop a Project Budget

Personnel Budget

Using your timeline and activity worksheets, figure out the personnel and FTE required for your project in the following way.

1. Select one position and determine the activities that position will do.

   For instance, for our sample project, Your Library for Life, the Library Assistant will:

   - Prepare handouts and research guides
   - Schedule speakers, workshops, and programs
   - Implement pre- and post-surveys
   - Calculate survey results
   - Record focus groups
   - Register people for classes

2. Determine the amount of time the position will be spending on these activities over the duration of the project and calculate the cost of the salary to cover that amount of time.

   For example, the Library Assistant will be doing the above activities throughout the entire 12-month period of the project, and we can estimate that this will take the Library Assistant an average of eight hours a week. Since the Library Assistant works 40 hours a week, this is one-fifth, or .20 FTE of the Library Assistant's time. The Library Assistant's full-time salary is $30,000 per year; therefore, the cost to the project for the Library Assistant's salary is $6,000.

3. Calculate the cost of benefits for your project personnel, and make sure to add that cost to the project budget. Your personnel department will be able to tell you this figure or percentage.

   For example, if the cost of benefits to the organization is 23 percent of the employee's salary, for .20 ($6,000) of the Library Assistant's salary, that is $1,380. Therefore, the total cost to the project for the .20 FTE Library Assistant for the 12-month duration of the project is $6,000 (salary) + $1,380 (benefits) = $7,380.

Go through the same process for all project personnel. Then create a personnel budget for your project using the Personnel Budget Template on page 201 in the Toolkit. Don't forget to include fringe benefit costs for all personnel, and make sure to include or designate a project manager. Figure 3.5 shows a Personnel Budget for Your Library for Life.

Cautionary Note: If library staff will be working as project personnel, you must decrease their current job duties and responsibilities to allow for the additional project duties they will be taking on before they begin working on the funded project. For instance, if the Library Assistant above currently works a 40-hour week, he already has job duties that take 40 hours a week to do. You must take away some of those job

Figure 3.5. Sample Personnel Budget			
Your Library for Life			
Position	**Salary**	**Benefits (23%)**	**Total**
.05 FTE Library Director	$3,750.00	$862.50	$4,612.50
.20 FTE Library Assistant	$6,000.00	$1,380.00	$7,380.00
.30 FTE Reference Librarian	$15,000.00	$3,450.00	$18,450.00
.05 FTE Circulation Clerk	$1,350.00	$310.50	$1,660.50
.25 Library Technician	$6,750.00	$1,552.50	$8,302.50
TOTAL PERSONNEL COSTS	**$32,850.00**	**$7,555.50**	**$40,405.50**

> When asked what she would do differently, Karen Yother, Youth Service Coordinator responded, "I would ask for more staff. We hit the ground running and could have used at least 2 more staff to run this program."
>
> —"From Your Library" Kootenai-Shoshone Area Libraries, Hayden, ID (see Library Grant Success Stories, pp. 184–185)

> The most difficult part of the grant process was estimating how much money to request for signage. In addition, it was necessary to anticipate every single kind of sign we would need in an eight-sided library lobby.
>
> —"New Library Signage" Columbia County Library, Magnolia, AR (see Library Grant Success Stories, pp. 148–149)

duties (by delegating to other staff or hiring another staff person) so they can add the additional project duties. You cannot simply pile more work on a person who is already working a full-time job. This can be a setup for failure (for the project and for the staff member), and will ensure that a staff person will not want to participate in any more library grant projects in the future. Expecting staff to assume additional work because a project is funded is a common pitfall that must be avoided. This practice also sends a message to the larger organization that you will pile more work on your staff without compensating them. When things get tough economically, they will remember the library as a place to save money by reducing staff because the remaining staff will be happy to do more work without being compensated.

Non-personnel Budget

Next, determine the cost for items other than personnel such as marketing, equipment, space rental, and supplies. Develop a Non-personnel Budget for your project using the Non-personnel Budget Template on page 202 in the Toolkit. See Figure 3.6 for a sample Non-personnel Budget for Your Library for Life.

Create your project budget by combining the Personnel Budget and the Non-personnel Budget, and add the total costs from each to determine the total project cost. Record the total cost of your project in #9 on your Project Planning Worksheet.

Incorporating Match and In-Kind Funding into the Budget

When your library, your partners, or other grants have already committed funds, personnel, equipment, space, or other items to support a project, it is important to include this information in your project budget. This serves several purposes: (1) you can easily see what parts of your project have already been funded and what parts have not yet been funded; (2) it will be easier to spot a funding opportunity when you know the amount you need and exactly what it will fund; and (3) you can pitch

Figure 3.6. Sample Non-personnel Budget		
Your Library for Life		
Item	**Description**	**Cost**
Marketing		
Brochure	10,000 for $1,000.00	$2,000.00
Newspaper ads	$90.00 for quarter page x 6	$540.00
Equipment		
Projector		$3,000.00
Copying Costs		
Handouts, research guides	5,000 @ $.05/copy	$250.00
Supplies		
Prizes		$200.00
Office supplies	$50.00/month x 12	$600.00
Printer cartridges	100 @ $30.00 each	$3,000.00
Paper	100 reams @ $2.00/ream	$200.00
Space Rental		
Computer classroom	600 sq. ft. @ $200.00/month x 12	$2,400.00
TOTAL NON-PERSONNEL COSTS		**$12,190.00**
TOTAL PERSONNEL COSTS		**$40,405.50**
TOTAL PROJECT COST		**$52,595.50**

your project idea in the community, focusing on the portion you still need to fund. If you have multiple sources of funding like this, it will be helpful to create a "working" budget that incorporates them all (see sample in Figure 3.7). Eventually, when you submit a budget with your proposal it will need to show all the sources of funding for your project.

Step 12: Create an Evaluation Plan

You must now determine how you will measure the effectiveness of your project in reaching your stated objectives and outcomes. How will you measure your progress? How will you measure your successes? How will you measure a change in behavior? How will you decide what adjustments need to be made to facilitate the success of your project as it progresses?

It is important to understand why you must conduct an evaluation and why an evaluation plan is a necessary part of your project plan.

Figure 3.7. Sample Working Budget

Your Library for Life

PERSONNEL BUDGET

Position	Total Cost	Match	Amount Requested
.05 FTE Library Director	$4,612.50	$4,612.50	
.20 FTE Library Assistant	$7,380.00		$7,380.00
.30 FTE Reference Librarian	$18,450.00	$9,225.00	$9,225.00
.05 FTE Circulation Clerk	$1,660.50		$1,660.50
.25 Library Technician	$8,302.50	$4,151.25	$4,151.25
TOTAL PERSONNEL COSTS	**$40,405.50**	**$17,988.75**	**$22,416.75**

NON-PERSONNEL BUDGET

Item	Total Cost	Match	Amount Requested
Marketing	$2,540.00		$2,540.00
Equipment	$3,000.00		$3,000.00
Copying Costs	$250.00	$250.00	
Supplies	$4,000.00	$2,000.00	$2,000.00
Space Rental	$2,400.00		$2,400.00
TOTAL NON-PERSONNEL COSTS	**$12,190.00**	**$2,250.00**	**$9,940.00**
TOTAL PROJECT COSTS	**$52,595.50**	**$20,238.75**	**$32,356.75**

Projects are undertaken to have an impact. Evaluations are conducted to show the success of a project's impact, and they can also point out improvements you can make in the project design.

Evaluation Types

Some funders prefer that you conduct evaluations throughout the life of the project rather than (or in addition to) evaluating the project at its end. These are called formative evaluations. The theory is that ongoing evaluations will enable project staff to measure the success of the project while it is being carried out and make needed adjustments throughout the life of the project to ensure its overall success. Some funders ask for one evaluation at the very end of the project that reports all accomplishments. This is known as a summative evaluation and stresses the outcome of the project.

A quantitative evaluation answers the question, "How much did you do?" Examples include: how many people attended a class, what skills did students learn, what was the cost to the project per student? Quantitative evaluations require obtaining and analyzing data over a large number of cases. Methods for collecting quantitative data include pre-tests and post-tests, questionnaires and surveys. Qualitative evaluations tell the project's story by communicating the participant's stories. They collect and examine data in greater depth on a smaller scale. Qualitative methods include interviews, case studies, observation, and documentation reviews telling what happened when, to whom, and with what consequences.

Your funder may require you to conduct only a summative evaluation at the end of the project. Don't limit your evaluation to the type required by the funder. Decide on an evaluation approach that serves the needs of your customers and that will best measure the success of your particular project. For some projects, you might want to conduct formative and summative evaluations, or qualitative and quantitative evaluations.

Outcome-Based Evaluation

Outcome-based evaluation (OBE) is an evaluation methodology that many government agencies and larger organizations have increasingly adopted for their programs and focuses on measuring the effect of a project on the people it serves (outcomes) rather than on services (outputs). Outcome-based evaluation methods can be used at many points in a project to provide indicators of a project's effectiveness, and they provide a greater degree of public accountability. Critical feedback is given about what is working, what needs to be changed, and how a program can be improved.

Outcome-based evaluation measures results, making observations that demonstrate change, and systematically collects information about specific indicators to show the extent to which a project achieves its goals.

As you recall, an outcome is a measure of change that benefits the people served by your project, such as achievements or changes in skill, knowledge, attitude, behavior, condition, or life status. Examples of outcomes include the following:

1. Library customers will know about the electronic resources available in the library. (Change in knowledge)

2. Teen library users will view the library as a place to attend rock concerts and gaming events. (Change in attitude)

3. Assistive technology will enable people with disabilities to use library resources to improve their quality of life. (Change in condition)

4. Mature adult customers will use library computers to stay in touch with family and friends. (Change in behavior)

5. The ability of the unemployed to find jobs will be increased due to job-finding resources in the library. (Change in life status)

Methods for Collecting Evaluation Information and Data

Your objectives themselves will determine the types of information you need to collect. For instance, if an objective states that 20 percent more mature adults will find information that meets their needs during a visit

> Planning programs is easy for librarians. Evaluating programs in a meaningful way was much harder. Outcome-based evaluation helped us focus on the long-term measurements and success of our series.
> —"Neighbors Connecting" Ocean County Library, Toms River, NJ (see Library Grant Success Stories, pp. 150–151)

to the library or the library's website, you will have to ask mature adult library visitors if they found the information they needed as they leave the library or website. In this case a survey or questionnaire is the most appropriate tool for collecting this information.

There are many ways to collect evaluation information and data. Evaluation instruments can include questionnaires and surveys; interviews; documentation review; observation; focus groups; or case studies. It is important to use the proper evaluation instrument to measure your results. Decide which measurement instrument is most appropriate to get the strongest data specific to your project objectives.

Questionnaires or Surveys

You can get much information quickly and easily from many people in a non-threatening way using questionnaires and surveys. People can complete them anonymously, they are inexpensive to administer, and you can administer them to many people. It is easy for you to compare and analyze results and you can get lots of data. Information gathered from surveys is only as good as the questions you ask, so you might want to consult an experienced surveyor as you design the questions. There are many survey and questionnaire instruments that have already been designed that you can use as templates; however, make sure to customize them to your project. The shorter a survey is, the easier it will be for a busy customer to complete. Be sure to provide confidentiality to your survey participants. Reassuring your participants that their survey responses will be kept confidential and anonymous might help improve your response rates. Usually, asking participants to reveal their personal information like name, address, and phone number on a survey will reduce response rates.

Interviews

Use interviews when you want to fully understand someone's impressions or experiences, or learn more about their answers in surveys or question-naires. Interviews give you the opportunity to get the full range and depth of information, they give you the opportunity to develop a rapport with the interviewee, and you can be flexible with your questioning. This method provides subjective data since it is based on opinions that may not reflect the true success of the project. It is a very time-consuming process, but it may yield future partners and project ideas. Interviews can add valuable information for outcome-based assessments because they may reveal changes in a person's change in behavior, attitude, skill, life condition, or knowledge.

Documentation Review

Use documentation reviews when you want an impression of how your project is operating without interrupting the project. This method is comprised of reviewing project statistics, memos, minutes, etc. Because this method does not measure changes in people's behavior, skills, knowledge, attitudes, condition, or life status, use it only as a supplement to instruments that do measure these things.

Observation

By observing a project, you can gather accurate information about how it actually operates, particularly about the process. You view the operations of a project as they are actually occurring.

Focus Groups

Focus groups allow you to explore a topic in depth through group discussion. They can provide very honest and useful information, you can get reactions to an experience or suggestion, and you can gain an understanding of common complaints. Focus group members can be organized into manageable numbers. If the participants are comfortable, they may give very helpful feedback. This is an efficient way to get key information about a project and you can quickly and reliably get impressions. You will need to have a facilitator for each group, and organizing and scheduling focus groups can take a lot of time. This information is subjective, and it could be time-consuming to compile the data.

Case Studies

Use case studies to fully understand or depict a customer's experiences as a participant in your project's input, process, and results. This is a powerful way to portray to outsiders the impact your project has had on individuals, and may be the best way to convey something like change in condition of life. Case studies are very time-consuming, and they are difficult to collect, organize, and describe.

Writing an Evaluation Plan

You can incorporate outcome-based evaluation into library planning and grant proposals by devising evaluation plans for your projects in the planning stage. This strategy naturally informs the library and community in measurable terms of the impact on customers as well as prepares the evaluation section of your grant application well before the deadline. Participants who follow this results-oriented approach to one particular library project will discover that, although it may require more time, energy, and resources, it can lead to more focused and successful programs and services. Once an initial project has been designed and implemented in this fashion, the methodology can be applied to other library projects. And in the course of a few years, most of the significant projects will be measurable in terms of customer benefits.

The key to writing an evaluation plan is to first have objectives that are measurable—the two are intertwined. If the objectives are written in vague terms and can't be measured, the evaluation section will be vague and weak. With measurable objectives, the evaluation section will become a natural extension of the objectives, and will be relatively easy to compose. It might help to think of objectives as the purpose of your project, the "things" that are left when the project is over. Usually, objectives are written in terms of increases and/or decreases.

For example, specific types of skills, such as problem solving, will show an increase while undesirable behaviors, such as truancy, will show a decrease.

If you have worked through the project planning process to this point, you already have all the information you need to easily develop an evaluation plan. Figure 3.8 shows a Sample Evaluation Plan for Your Library for Life. Use the Evaluation Plan Template in the Toolkit on page 203 to plan your project evaluation plan.

Figure 3.8. Sample Evaluation Plan		
Your Library for Life		
Objective	**Evaluation Method**	**Timeline**
20 percent more mature adults will find information that meets their needs during a visit to the library or the library's website.	Surveys will be conducted when mature adult community members leave the library or the library's website. This will be done prior to the implementation of the project, during the project and at the conclusion of the project. Pre-tests and post-tests will be administered to mature adult community members taking classes to determine the impact of the class on their success in finding information.	March–June September/October
Mature adult library customers will be able to meet 50 percent more of their information needs and requests online.	Surveys will be conducted on the website to determine how many requests were made online by mature adult community members. This will be done prior to the implementation of the project and at the conclusion of the project to determine the percentage change. Pre-tests and post-tests will be administered to mature adult community members taking technology classes to determine their success in using information technology to answer questions.	January December
85 percent of mature adult community members will find library services valuable and applicable to their lives.	Interviews will be conducted with mature adult customers to determine the value of library services in their lives. Case studies will be prepared for appropriate cases. Surveys will be conducted in classes and at programs. Focus groups will be held.	January–December
25 percent more mature adult community members will determine that library programming improved their quality of life.	Questionnaires will be issued at the end of each program. Focus groups comprising of program attendees will be held. Individual program participants will be interviewed two weeks after they attended a program. Case studies will be prepared for appropriate cases.	June–December
40 percent of the adult population over 55 will be registered library borrowers.	Census data will be analyzed to determine the number of people over 55 in the community, and library statistics will show the current percentage that are registered prior to the project. The data will be analyzed at the end of the project to determine the change.	January December

Key Considerations for Writing an Evaluation Plan

Consider the following key questions when you are designing a project evaluation:

1. What is the purpose of the evaluation, i.e., what do you want to measure as a result of the evaluation?

2. Who are the audiences for the evaluation results, e.g., funders, government, board, staff, partners, other libraries, and potential partners?

3. What kinds of information do you need to measure your progress, the strengths and weaknesses of the project, impact on customers, or how and why the project failed?

4. What sources will you use to collect the information, e.g., staff, customers, program documentation?

5. How can the information be collected, e.g., questionnaires, interviews, observation, conducting focus groups?

6. When do you need the information?

7. What resources are available to collect the information?

Now record your evaluation methods in #11 of your Project Planning Worksheet.

Congratulations! Your Project Plan is complete.

Organizing the Grant Team

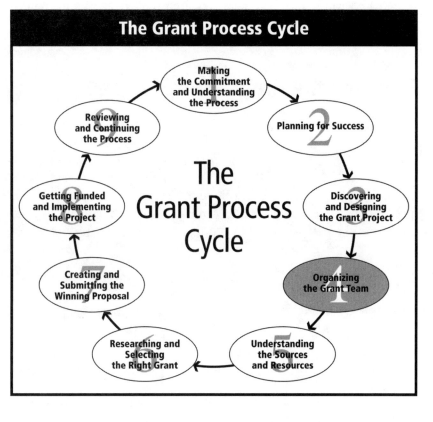

Overview

As we discussed in Chapter 1, the library's leadership and staff must be committed to the entire process of planning and implementing grant opportunities. A grant team is necessary so that the library's grant work is supported by the entire library and not driven by just one individual. No matter the size of your library, it is possible to have a team working on grants by involving board members, volunteers, and community representatives. Library leadership and staff should be included on the grant team, especially if they will be implementing the grant projects. Continuing to involve your community members who are on library planning or project committees can also be beneficial. A grant coordinator must be responsible for overseeing the entire process. Depending on your library's size, your grant team may consist of just a few people, or your library may be large enough that you can have one person concentrate specifically on each responsibility. Creating a grant team will generate ownership, buy-in, support, and the implementation, follow-up, and sustainability necessary for successful grant projects.

By utilizing the skills and talents of staff and volunteers, an effective funding program can be developed that expands the ability of the library to pursue and secure grant and donor funds. Teams are always stronger than individuals as the more people involved increases the amount of skills, ideas, energy, momentum, and time available. Teams enable multiple perspectives, a variety of experiences, and a broad skill set. The more people who will brainstorm ideas, research funders and grants, check rough drafts, edit the finished proposal, share contacts, and give their varied opinions, the less daunting the work of the grant team.

Selecting the Grant Team Members

Solicit help early on and throughout the process, and the ideas generated and time saved will ensure success and lessen stress. Selecting the right number of people to complete the team is important. Keep the team as small as possible while still bringing in all the necessary skills. The smaller the group, the easier it will be to manage and keep focused on specific tasks. These team members will be vested in the grant process, and more likely to contribute support when the grant proposals are funded.

Grant Team Member Skills

The following skills are needed for grant work. Don't worry if you are working on a grant by yourself and aren't experienced in all these areas. We've often worked on grant proposals with just one or two primary people, but additionally sought input from other individuals skilled in specific areas, for example, budgeting.

The following are some of the qualities to look for in team members:

- Organizational awareness: know your library
- Community awareness: know your users
- Planning: creating goals, objectives, timelines
- Project development: from problem to solution
- Project management: overseeing the implementation
- Coordination and organization
- Initiative: "do-it-yourselfers"
- Information gathering and research

The staff must be passionate about the topic and willing to work collaboratively during the entire time of the project from the first ideas through the implementation of details.
—"From Anne Frank's Story to Your Story: Creating History One Person at a Time" Ela Area Public Library District, Lake Zurich, IL (see Library Grant Success Stories, pp. 174–177)

- Fiscal or budget development experience
- Partnership building
- Superior writing abilities
- Excellent editorial skills
- Time management
- Resource management
- Storytelling experience
- Awareness to detail
- Technology skills
- Ability to communicate with funders
- Capability as a library champion
- Sense of fun and dedication

Team Member Titles and Responsibilities

Just as each library is very different due to demographics, politics, and social influences, grant teams are also varied and should reflect your library's community. These are possible team member titles and responsibilities, but your team should be a good fit for your library, and may have a different structure.

Director/Leadership

These team members should include representatives of senior library management and act as sponsors to maintain support and encouragement for the library grant work. They can help remove internal barriers and be spokespeople in support of the team. You should also include team members who are liaisons with governing authorities, such as your city, university, school, etc., depending on your particular library environment. This is a great way to develop relationships with those who influence your budget and will ensure that your library is involving your community leaders.

Staff and Board Representatives

It is very important that the library board and staff are aware of the library's grant activities. This is crucial for maintaining buy-in and also for obtaining a united and supportive group. It is important that they are informed and if contacted by a funder that they can articulate the library grant work and how it connects with the library's mission. They can also help establish relationships with partners or may personally know staff from funding agencies. While you certainly don't have to "know someone" to get grant funding, it doesn't hurt!

Grant Coordinator

A grant coordinator is responsible for the performance of the team and is the main point of contact with the funding organizations and partners. The coordinator allocates all grant tasks and promotes good communication among all team members. They ensure that team members are aware of and meet all deadlines, and organize periodic meetings. More grant coordinator responsibilities are detailed later in this chapter on pages 68–69.

Grant Project Directors

In larger libraries or in those managing many grant projects, project directors may assist the grant coordinator. Each project director would manage one specific grant project. The project directors must be self-motivated and devoted to the project goals, as they are responsible for leading the project once it is funded.

Implementation Team

These are the individuals, often frontline staff, who will be responsible for performing the project work. They will implement and help monitor and evaluate the project. They need to know their responsibilities, including grant stipulations and reporting requirements. The library must be committed to the projects and support any necessary scheduling adjustments to their workloads. These individuals should be identified and included in the planning process. This team may be headed by a project director.

Community Advisors

These are representatives of key stakeholder groups in your community who contribute their perspectives and are aware of community needs. It is important to make it clear that their role is advisory only; they should be aware they are not charged with making decisions or representing the library without authority. Funders will be pleased to see there are advisors on your team as this shows the library is not acting in isolation from the community. Including members from the population to be served by the grants will be another appealing factor to the funders, and also helpful to ensure your planning will be beneficial to the target audience. Community advisors can also assist when it is time to market your new service, building, or other grant project.

Researcher

This individual will help identify applicable grant sources, compile library data and history to be used in the grant application, and investigate related efforts by other community groups. They may also research possible partners. They will compile all information on specific grant opportunities and can also track and organize information on potential funders. A researcher can also help with developing draft budgets, determining costs based on resources needed. This can be an excellent position for a volunteer member, and we've even seen libraries use high school or college students to help with this type of research.

Writer

This person will write and compile the actual proposal, from cover letter to narrative to evaluation. For some libraries, this may be a team effort, with several people contributing to different sections of the proposal, but one person should be responsible for the final compilation to ensure that the writing flows and that each part fits together into a well-arranged plan. The writer may also be the person who gathers anecdotal evidence of needs, such as stories about library patrons who will be served by the grant project. This person may also be responsible for writing and submitting follow-up reports.

Subject Matter Experts

Subject Matter Experts (SMEs) provide specialized expertise at various phases or steps in the grant process. This could be a systems librarian or other technology expert, for library grants that involve technology. Fiscal agents or whoever will be managing the awarded funds should also be included. They will understand current budget cycles and any stipulations regarding accepting grant funding. This isn't always as simple as you may think, and you will need to be certain your library can accept and utilize the funding. You wouldn't want to find out you can't receive funds after all your hard work. It is also helpful to have a legal expert and an architect whom you can consult with if necessary, depending on your grant project needs.

Partners

Your team should include a representative from each of your partnering organizations. Involving them early on will ensure that they are fully vested in the entire process and that they are aware of their role in any grant projects. One funder told us that after awarding a grant to a library, the funder discovered that the library had not previously contacted the partners named in their proposal that were essential to the grant project. The library said they didn't want to get the partners' hopes up until they were sure the grant would be funded. When the partners were contacted, they declined to participate since they had not been consulted previously. What a way to learn a lesson!

Hiring a Professional Grant Writer or Researcher

You may want to hire a professional grant writer if you don't have anyone with grant experience on your staff, or if you are short on staff time. Although it may seem cost prohibitive to be spending money on getting money, it could be useful to have someone with experience write a first proposal or even complete a more involved federal RFP. You could then use this proposal as a learning opportunity and use some of the information in other grant writing. The grant writer could take care of some of the more difficult or time-involved sections of the grant, which are often asked for by all funders. Examples include the organizational background and overview, the community demographics, the description of needs, and the evaluation methods. Or you could hire someone to do research on funding sources. Searching grant directories and databases does take time and this could be another skill your organization could eventually develop internally.

There are several very important things to consider when seeking outside assistance with grants. The job of a grant consultant/writer is to assist those who are seeking grants. Do not be tempted to have the grant writer completely plan and design your project and write your proposal for you. This will result in a project that the grant writer supports but may not be something you and your staff can or want to do. Hiring or relying on an outside grant consultant does not relieve the library from devoting time to planning a project and overseeing the proposal design and writing.

You will need to have planning meetings with your consultant. It is vital to the success of the future project that all stakeholders have input into the projects being designed. Even if you hire a consultant, grant work still takes time. You will also need to review proposal drafts and give feedback along the way to ensure the project represented fits the library's vision.

Remember that grant-writing consultants are professionals and skilled in the grant-writing business. Most outside consultants will require an hourly fee to write your proposal just as doctors, attorneys, and accountants charge for their expertise. Never pay a grant writer a percentage of the awarded grant. Most funders will not allow the grant writer's fees to be included in a requested grant budget. No grant writer is successful all the time, so be wary of consultants who promise a winning proposal.

Using Volunteers

Instead of paying someone to write proposals or research grants, you could solicit volunteers. You may find a retiree in your community who has spent a career obtaining grants and would love to give back to their local library and community with their valuable skills. Volunteers can do research, proofread, or even write parts of the proposal. Or you may have a college or university that requires internships. One high school in South Dakota taught their students to write grants for the libraries—and they were successful. What a great learning opportunity for the students! In Angel Fire, New Mexico, a volunteer grant writer wrote almost one grant a month for a year for her small library's new building project and was awarded seven of the grants. She said the first one took the most time, but after that the work went faster, as some of the information could be replicated (Gerding, 2003: 16).

You should interview volunteers just as you do paid staff and you should have clearly written job responsibilities. Review their writing samples and check references. The grant proposal will represent your agency, and you want someone credible on your team.

Ongoing Grant Coordinator Responsibilities

While grant coordinators probably have other job responsibilities, it is critical that they set aside a certain amount of time each week to fulfill their role as grant team leaders. Here are several of the ongoing tasks for which they are responsible:

- Monitor the overall progress of the grant team. It's critical that they are available to help team members when needed. They should check in with each participant periodically to see if they can provide guidance. This will help in solving minor issues before they become major problems that could jeopardize the project's success.

- Maintain a written schedule or timeline for the research and projects that can be adjusted and updated as work proceeds. They should track all due dates, tasks, and individual responsibilities. Coordinators plan backward from the date the grant proposals need to leave the library to meet the grant deadline. This includes scheduling enough time to write, review several drafts and to fill out any required forms, including signature pages. Some grants and some organizations, such as universities, require approval before the library submits a proposal and that will present its own set of internal deadlines. Proposals often require support letters and other attachments. Enough time must be allowed to copy, collate, and send the proposal. Each team member should be provided with a copy of the timeline.

- Schedule the meeting dates, describe the activities to be accomplished, and assign responsibilities for each meeting.

- Keep all leadership updated. It is easy to become so consumed with managing a team that you forget to let your own supervisors know how the initiative is progressing. Regular updates should be made to library leadership and board members.

- Communicate and provide as much support as possible. All team members should be provided with all the information they need. This may be in the form of training (research, writing proposals, etc.), or informational sessions led by other staff members who have worked on recent grants. The role of the finance department should be fully explained. The team should be able to identify and familiarize itself with all resources, to brainstorm about possible departmental or community collaboration on grant projects, and have all the support they need.

- Help move the draft budget through the appropriate channels of approval.

- Oversee submission of final grant proposals, verifying all components are included and ensuring all team members are informed, and all dates are confirmed. Verify that the grant was received and answer all questions from the funder through the review process.

- Evaluate and review the grant if awarded. Coordinate all grant reports and give updates to library management and funders.

Grant Team Meetings

Gathering your grant team periodically is essential. A team is a group of people with interdependence, aiming for a specific goal. So once you have identified the members of the team, you are ready to actually bring

We used the PLA Planning Process and the forms from Managing for Results to keep the planning team on track. Starting by analyzing community needs, having representation from target group, and moving through the process is an excellent way to keep things moving!
—"Bridging the Gap"
Athens Regional Library System
Success Story
(Gerding and MacKellar, 2006: 167)

these individuals together to form a team. And we don't just mean getting everyone together in one room. When having grant team meetings, keep in mind these **five teamwork fundamentals** identified in *Visualizing Project Management* (Forsberg, Mooz, and Cotterman, 1996: 31).

1. Common goals
2. Acknowledged interdependency and mutual respect
3. A common code of conduct
4. Team spirit and energy
5. Shared rewards

Grant teams share the rewards of the grant project's purpose, fulfilling the library's mission, sharing innovative ideas, and networking. A shared vision and a sense of belonging to an appreciated, valuable group can be very rewarding and can boost staff morale.

Initial Informal Meeting

Team members need to know the team goals, and they should be able to put them in their own words. The grant coordinator should start with an initial informal meeting or one-on-one conversation with each team member to discuss his or her skills and how those abilities will be used by the team. This is particularly useful in a large library, when working with people from areas of the library who don't normally work together. This meeting should also include determining how much time the employee will have to devote to the team and what tasks and reports will be required. The discussion should be upbeat and organized, with all facets of the grant work and project explained, including their individual roles, while encouraging their ideas and input. They should understand what the team will be doing and confirm that they want to be a part of the grant effort.

The First Team Meeting

Once the grant coordinator has met with each team member individually, the team should have its first meeting. This meeting should include a review of the goals, any current RFPs being considered, a timeline of all deadlines, and a discussion of available resources. Each person's responsibilities should be clearly identified, while making sure everyone knows that the process will not be micromanaged. By giving team members a degree of freedom in how they do their jobs, productivity will ultimately increase. Mutual respect is essential for the team to be most effective. By sharing the strengths that each team member is bringing to the group, progress can be made toward this essential team element.

These meetings don't need to be formal or boring, but they should be organized, with a set agenda. This demonstrates that you value team members' time. Bringing snacks and encouraging a warm environment will help with teamwork as well. A summary of the meeting's goals should be distributed before the meeting. In addition to providing team members with a valuable reference, promptly distributing the summary will help convey the importance of the grant work. The grant coordinator should provide a written schedule or timeline for the grant work that can be adjusted and updated as work proceeds.

You can establish common rules of behavior such as: no interrupting, no gossiping, requiring a representative to be sent if the team member must miss a meeting, acknowledging that all ideas will be listened to, etc. Having the team decide on and agree to these rules can help establish a sense of teamwork.

The team must be empowered and know that together they will produce something greater and more significant than could be achieved alone. Team members should work together and be willing to do what must be done to get the grant submitted on time. Each member must be committed and accountable for actions, or lack of action. Don't forget to celebrate each milestone, and thank each person for individual contributions along the way.

Elevator Speech

The library's leadership, the grant team, the board members, and the trustees should have an elevator speech. You might want to incorporate this topic into a team meeting. An elevator speech is a few sentences used to respond when asked, "Why do you volunteer for, work for, or donate to the library?" When anyone asks about the library it is an OPPORTUNITY to be certain that the correct message gets out to the public. Take time in a grant, staff, volunteers, and/or board meeting to find out what each person who represents the library says when asked this question (or when asked "What do you do besides read books all day?"). Have everyone share the elevator speeches. Then, together, talk about what is best about them and what could be clarified or improved. No one needs to memorize a monologue that is repeated like a robot. Everyone should be encouraged to talk from the heart. Your library does make a difference in your community, so how can those benefits be described? The elevator speech should be no more than a few sentences. Every time anyone asks about the library, all representatives should take that opportunity to get the library, its work, and its successes into one more community member's mind. You never know if you may be talking to a future grant reviewer, future volunteer, or a potential major contributor!

Implementation and Resources

More funding is available for projects than for operating expenses, so you must be certain that your library can afford the amount of staff time and expense required in grant work. It isn't just depositing the checks, after all. You must have the resources to carry out the project and to do the necessary follow-up and promotion. Writing a proposal takes time, but implementing a project will take even longer. If you are overwhelmed with the time needed for the initial planning and design of a grant proposal, look into how you can free up the necessary time to devote to a project if the proposal is successful.

Some resources needed by the grant team include the following:

- Space: Ideally a primary place should be provided for the team to organize materials and concentrate on writing, making phone calls to funders, etc. This could range from a few file folders to a closet (actually done by one librarian), to a separate grants/development office.

- Print and online resources: See Chapter 5 for recommendations of resources and locations of Foundation Center Cooperating Collections that have grant collections.

- Computer for organizing research, performing searches, sending e-mail, and writing grant proposals.

- Copier, printer, postage meter, telephone, and any other office equipment.

- Ongoing professional development, including training and funder meetings, including time and travel expenses.

- Staff who will be involved in the entire cycle.

- Time—the most important resource of all, besides staff.

Few libraries have full-time development staff that can devote their days to researching grants, contacting funders, writing proposals, and completing evaluations. Instead, most librarians wear many hats, and grant seeking is just one of many responsibilities. One complaint we hear from librarians is that they wish they had more time. By forming a team to work on grants, you can divide and conquer. If you only have one hour a week to devote to grants, you may find yourself staying up late at night, and working extra hours to get your proposals in on time. But if you can gather a team of staff and/or volunteers who can each give one or two hours a week, the math is simple—you suddenly have the needed time. This team will build collaboration within your organization, and they also have the potential to increase their own leadership skills, which in turn can boost their confidence and commitment to the library.

Understanding the Sources and Resources

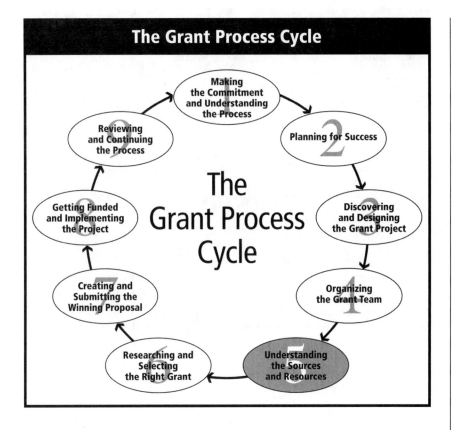

So far, we have explained the grant process and the importance of committing yourself to it, how to plan for success, including planning a specific project based on your community's needs, and how to organize the grant team. Now, it's time to take a look at the different funding sources to consider and the resources you will be using to locate the grant that is just right for the library project you are planning.

For the purposes of this chapter, a "source" is the origin of the funding—the funder or grantor. There are two major types of funding sources—government and private. In this chapter we explain the categories

Library Grants
BLOG

within each major type, providing examples of sources that are likely to fund library projects. Then we present a general overview of some "resources" or tools you will use to locate the funding source that best matches your project. This information can be overwhelming at first, but once you get the basic idea, it will all fall into place. If you want to get started on the fast track and see what grants are out there for libraries right now, read about our Library Grants Blog in the Resources section of this chapter.

Funding Sources for Grants

To help you organize your research, it is useful to understand that there are two basic grant types: government and private. Within each type are several categories, as illustrated in Figure 5.1.

Figure 5.1. Types of Funding Sources	
Government	**Private**
• Federal government • State government • Local government (county, city, town, village, municipality)	• Foundations and non-profits • Corporations and corporate foundations • Clubs and organizations • Professional and trade associations

Government Funding Sources

Federal Government Sources

The federal government awards billions of dollars annually for research and development, facilities improvement, demonstration and model projects, and grants covering a broad range of educational and social reforms and initiatives designed to carry out the purposes established by federal legislation. The federal government issues two kinds of grants: (1) discretionary and (2) formula (or block) grants. Discretionary grants are awarded directly to grantees by a federal agency; formula (or block) grants put federal money into the hands of states, cities, or counties for them to distribute. Libraries can apply for either kind; however, state or local governments award formula and block grants.

The federal government is the largest source of grant funding in the United States, and each governmental department, bureau, or office has its own unique and separate priority list and grant guidelines. There are hundreds of federal government grant programs managed by a wide variety of departmental bureaucracies. Grant guidelines for federal government agencies are highly competitive and they can be very complex.

The following U.S. federal government agencies fund projects of interest to libraries, information clearinghouses, archives, technical information services, and their partners and collaborators:

U.S. Department of Agriculture

Cooperative State, Research, Education, and Extension Service's (CSREES) (www.csrees.usda.gov/fo/funding.cfm) unique mission is to advance knowledge for agriculture, the environment, human health and well-being, and communities by supporting research, education, and extension programs in the Land-Grant University System and other partner organizations. CSREES helps fund research at the state and local level and provides program leadership in these areas.

Rural Development Community Connect Grant Program (www.usda.gov/rus/telecom/commconnect.htm). The Community-Oriented Connectivity Broadband Grant Program is designed to provide financial assistance to furnish broadband service in rural, economically challenged communities where such service does not currently exist. Grant funds may be utilized to deploy broadband transmission service to critical community facilities, rural residents, and rural businesses and to construct, acquire, or expand, equip, and operate a community center that provides free access to broadband services to community residents for at least two years.

U.S. Department of Education

The Department of Education (ED) (www.ed.gov/fund/landing .jhtml?src=rt) administered a budget of $62.6 billion in regular FY 2009 discretionary appropriations and $96.8 billion in discretionary funding provided under the American Recovery and Reinvestment Act of 2009, and operated programs that touched on every area and level of education. The department's elementary and secondary programs annually serve nearly 14,000 school districts and approximately 56 million students attending some 98,000 public schools and 34,000 private schools. Department programs also provide grant, loan, and work-study assistance to more than 13 million postsecondary students.

The following ED offices administer grants of potential interest to libraries:

Institute of Education Sciences (IES) (www.ed.gov/about/offices/list/ies/index.html) compiles statistics, funds research, evaluations and information dissemination; and provides research-based guidance to further evidence-based policy and practice.

Office of Innovation and Improvement (OII) (www.ed.gov/about/offices/list/oii/index.html) makes strategic investments in innovative educational practices through 24 discretionary grant programs to states, schools, and community and non-profit organizations. It also leads the movement for greater parental options and information on education.

Office of Elementary and Secondary Education (OESE) (www.ed.gov/about/offices/list/oese/index.html) provides financial assistance to state and local education agencies for both public and private preschool, elementary, and secondary education. Working together with these and other education partners, the OESE promotes and supports equal educational opportunities and educational excellence for all students.

Office of English Language Acquisition, Language Enhancement, and Academic Achievement for Limited English Proficient Students (OELA) (www.ed.gov/about/offices/list/oela/index.html) administers programs designed to enable students with limited English proficiency to become proficient in English and meet challenging state academic content and student achievement standards.

Office of Postsecondary Education (OPE) (www.ed.gov/about/offices/list/ope/index.html) directs, coordinates, and recommends policies for programs that are designed to provide financial assistance to eligible students; improve postsecondary educational facilities and programs; recruit and prepare disadvantaged students for postsecondary programs; and promote the domestic study of foreign languages and international affairs, research, and exchange activities.

Office of Special Education and Rehabilitative Services (OSERS) (www.ed.gov/about/offices/list/osers/index.html) assists in the education of children with disabilities and the rehabilitation of adults with disabilities and conducts research to improve the lives of individuals with disabilities regardless of age.

Office of Vocational and Adult Education (OVAE) (www.ed.gov/about/offices/list/ovae/index.html) works to ensure that all Americans have the knowledge and technical skills necessary to succeed in postsecondary education, the workforce, and life. Through the Preparing America's Future initiative's comprehensive policies, programs, and activities, OVAE is helping reform America's high schools, supporting America's community colleges, and expanding America's adult education programs. These efforts will transform the federal role, sparking state and local reform efforts.

U.S. Department of Health and Human Services

Administration for Children and Families (ACF) (www.acf.hhs.gov/grants) is a federal agency funding state, territory, local, and tribal organizations to provide family assistance (welfare), child support, child care, Head Start, child welfare, and other programs relating to children and families. Actual services are provided by state, county, city, and tribal governments, and public and private local agencies. ACF assists these organizations through funding, policy direction, and information services.

Health Resources and Services Administration (HRSA) (www.hrsa.gov/grants) is charged with increasing access to health care for those who are medically underserved. HRSA's programs are designed to increase access to care, improve quality, and safeguard the health and well-being of the nation's most vulnerable populations.

National Library of Medicine (NLM)
(www.nlm.nih.gov/grants.html) provides the following grants and fellowships to organizations and individuals: research grants, awards supporting career development and training, fellowship programs at NLM; support for outreach initiatives to improve access and eliminate health disparities; and trans-NIH programs and initiatives supported by NLM. NLM has a vital interest in information management and in the enormous utility of computers and telecommunication for improving storage, retrieval, access, and use of biomedical information. NLM provides extramural support through grants-in-aid and, less commonly, contracts.

National Network of Libraries of Medicine (NN/LM)
(nnlm.gov/funding/) advances the progress of medicine and improves the public health by providing all U.S. health professionals with equal access to biomedical information and improving the public's access to information to enable them to make informed decisions about their health. NN/LM is coordinated by the National Library of Medicine and carried out through a nationwide network of health science libraries and information centers. Grants are offered by each region in the network and focus on access to health information through outreach, professional development, technology, and training, for example.

U.S. Department of Justice

Office of Juvenile Justice and Delinquency Prevention (OJJDP)
(ojjdp.ncjrs.org/funding/funding.html) provides funding to states, territories, localities, and private organizations, including faith-based institutions, through formula and block grants and discretionary grants to prevent and respond to juvenile delinquency and victimization.

Institute of Museum and Library Services

Institute of Museum and Library Services (IMLS)
(www.imls.gov/applicants/name.shtm) is the primary source of federal support for the nation's 122,000 libraries and 17,500 museums. The Institute's mission is to create strong libraries and museums that connect people to information and ideas. IMLS grants are available for archives, federally recognized Native American tribes, historical societies, libraries, museums, non-profits that serve Native Hawaiians, professional associations, regional organizations, state library administrative agencies, state or local governments, and public or private non-profit institutions of higher education. Every year the IMLS allocates Library Services and Technology Act (LSTA) funding to state library agencies for distribution to libraries throughout each state using a population-based formula. (*See* State Library Agencies in the following section, State and Local Government Sources.)

National Endowment for the Arts

National Endowment for the Arts (NEA)
(www.nea.gov) is a public agency dedicated to supporting excellence in the arts; bringing the arts to all Americans; and providing leadership

in arts education. The NEA is the nation's largest annual funder of the arts, bringing great art to all 50 states, including rural areas, inner cities, and military bases.

National Endowment for the Humanities

National Endowment for the Humanities (NEH) (www.neh.gov/grants) is an independent grant-making agency of the United States Government dedicated to supporting research, education, preservation, and public programs in the humanities.

National Historical Publications and Records Commission

National Historical Publications and Records Commission (NHPRC) (www.archives.gov/nhprc/announcement/) is the grant-making affiliate of the National Archives and Records Administration (NARA). The NHPRC promotes the preservation and use of America's documentary heritage essential to understanding our democracy, history, and culture. Each year Congress appropriates up to $10 million for grants to support the nation's archives and for projects to edit and publish historical records of national importance.

National Institute for Literacy

National Institute for Literacy (www.nifl.gov/nifl/grants_contracts.html) provides leadership on literacy issues, including the improvement of reading instruction for children, youth, and adults. In consultation with the U.S. Departments of Education, Labor, and Health and Human Services, the Institute serves as a national resource on current, comprehensive literacy research, practice, and policy.

State and Local Government Sources

Some federal funding is passed directly to states, counties, or local governments for their use or for redistribution through formula (or block) grants. A state or local government entity may acquire a grant of their own which requires others to perform part of a project's scope of work. In this case, the local government will issue a Request for Proposals (RFP) for services or products. Libraries may be eligible for a formula or block grant, or may respond to an RFP to perform work on a state formula or block grant.

State Library Agencies

State Library Agencies are one example of a state government source that offers grants to libraries using federal funds received as formula grants. Library Services and Technology Act (LSTA) funding, the only federal funding exclusively for libraries, promotes access to information resources provided by all types of libraries. Every year the Institute of Museum and Library Services (IMLS) allocates LSTA funding to state library agencies for distribution to libraries throughout each state using a population-based formula. Applicants for this grant program must be one of the 59 State Library Administrative Agencies that may use the appropriation to support statewide initiatives and services by conducting competitive subgrant competitions or cooperative agreements for public, academic, research, school, and special libraries in their states. LSTA priorities specify that each state develop the goals and objectives for its five-year plan to strengthen the efficiency, reach, and effectiveness of library services in their state. Check with your State Library about the availability of LSTA funds in your state on its website. LSTA funding has increased over the past several years, and continues to be a good source of funding for most libraries. The 2009 Omnibus Appropriations bill included $171,500,000 for the Grants to State Library Agencies program within the LSTA, an increase of more than $10 million from 2008. In 2010, the president proposed a 0.5 percent increase in LSTA funding for the nation's libraries.

State Humanities Councils, Arts Councils, Cultural Services Agencies, and Departments of Education

Investigate grant opportunities available through other state, county, or city agencies and departments that may fund your project, such as Humanities Councils, Arts Councils, Cultural Services Agencies, and Departments of Education.

Private Funding Sources

Foundations

Foundations exist to support specific ideals that inspired the creation of the foundation. Billions of dollars are granted annually by foundations to help schools, communities, libraries, and other non-profit organizations reach their goals. Community foundations are foundations in communities that distribute funding for many different funders in their communities, such as small foundations, businesses, corporations, organizations, or individuals.

Corporations

Corporations offer many opportunities in the form of partnerships, material resources, mentors, expertise, and funds to schools, communities, libraries, and other non-profits. Corporations are generally interested in establishing their names and relationships within the communities in which they operate. Commercial enterprises are driven primarily by their desire for public recognition.

Clubs and Organizations

Local clubs and organizations such as the Rotary Club, Kiwanis, Civitan, Elks, and the Junior League provide support for local projects and programs. Motivated to help local communities through service, materials and financial investments, these local funding opportunities are usually not widely advertised or promoted. It may require some networking on your part to discover them.

Professional Associations

Professional associations often make grant funds available to members of their association or organization that carry out missions that are compatible with the interests of the professional organization.

Resources for Finding Grant Opportunities

Library Grants Blog (librarygrants.blogspot.com). This is a free website that we maintain, regularly posting new grant opportunities for libraries. Our website is different from others because we post only grants that invite libraries to apply. We've done the hard work for you! Reading our blog is a great way to get started looking for grants and to get an idea about what kinds of grants are out there and what funders are looking for. We focus on grants of interest to a national audience, updating the listing often, so that what you find there will be grants that are currently open. Follow the links in our postings to the actual grant announcements, application guidelines, and eligibility requirements. Visit our blog or subscribe to the RSS feed, and you will be notified about grants as soon as we find out about them.

The resources or tools you will use to identify funding opportunities are available in a variety of formats. Grant opportunities are compiled and listed in print directories, online databases, CD-ROMs, websites, print and electronic newsletters, and e-mail discussion groups. Here we provide a general overview of the available resources; however, remember that there may be resources specific to the topic of your project or your geographical region that are beyond the scope of this overview. You must do the research necessary to uncover these resources.

You will use many resources in the course of your grant research. There is not one directory or database that will contain all the funding opportunities available to fund your project. Some of these resources are costly; however, you should be able to find them in your state library, a nearby college or university library, the reference collection in a nearby large public library, the web, or your local community foundation.

Government Funding Resources

Today, you can find most federal grant opportunities on the Internet. Grants.gov is the unified central location for accessing all annual grant funds available through the federal government.

Federal Government

The *Catalog of Federal Domestic Assistance* (*CFDA*) (www. cfda.gov) provides a full listing of all federal programs available to state and local governments; federally-recognized Indian tribal governments; territories, and possessions of the United States; domestic public, quasi-public, and private profit and non-profit organizations and institutions; specialized groups; and individuals. The CFDA is disseminated electronically via its website at www.cfda.gov. A printable version is available for downloading at their website.

Grants.gov (www.grants.gov) is a central storehouse for information on more than 1,000 grant programs, providing access to approximately $500 billion in annual awards. Here you can electronically find and apply for competitive grant opportunities from all 26 federal grant-making agencies. Grants.gov also supports electronic applications that can be downloaded and provides online user support tools and personalized assistance. Grants.gov offers e-mail subscriptions notifying subscribers about new grant opportunity postings and updates. Notices can be customized based on advanced criteria. RSS feed also available.

Federal Agency Websites. Most federal agencies devote a section on their websites for announcing currently available grants. Look for a button near the top of the agency's homepage labeled "Grants" or "Grant Applicants," or perform a search for "Grants" using the site's search box.

The *Federal Register* (www.gpoaccess.gov/fr/index.html) is the official daily publication of U.S. federal agency information, including notifications and announcements of grant opportunities by federal agencies and organizations. A Notice of Funds Availability (NOFA) lists the application deadlines, priorities, eligibility requirements, and places where you can get more help in applying for program funds. Because some agencies have discontinued NOFAs in the *Federal Register*, also check the websites of federal agencies for available grants and full information.

Primary Source (www.imls.gov/news/source.shtm), the IMLS newsletter, contains brief articles which alert readers to new information about grants and other news.

The **TGCI** *Federal Register* **Grant Announcements** (www.tgci.com), an alert service provided by The Grantsmanship Center (TGCI), draws announcements from TGCI's daily search of the *Federal Register*. Registration is free.

State and Local Government

Check your state and local government websites regularly for RFPs and subgrant offerings. Make contact with key officials in departments that are likely to fund a project like yours, should they have funding. Ask to be notified if funding becomes available.

State Library Agencies. Check your state library agency's website often for grant opportunities. You can find your state library's website at www.publiclibraries.com/state_library.htm.

State Humanities Councils, Arts Councils, Cultural Services Agencies, and Departments of Education. Investigate grant opportunities available through state, county, or city agencies and departments by checking their websites. You can find them using the following links.

- Your State Humanities Council
  (www.neh.gov/whoweare/statecouncils.html)
- Your State Arts Council
  (www.nasaa-arts.org/aoa/saaweb.shtml)
- Your State Department of Education
  (wdcrobcolp01.ed.gov/Programs/EROD/org_list.cfm?
  category_ID=SEA)

Private Funding Resources

Foundations

The Foundation Center (fdncenter.org) is the largest producer of directories and databases of grant-giving foundations. The Center publishes print and electronic directories by subject, foundation name, geographic region, and grants previously funded. Their subject directories cover topics such as aging, arts and culture, children and youth, education, employment, environmental protection and animal welfare, public health, housing, libraries and information services, information technology, and religion, religious welfare, and religious education.

FC Search, the Foundation Center's database on CD-ROM, features a comprehensive listing of active U.S. foundations and corporate giving programs and their associated grants. It includes a Grantmaker File of more than 80,000 records, and a Grants File with more than 388,000 grants awarded by the nation's largest funders. You may also link directly to the websites of more than 6,000 of the nation's top foundations as well as more than 3,300 corporate websites. Go to foundationcenter.org/getstarted/tutorials/fcsearch_tour/index.html for a tour.

The **Foundation Center's Cooperating Collections** (foundationcenter.org/collections) are free funding information centers in libraries, community foundations, and other non-profit resource centers that provide a core collection of Foundation Center publications and a variety of supplementary materials and services useful to grant seekers. There is at least one Cooperating Collection in each state plus Australia, Brazil, Mexico, Nigeria, South Korea, and Thailand. Core collections include *The Foundation Directory Online Professional* and *Foundation Grants to Individuals Online* as well as a wide range of print resources.

Foundation 1000 offers comprehensive information on the 1,000 largest foundations in the United States. Profiles include grant maker program interests, purpose statements, application guidelines, names of key officials, in-depth analysis of grant programs, and extensive lists of sample grants.

Foundation Directories list key facts and provide descriptions with key facts for the nation's top 20,000 foundations.

Foundation Directory Online (www.fconline.fdncenter.org) is available from the Foundation Center and offers five subscription plan levels starting at $19.95 per month. Includes up to four databases of grant makers, companies, grants and 990s and up to 53 search fields including keyword searching. Includes over 98,000 U.S. foundations and corporate donors, 1.6 million recent grants and more than 400,000 key decision makers. The *Foundation Directory* is also available through DIALOG File 26.

Foundation Grants Index compiles grant records found in the Foundation Directory Online. An average of 10,000 new grants per month are added. DIALOG File 27.

Foundation Grants for Preservation in Libraries, Archives, and Museums lists 1,944 grants of $5,000 or more awarded by 488 grant makers, from 2004–2009. It covers grants to public, academic, research, school, and special libraries. Published by the Foundation Center and the Library of Congress. Downloadable at www.loc.gov/preserv/foundtn-grants.pdf.

Grant Guides provide you with descriptions of actual foundation grants of $10,000 or more awarded in various subject fields. These guides will help you identify funders in your field and track grants awarded to organizations similar to yours.

Grants for Information Technology covers current foundation giving in the field. Describes more than 3,600 grants worth more than $600 million from over 500 foundations. Digital edition.

Grants for Libraries and Information Services reveals the scope of current foundation giving in the field. Describes more than 2,800 grants of $10,000 or more, worth in excess of $527 million from more than 700 foundations. Digital edition.

Guide to U.S. Foundations, Their Trustees, Officers, and Donors contains crucial facts about U.S. grant-making foundations. Each foundation entry includes contact information, current assets, annual contributions, names of trustees, officers, donors, and more.

Philanthropy News Digest (PND) (foundationcenter.org/pnd/info/about.jhtml), a daily news service of the Foundation Center, is a compendium of philanthropy-related articles and features culled from print and electronic media outlets nationwide.

RFP (Request for Proposals) Bulletin (foundationcenter.org/pnd/rfp) is a roundup of recently announced RFPs from private, corporate, and government funding sources. Each listing provides a brief overview of a current funding opportunity offered by a foundation or other grant-making organization, along with the date the RFP was posted and the deadline. Published weekly.

Corporations

Corporations often create corporate foundations for the purpose of granting money for specific projects. Corporations also give directly to projects. Check the foundation resources above for corporate foundations as well as the following resources for additional corporate foundations and corporate direct giving programs.

Corporate Giving Directory: Comprehensive Profiles of America's Major Corporate Foundations & Corporate Giving Programs provides complete profiles of the 1,000 largest corporate foundations and corporate direct giving programs in the United States, representing nearly $5.6 billion in cash and non-monetary support annually. Information Today, Inc.

Corporate Giving Online is an online database of corporate donors that support non-profit organizations and programs through grants as well as in-kind donations of equipment, products, professional services, and volunteers. Go to foundationcenter.org/getstarted/tutorials/corporate/ for a tour.

Corporate Philanthropy Report includes corporate grant information, funding opportunities, insight on who's funding what, including contact names and phone numbers. Also provides advice on how to take advantage of corporate giving opportunities. LRP Publications.

National Directory of Corporate Giving includes detailed portraits of close to 3,000 corporate foundations and 1,300 direct giving programs; application guidelines; key personnel; types of support awarded; giving limitations; and financial data including assets, annual giving, and the average size of grants; and more than 9,000 sample grants. Foundation Center.

Investigate websites of corporations operating in your geographic area, looking for links to "community involvement" or "community giving." Many corporations devote entire sections of their websites to explaining what they fund in their communities and how to apply. You may even find an online application that you can submit electronically.

Visit your local community foundation and ask to see the information they have about corporations in your area that fund local projects. You may find annual reports or other compilations that include descriptions of the corporation's granting interests and grant-making history. Don't forget to check local finding directories specific to your state or geographical region for corporate funding opportunities.

Clubs and Organizations

Funding opportunities available through local organizations are not widely advertised. This is where your networking and people skills will come in handy. Ask friends, neighbors, and family members who are involved in local organizations what their organizations support. Mention your idea or project to them and inquire about the possibility of presenting it to the organization. Ask if they know any other local organizations that support ideas or projects like yours.

Research your local community directory at these sites:

- Foundation Center: fdncenter.org/getstarted/topical/sl_dir.html

- Michigan State University's list of service clubs and civic organizations that provide funding: www.lib.msu.edu/harris23/grants/servicec.htm

Your yellow pages, friends, and staff may also help identify local clubs and organizations that provide funding.

Professional Associations

Investigate your state, regional, and special library associations, including divisions, special interest groups, chapters, and library foundations. Your state library association can be found at www.ala.org/ala/aboutala/offices/cro/chapters/stateandregional/stateregional.cfm. The American Library Association, Public Library Association, Special Libraries Association, and American Association of School Librarians offer many grant, award, scholarship, and fellowship opportunities.

Community Foundations

Visit your local community foundation and talk to the staff there. Tell them about your project idea and ask if there are any grants through the community foundation that fund projects like yours. Establish a relationship with these people and check in with them periodically. When funding becomes available for projects like yours through the community foundation, they will contact you about applying. Community foundations often have solid collections of materials about writing proposals; print, electronic, and local directories of funding sources; and offer classes for community members about their funding and resources. You will find extensive information about local corporations and foundations that you may not find collected in any other place. You can find your local community foundation using the Community Foundation Locator from the Council on Foundations (www.cof.org/Locator/index.cfm?menuContainerID=34&crumb=2).

Other Resources

Annual Register of Grant Support is a comprehensive directory that provides details on more than 3,200 major grant programs offered by traditional corporate, private, and public funding programs as well as lesser-known non-traditional grant sources such as educational associations and unions. Information Today, Inc.

Big Book of Library Grant Money 2007: Profiles of Private and Corporate Foundations and Direct Corporate Givers Receptive to Library Grant Proposals profiles foundations and corporate grant makers that have made grants to libraries or have listed libraries as typical recipients. Taft Group.

Foundation Reporter provides important foundation contact, financial, and grants information. This resource covers the top 1,000 private foundations in the United States that have at least $10 million in assets or have made $500,000 in charitable giving. Information Today, Inc.

LIBRARY ASSOCIATIONS

American Library Association
- **ALA Awards and Grants** www.ala.org/ala/awardsgrants/index.cfm
- **American Association of School Librarians Awards and Grants** www.ala.org/ala/mgrps/divs/aasl/aaslawards/aaslawards.cfm
- **Association for Library Service to Children** www.ala.org/ala/mgrps/divs/alsc/awardsgrants/index.cfm
- **Association for Library Collections and Technical Services** www.ala.org/ala/mgrps/divs/alcts/awards/index.cfm
- **Association of College and Research Libraries** www.ala.org/ala/mgrps/divs/acrl/awards/index.cfm
- **Association of Specialized and Cooperative Library Agencies** www.ala.org/ala/mgrps/divs/ascla/asclaawards/index.cfm
- **Library Leadership and Management Association** www.ala.org/ala/mgrps/divs/llama/llamaawards/default.cfm
- **Reference and User Services Association** www.ala.org/ala/mgrps/divs/rusa/awards/index.cfm
- **Young Adult Library Services Association** www.ala.org/ala/mgrps/divs/yalsa/awardsandgrants/yalsaawardsgrants.cfm

Public Library Association www.pla.org/ala/mgrps/divs/pla/plaawards/index.cfm

Special Libraries Association www.sla.org/content/learn/scholarship/index.cfm

American Association of School Librarians (a division of ALA, *see* above)

Grants for Libraries E-News Alerts
(west.thomson.com/signup/newsletters/209.aspx) is a free weekly e-mail newsletter that provides timely information on new grant opportunities and funding programs for libraries.

Grants for Libraries Hotline
(west.thomson.com/productdetail/139015/40560036/product detail.aspx#) offers 12 monthly issues that describe grant opportunities for libraries and librarians, as well as opportunities in the field of education. Print with weekly e-mail updates. West.

Private Grants Alert (www.cdpublications.com) offers 12 issues per year that provide grant opportunities from foundations, corporations, and individuals; details about preparing letters of intent and applications; grant seeking and proposal writing advice, and more. Print and online versions are available. CD Publications.

Local Funding Directories. Your state and local funding directories are invaluable resources for finding foundations and corporations that limit their giving to your geographic area. Find your local directory in *State and Local Funding Directories: A Bibliography* at fdncenter .org/learn/topical/sl_dir.html.

The Grantsmanship Center (www.tgci.com/funding/states.asp) maintains information about your state's foundations, community foundations, corporate giving programs, and the top 40 foundations that give in your state.

Researching and Selecting the Right Grant

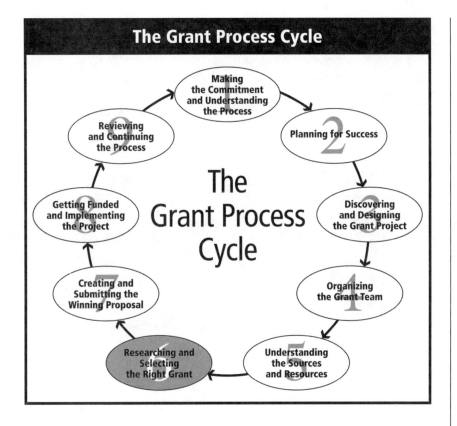

Now that you have a well-planned project, you know about the different grant sources, and you understand what resources are available for identifying grant funders, it is time to research and select funders that fund projects just like yours.

First, let everyone know that you are seeking funding and tell them about your project idea. Tell library staff, board members, the city council, family and friends, and local business leaders. You never know who might be on a foundation's board or know someone who is a board member for a foundation that has just the right funding for your project.

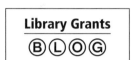

Library Grants
ⒷⓁⓄⒼ

When first thinking about applying for a grant, we spoke with Idaho Commission for Libraries about grants that may be available to us. There were several traditional grants including *Read to Me* and LSTA, however the timing and purpose of the new Wal-Mart Mini Grants were perfect for our project.

—"ELL Storytime Project"
Boise Public Library, Boise, ID
(see Library Success Stories, pp. 186–188)

Some other things you can do to find the right funder are also covered in this chapter:

- Do thorough research.
- Read publications like newsletters, journals, and local newspapers for funding opportunities.
- Subscribe to the Library Grants blog (librarygrants.blogspot .com).
- Subscribe to other grant-related RSS feeds and electronic discussion groups.
- Contact other libraries in your area that have received grants.
- Talk with potential funders about their interests and priorities.

Doing the Research

Internet and library research is usually the easy part for librarians. We have an advantage when it comes to doing grant research because we are trained to effectively use reference materials and electronic resources. Not only do we have the skills it takes to find information, we are a persistent group who will find information wherever it may be, and however deeply it is buried. We're naturals. So, let's put our valuable information-finding skills to work and find the grant that will fund our project to meet the needs of our communities.

Here are some tips for you to think about while you do your research:

- Translate your project into the language used by the resources and funders.
- Work from the general to the specific.
- Record what you find.
- Keep your research organized.

Translate Your Project into the Language Used by Resources and Funders

When identifying keywords describing your project, remove any mental barriers you may have about libraries and what libraries traditionally do. Eliminate stereotypes and think big. Be generous and open-minded about choosing terms, and avoid narrowly defining your project for now. Funders and resource compilers may not even think of libraries when they are writing profiles, defining areas of focus, or composing calls for proposals. For instance, if a funder is interested in awarding grants for children's performances, they may not know many libraries have programs that include children's performances. In a case like this, "library" would not appear as a keyword in the entry, but "children," "theater," and "performance art" would. If you only search for "library" you will miss this potential funder. Make sure to uncover every possible match by thinking broadly when it comes to keywords describing your project. Include synonyms, alternate spellings, and multiple terms with similar meanings.

Stay in this frame of mind when you are deciding which resources to search. Of course, you will want to use library-specific resources like *Grants for Libraries and Information Services*, *The Big Book of Library Grant Money* (Taft Group, 2007), *Grants for Libraries Hotline* and the Library Grants blog; however, don't overlook other subject guides such as the *Grants for Arts, Culture, and the Humanities* if your project involves an art exhibit, humanities program, or cultural performance. Consult *Grants for People with Disabilities* if people with disabilities will benefit from your project. Thoroughly search for local or lesser-known specific funding resources that may help you in your search for a grant. Examples of these are the *Everything Technology: Directory of Technology Grants* and the *Directory of Grants for Native American Tribes and Organizations*.

Spend some time examining each resource to understand the unique terms used in the resource and how the resource defines terms. Definitions are usually included in a glossary, appendix, or user's guide. Be clear on how a resource defines different kinds of grants and use exactly those terms to narrow your search in that resource.

Understand the Different Kinds of Grants

Before you begin your research, familiarize yourself with the terminology used for different kinds of grants. If you understand what these kinds of grants fund you will save yourself time by researching only grants that are appropriate for your project and your library.

- **Block Grant**: A federal grant awarded to state or local governments for a specific need or issue. Local and state governments then set specific grant guidelines within their own jurisdictions and make smaller grants to local agencies and non-profits.

- **Capacity-Building Grant**: Grants that help agencies and non-profits strengthen their internal operations so that they can be more effective/efficient in fulfilling their missions.

- **Capital-Building Grant**: "Bricks and mortar" funding used to purchase land and construct, renovate, or rehabilitate buildings and facilities. These grants may also fund major equipment purchases or endowments.

- **Challenge Grant**: A grant promised to awardees on the condition that they raise additional funds from other sources to reach a specific fundraising goal.

- **Discretionary Grant**: Federal or state grants that are awarded directly to community organizations, schools, and/or local governments.

- **Emergency Grant**: Grants made to help an agency through an extraordinary short-term or unexpected financial crisis.

- **Formula Grant**: Non-competitive grants awarded by federal or state governments to lower levels of government based on a predetermined formula to address specific needs.

- **General Operating Support Grant**: Funding for the general purpose or work of an organization such as personnel, administration, and other expenses for an existing program.

- **Matching Grant**: A grant that requires awardees to provide a certain amount and funders to provide the rest. For example, a 1:1 match means that the funder and the library each provide half of the cost of the project.

- **Project/Program Grant**: Funding for a specific initiative or new endeavor, not for general purposes.

- **Research Grant**: A grant that supports a specific research project or issue.

- **Seed Grant**: Funding designed to help start a new project or charitable activity, or to help a new organization in its start-up phase.

- **Technology Grant**: A grant that provides funding for a technology project, including equipment.

Work from the General to the Specific

Broad Research

First, record the goals, objectives, and activities of your grant project on a Keyword Worksheet. You can take this information directly from the Project Planning Worksheet you completed in Chapter 3. Bring together your grant team to develop a comprehensive list of keywords that describe your project. Think of broad, narrow, and related terms. Start with general keywords like "library," "libraries," or "information." Then think of words more specific to your project, yet still broad, like "technology," "resources," "services," or "instruction." Incorporate the keywords you already identified on your Project Planning Worksheet. Don't forget to include variations on words and synonyms.

Do a team brainstorming activity or work in small groups. Team members might be given ten minutes to write down keywords on their own Keyword Selection Worksheets first. Record the keywords your team selects on one Keyword Selection Worksheet that you will use throughout your grant research to keep you on track and headed in the right direction. Figure 6.1 shows an example of a completed Keyword Selection Worksheet for the project we designed in Chapter 3, Your Library for Life. See page 204 in the Toolkit section for a Keyword Selection Worksheet you can copy and use for your own team activities and research.

Use these keywords to do your broad research in all the general resources appropriate for your project, such as national directories and grants databases for government, foundation, corporate, and local funders. If more than one person will be doing the research, each person can work from a copy of the same Keyword Selection Worksheet.

Figure 6.1. Sample Keyword Selection Worksheet

Project: Your Library for Life	Keywords
Goals: By addressing library services for mature adult community members this project will: 1. Facilitate access to the library's resources and services by mature adult customers. 2. Respond to the lifelong learning, leisure, and changing information needs of the community's mature adult population.	Mature adults Aging Senior citizens, seniors Older adults Resources Services Community, communities, community members Library, libraries Lifelong learning Continuing education Class, classes Instruction Training Education Teach Learning Leisure Information Online Information technology Technology Computers Programs, programming Economy Library patrons, library users, library customers
Objectives: 1. 20 percent more mature adults will find information that meets their needs during a visit to the library or the library's website. 2. Mature adult library customers will be able to meet 50 percent more of their information needs and requests online. 3. 85 percent of mature adult community members will find library services valuable and applicable to their lives. 4. 25 percent more mature adult community members will determine that library programming designed to help them in tough economic times improved their quality of life. 5. 40 percent of the adult population over 55 will be registered library borrowers.	
Outcomes: 1. The ability of mature adult community members to research their questions using information technology in the library will increase their ability to make informed choices. 2. Mature adult community members will be knowledgeable about the information technology available in the library, and they will know how to use it to improve their quality of life. 3. Mature adults in the community will be able to use the library's website to find information that will improve their quality of life. 4. Mature adult customers will gain knowledge as a result of library programs and seminars that will improve their condition.	
Activities and Action Steps: Advertise classes and programs, information technology resources and services. Create a brochure. Create advertisement. Recruit older adults. Develop a public awareness plan and marketing strategy. Hold public awareness activities. Develop curriculum. Teach classes. Design and implement pre- and post-tests/surveys. Develop standardized research guides. Update and enhance website. Develop a plan to spotlight library materials in areas heavily used by older adults. Conduct a needs assessment. Conduct focus groups. Develop a collection development plan. Collaborate and partner. Plan programs. Assess barriers. Evaluate ADA compliance.	Public awareness Marketing Brochure Advertisement Public awareness Curriculum Classes Training Instruction Teach Computers Website Online Classroom Computer lab Tests Research guides Displays Collection development Disabilities Americans with Disabilities Act (ADA)

Narrowing Your Search

As you narrow your research, you will use more specific resources such as electronic databases, local directories, and subject directories. Databases allow you to combine multiple fields in one search, and they often will provide more in-depth information about targeted funding sources. Make yourself aware of what is available in the various resources you are using and take full advantage of the information provided. Local funding directories list funders that limit their grant giving to your geographic area, as well as local corporate giving programs and small corporate grants that may not appear in the national directories. Likewise, subject directories may include funding sources just right for your project that may not be included in the national directories due to their size. As you narrow your search, you will begin to see some real funding possibilities. This part of your research can be time-consuming; however, this is an important part where you will find the right funder for your project. So, dig in!

As you examine the funder entries in the broad research resources, compare your project keywords on the Keyword Selection Worksheet with a potential funder's purpose; field of interest or focus; and the type of support given. Decide whether a funder is a good match based on how relevant the information in the entries is to your project.

Record Your Findings

When you identify a likely funder, record the information about the funder on a Funder Summary Worksheet (see page 205 in the Toolkit section). Don't scrutinize too much at this point; make a worksheet for any funder that is a possibility. If you do this faithfully during the course of your research, when you finish, you will have a healthy pile of Funder Summary Worksheets chock-full of important information about funders that are "good matches" for your grant project. These worksheets hold your research "notes," providing the information you will need to move ahead while reducing the chance that you will miss some vital information you forgot to write down.

Organize Your Research

Look carefully through your Funder Summary Worksheets and prioritize them. If, as you look at these worksheets again, you determine that some are definitely not good matches, file them away. They were close enough for you to start a worksheet, and they may be on target for a future project. If you have questions on some, or need further clarification on whether a funder may be interested in a project like yours, contact the funder. By now you are very familiar with the foundation, agency, or corporation; therefore, you will be asking intelligent, informed questions. Use this initial contact to develop a rapport with the contact person. He or she is usually happy to answer your questions and work with you, and will be pleasantly surprised at how much you already know from the research you have done. After this contact, you will know whether to place the worksheet in the "go" or "no go" pile.

The worksheets in the "go" pile represent the funders you will approach for a grant. Start a separate file for each funder. Here you will keep the worksheet, a record of contacts, phone notes, correspondence, grant announcements, etc.

Researching Government Resources

Grants.gov (www.grants.gov)

Grants.gov includes all discretionary grants offered by the 26 federal grant-making agencies and it is your best bet for an initial broad search for federal grants awarded directly to community agencies and organizations, schools, and libraries. Go to the main Grants.gov page and click on "Find Grant Opportunities." Figure 6.2 shows the Grants.gov main search screen.

To search for a grant opportunity you do not need to register at the site; however, if you want to apply for a grant you must register. This can take three to five business days, so if you think you might be applying, register early. From the main search screen, you can do the following:

Figure 6.2. Grants.gov Main Search Screen

- Do a Basic Search by keyword, Funding Opportunity Number (FON) or Catalog of Federal Domestic Assistance (CFDA) number.
- Browse by category of funding activities.
- Browse by the agency offering grants.
- Do an Advanced Search using more specific criteria.

Select Basic Search and enter broad keyword term(s) in the Keyword Search box. Then click on "Search" and take a look at the results (see Figure 6.3). Take note of the closing date column. The deadlines for many grants in your results list may have already closed. If you click on the Closing Date column you can arrange your results by closing date in descending order, thereby showing the open opportunities at the top of your list. From your results list using any search mode on Grants.gov, you can click through to the original.

The Basic Keyword Search searches grant titles and synopses only. If you aren't satisfied with your results, then from the main search page, you may select "Browse by Category" or "Browse by Agency" to do your broad search. When you use "Browse by Category" or "Browse by Agency," your results list will be shorter and easier to browse; however, you may miss an opportunity offered by an agency or a category you inadvertently overlooked. When you use Browse by

Figure 6.3. Grants.gov Results Screen

GRANTS.GOV℠

Contact Us   SiteMap   Help   RSS   Home

Home > Find Grant Opportunities > Search Grant Opportunities > Search Results

FOR APPLICANTS

Applicant Login

Find Grant Opportunities

  Basic Search

  Browse by Category

  Browse by Agency

  Advanced Search

  Email Subscription

Get Registered

Apply for Grants

Track My Application

Applicant Resources

Search FAQs, User Guides and Site Information

APPLICANT SYSTEM-TO-SYSTEM

FOR GRANTORS

ABOUT GRANTS.GOV

HELP

CONTACT US

SITE MAP

Search Results

New Search

Sort: Relevance, Descending   Sort by Open Date   Sort by Relevance   Results 1 - 20 of 353

Close Date	Opportunity Title	Agency	Funding Number	Attachment
08/04/2009	Arizona Trails Development and Maintenance	Department of the Interior	BLM-AZ-RFA-09-1364	RFA New Award ,
08/06/2009	CHILDREN'S HEALTH INSURANCE PROGRAM REAUTHORIZATION ACT (CHIPRA) OUTREACH AND ENROLLMENT GRANTS CYCLE I	Centers for Medicare & Medicaid Services	HHS-2009-CMS-CHIPRA-0008	CONFIDENTIAL ,
10/06/2009	Digital Humanities Start-Up Grants	National Endowment for the Humanities	20091006-HD	
12/10/2009	Spinal Cord Injury Research Program Advanced Technology Therapeutic Development Award	Dept. of the Army -- USAMRAA	W81XWH-09-SCIRP-ATTDA	Principal Investigator ,
04/14/2009	DOD Neurofibromatosis Exploration ? Hypothesis Development Award	Dept. of the Army -- USAMRAA	W81XWH-09-NFRP-EHDA	Principal Investigator , Program Announcement ,
07/31/2009	BLM WY Amphibian Batrachochytrium Dendrobaditis PCR Testing and DNA Collection	Department of the Interior	BLM-WY-RFA09-9006	RFA New Award ,
11/02/2007	Woody Biomass Utilization Grant Program	Forest Service	USDA-FS-2008-01	1 GRANT APPLICATION PACKAGE Request for Proposals ,
08/05/2009	Montana Education and Weed Awareness	Department of the Interior	BLM-MT-NOI09-1076	UNITED STATES ,
07/16/2009	San Simon Watershed Assessment	Department of the Interior	BLM-AZ-NOI-09-1291	NOI New Award ,
01/30/2009	Federal Motor Carrier Safety Administration Fiscal Year 2009 Safety Data Improvement Program Grant Opportunity	DOT/Federal Motor Carrier Safety Administration	FMCSA-SADIP-2009-01	SAFETY DATA IMPROVEMENT PROGRAM GRANT DESCRIPTION ,

Agency, remember to look at all federal government agencies that fund libraries, clearinghouses, archives, and technical information services mentioned in Chapter 5, such as the Department of Education, Department of Health and Human Services, National Endowment for the Arts, National Endowment for the Humanities, Institute of Museum and Library Services, and the National Institute for Literacy. Most of these agencies, such as the Institute of Museum and Library Services have their own websites (see Figure 6.4) where they post the availability of grants, including guidelines, application and deadline information. Often, departmental websites offer more functionality for searching their grant opportunities. For instance, the IMLS site can be searched for available grants by grant name, institution, or project type.

To narrow your search on Grants.gov, use the "Advanced Search" option to combine multiple fields such as title keywords, dates, funding activity categories, funding instrument types, eligibility, agencies, and subagencies (see Figure 6.5). Here you can limit your search to "Open Opportunities," which is a big plus in narrowing your results.

For help with searching Grants.gov, refer to "Searching Grant Opportunities" at www07.grants.gov/section3/SearchingGrantOpportunities .pdf.

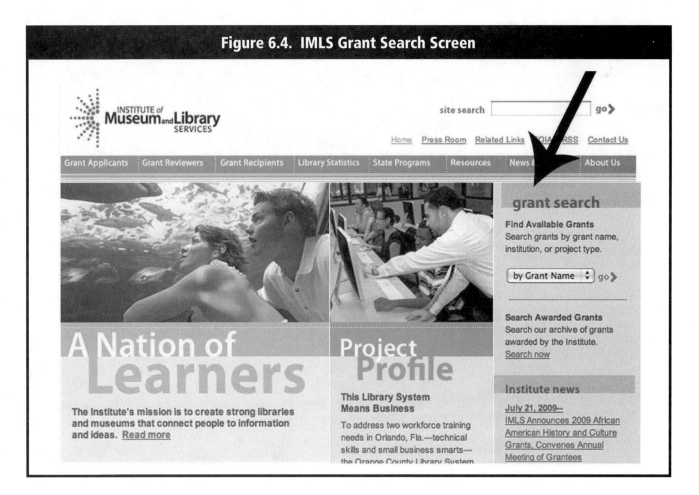

Figure 6.4. IMLS Grant Search Screen

Figure 6.5. Grants.gov Advanced Search Screen

Federal Register (www.gpoaccess.gov/fr/index.html)

Many federal grant opportunities appear in the *Federal Register* in the form of Notices of Funding Availability (NOFAs), Notices Inviting Applications, or Notices and Requests for Applications. To search for these announcements, start at the Federal Register "Advanced Search" page (www.gpoaccess.gov/fr/advanced.html) and check the boxes for: (1) the most recent volume and (2) "Notices" and a date range from three to six months ago to the present date. You can limit by inclusive dates to narrow your search; however, be careful with this. You don't want to limit too narrowly and miss finding applicable grants. The periods of time between notice announcements and submission deadlines vary widely among federal agencies. Enter your broad keywords in the Search box, and add the truncated keyword "fund*" to include funds, funding, and other variations on the word "fund" (see Figure 6.6). For

Figure 6.6. Federal Register Advanced Search Screen

GPO Access

Resources by Topic [Go] Site Search: advanced [   ] [Go]

LEGISLATIVE / EXECUTIVE / JUDICIAL   HELP / ABOUT

A-Z RESOURCE LIST / FIND A FEDERAL DEPOSITORY LIBRARY / BUY PUBLICATIONS

Home Page > Executive Branch > Federal Register > Advanced Search

Federal Register: Advanced Search

DATABASE FEATURES
- FR Main Page
- Browse
- Simple Search
- Advanced Search
- Retrieve an FR Page
- Search Tips
- About the FR

RELATED RESOURCES
- Regulations.gov
- Unified Agenda
- Code of Federal Regulations
- e-CFR
- List of CFR Sections Affected
- Search all Regulatory Applications
- All NARA Publications

ABOUT GOVERNMENT
Ben's Guide to U.S. Government

Select a Volume(s):

☑ 2009 FR, Vol. 74   ☐ 2004 FR, Vol. 69   ☐ 1999 FR, Vol. 64
☐ 2008 FR, Vol. 73   ☐ 2003 FR, Vol. 68   ☐ 1998 FR, Vol. 63
☐ 2007 FR, Vol. 72   ☐ 2002 FR, Vol. 67   ☐ 1997 FR, Vol. 62
☐ 2006 FR, Vol. 71   ☐ 2001 FR, Vol. 66   ☐ 1996 FR, Vol. 61
☐ 2005 FR, Vol. 70   ☐ 2000 FR, Vol. 65   ☐ 1995 FR, Vol. 60

Select a Section(s): (if desired)

☐ Contents and Preliminary Pages   ☐ Notices   ☐ Reader Aids
☐ Final Rules and Regulations   ☐ Presidential Documents ☐ Corrections
☐ Proposed Rules   ☐ Sunshine Act Meetings
                                   (before 3/1/1996)

Search by Issue Date: (if desired)

- Date Range (mm/dd/yyyy): From [   ] to [   ]
- Specific Date (mm/dd/yyyy): ⦿ ON ○ BEFORE ○ AFTER [   ]

Search: [   ] (Submit) (Clear) [Search Tips]

Maximum Records Returned: [50 ↕]

- The FR citation 60 FR 12345 refers to page 12345. To search by page, enter "page 12345" (in quotes) in the search terms box. FR pages start with page 1 with the first issue and continue sequentially until the end of the calendar year.
- To search by CFR citation, enter (in quotes) the title, the words *CFR* and *part*, and the part number. For example: "40 CFR part 55".
- To narrow a search, use the Boolean operators ADJ (adjacent), AND, OR and NOT. For example: "environmental protection agency" AND superfund.
- To find variations on words, truncation can be used. For example: legislat* will retrieve both legislation and legislative.

A service of the U.S. Government Printing Office.

more information, read the "Search Tips" for information on Boolean searching capabilities and truncation.

Remember, you are starting with a broad search, so your results may require major sifting. The good news here is that you may catch something that wouldn't appear if you had performed a narrow search first. The extra work up front is sometimes worth it in the long run. If your broad search yields an overwhelming amount of results, begin to narrow your search with additional keywords until your results list is manageable. Figure 6.7 illustrates the search results.

When you click on an entry, you will go straight to the corresponding *Federal Register* announcement. To view a sample *Federal Register* entry for an opportunity shown on the results in Figure 6.7, see this book's companion DVD. As you will see, the notice includes complete information including eligibility information, priorities, application and submission information, application review information, definitions, and who to contact if you have questions.

Catalog of Federal Domestic Assistance (CFDA) (www.cfda.gov)

There are many ways to navigate the CFDA website. One way is to look for "Find Programs" on the main page. Enter your keywords,

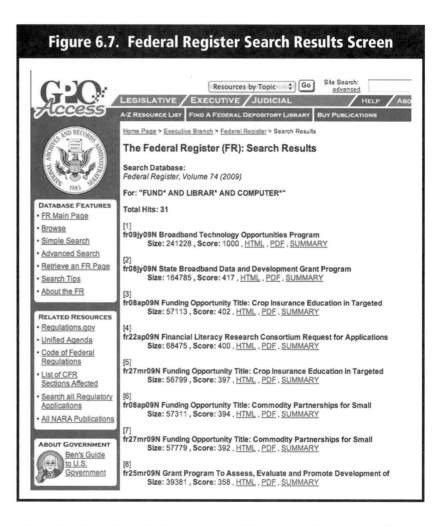

Figure 6.7. Federal Register Search Results Screen

select "Project Grants" for Assistance Type, and click on Search (see Figure 6.8).

Figure 6.8 shows a list of all federal programs that fund project grants and contain the entered keywords. Beware—these are not all active grant opportunities. You will be able to access information about a program on the CFDA site; however, to find out if a grant is currently available for the program you must click through to the agency website. (See the Toolkit section in this book and the companion DVD for an example of a program description on the CFDA website.)

The CFDA site is an excellent place to get an overall "big picture" view of federally funded grant programs in your area of interest. If you see a potential match that is not an active grant program, you can watch for an announcement on the *Federal Register* website, or periodically revisit the agency's website for new grant announcements. If you find a grant match that is active, fill out a Funder Summary Worksheet!

At the CFDA website you can search for formula grants, which are grants that funnel funds through state agencies. If you see a potential formula grant opportunity, follow through by contacting your state agency to inquire about applying for these funds. Using the Advanced Search form you can narrow your search by functional area, agency,

Figure 6.8. CFDA Search Results Screen

subagency, applicant eligibility, beneficiary eligibility, deadlines, type of assistance, and more.

Researching Foundation Resources

Grants for Libraries and Information Services is a good place to start your broad search for foundation grants. This Foundation Center publication, updated annually, contains descriptions of more than 2,800 recent grants to libraries and information services of $10,000 or more. Close to 700 foundations are represented. *The Big Book of Library Grant Money* (Taft Group, 2007) contains profiles of private and corporate foundations and direct corporate givers of grants to libraries. Remember to consult other subject-specific directories that match your project, such as arts and culture, children and youth, health, and education.

Once you identify possible funders, you can narrow your search by referring to the *Foundation Directory* and the *Foundation 1000* for more in-depth information about a particular foundation. The *Foundation Directory Online* is available free of charge as part of the Foundation Center's Core Collection at Cooperating Collections throughout the United States (foundationcenter.org/collections) and by subscription at various levels from the Foundation Center. Using this database, you can combine multiple criteria to narrow your search. When you identify a funder you may access detailed information about the funder including application information and the funder's IRS returns, or 990s.

A non-profit legally established in any state must obtain recognition as a charitable organization from the IRS so that contributions can be tax deductible. Most foundations apply for this 501(c)(3) status. The IRS requires foundations to make their information available by filing a Form 990. This form becomes a great source of information to the grant seeker as it provides information about the foundation's finances, the grants it gives, and who serves as board members, for example. Form 990s for foundations and community foundations can be searched at the Foundation Center's 990 Finder (tfcny.fdncenter.org/990s/990search/esearch.php). Guidestar (www.guidestar.org) also provides Form 990s for many tax-exempt organizations.

Websites of the foundations themselves are excellent sources of current information about a foundation, including its mission, what it is interested in funding, upcoming deadlines, application guidelines, recently funded projects, and contact information. You can find links to foundations by searching for a foundation at The Foundation Center's (foundationcenter.org/) main page.

Researching Corporate Resources

Many major corporations have created their own foundations and corporate giving programs. The *National Directory of Corporate Giving* is a good starting place as well as the corporations' websites. In general, corporations give to organizations in communities in which they operate. Go to the corporation's main webpage and look for a link containing the word "Community," for example, Community Involvement, Community Giving, and Community Outreach. Click on this link to find information about grants the corporation awards to community organizations. One example of a corporation that gives to communities is Target (see Figure 6.9).

Figure 6.9. Target Community Outreach Page

Community Outreach

Target gives 5% of its income to communities – over $3 million every week.

Company ▸ Community Outreach

Education

We play an active role in supporting education, especially early childhood reading and resources for teachers and classrooms.

More about education ▸

Arts + Culture

We sponsor programs, exhibits and performances that make artistic and cultural experiences more visible and accessible to families.

More about arts ▸

Social Services

To strengthen the communities we serve, we are dedicated to providing basic needs to families in crisis, supporting disaster relief efforts, and preventing family violence.

More about social services ▸

Target Grants

Find out if your program or project qualifies for a local store grant or a Target Foundation grant, and get application information.

Apply for a Grant ▸

Key Partners

American Red Cross   PTO Today, Inc.

Each corporate site is arranged differently, so you may need to explore a little to get to the information you need. If you have questions, contact the corporation's Community Outreach office. They are usually happy to talk to you about what they fund and where to find additional information.

Researching New Grant Opportunities

An important part of your research is staying up-to-date with new grant opportunities. Subscribe to some of these blogs, RSS feeds, e-mail notification services, and electronic newsletters; read periodicals; and participate in electronic discussion groups.

Blogs

A shortcut to finding library grants is available on the Library Grants blog, a free service we have offered since 2005. New grants are posted every month, and at times every week. We include the deadline, a brief description, and a link to more information. To save you time in grant seeking, we verify with every grant opportunity that libraries of some type are eligible to apply, we only include national or large regional grants, and we remove the listings once the deadlines have passed. All types of grants are posted. Visit us at librarygrants.blogspot.com and subscribe to the RSS feed.

E-mail Notification Services

The *Philanthropy News Digest RFP Bulletin* is a weekly roundup of recently announced Requests for Proposals (RFPs) from private, corporate, and government funding sources. Each RFP listing provides a brief overview of the funding opportunity as well as a link to the complete RFP. Subscribe to this and other electronic newsletters at the Foundation Center website (foundationcenter.org/newsletters/).

At Grants.gov you can receive notifications of new grant opportunity postings and updates by subscribing to various RSS feeds (www.grants .gov/help/rss.jsp) or e-mail notification services (www.grants.gov/ applicants/email_subscription.jsp).

You can subscribe to Grants.gov RSS feeds for the following:

- New Opportunities by Agency
- New Opportunities by Category
- Modified Opportunities by Agency
- Modified Opportunities by Category

Grants.gov e-mail notification services include the following:

- **All Grants Notices** sends you e-mail notifications of all new grant opportunities.
- **Grants.gov Updates** sends you updated information about critical issues, new tips, and other updates.
- **Notices Based on Advanced Criteria** sends you e-mail notifications based on specific criteria such as funding instrument type, eligibility, or subagency.
- **Notices Based on Funding Opportunity Number** sends you notifications based on Funding Opportunity Numbers (FON). A FON is a number that a federal agency assigns to its grant announcement.

Electronic Newsletters

Centered
www.tgci.com/newsletter/
A newsletter from The Grantsmanship Training Center offering tips, advice, and strategies on grantsmanship.

Grants for Libraries E-News Alerts

west.thomson.com/signup/newsletters/209.aspx

A free weekly e-mail newsletter that provides timely information on new grant opportunities and funding programs for libraries.

Philanthropy News Digest

foundationcenter.org/pnd

A daily news service of the Foundation Center, this is a compendium, in digest form, of philanthropy-related articles and features culled from print and electronic media outlets nationwide.

Primary Source

www.imls.gov/news/source.shtm

IMLS newsletter containing brief articles that alert readers to new information about grants and other news.

TGCI *Federal Register* **Grant Announcements**

www.tgci.com

An alert service provided by The Grantsmanship Center (TGCI) draws announcements from TGCI's daily search of the *Federal Register*. Registration is free.

Periodicals

Check your state library agency, large local library systems, college and university libraries, community foundations, and online databases for these periodicals.

Grants for Libraries Hotline

west.thomson.com/productdetail/139015/40560036/product detail.aspx#

Twelve monthly issues describe grant opportunities for libraries and librarians, as well as opportunities in the field of education. $213 (12 issues) with weekly e-mail updates.

Chronicle of Philanthropy

1255 23rd Street NW, Suite 700

Washington, DC 20037

philanthropy.com/section/Home/172

Includes a "New Grants" section. $72 per year (24 issues) with online and digital editions available

Electronic Discussion Groups

Charity Channel Forums (www.charitychannel.com) are online discussion groups where non-profit professionals join discussions on topics related to funding and other non-profit issues. There is an annual subscription fee.

Databases

If you are at an academic institution, investigate grants alert opportunities through your Grants and Contracts or Research Office. Subscription databases may include IRIS, InfoEd SPIN, GrantSelect, GrantWire, or GrantAdvisor Plus.

Researching Local Resources

It is very possible that many local grant opportunities may not be found while you are researching the national directories, websites, periodicals, and newsletters. Local research requires legwork, phone calling, networking, relationship building, and marketing your project idea. Here are some places for you to start your local research.

State or Local Funding Directories

Don't forget to search for local opportunities, starting with your local or state funding directory (fdncenter.org/getstarted/topical/sl_dir .html). State libraries and college and university libraries generally provide these types of funding directories and research tools.

Community Foundations

Visit your local community foundation to use their library or collection of information on local corporations and foundations. Talk to the people at your community foundation about appropriate funding sources for your project idea. Their business is to match funders with organizations like yours. Visit your community foundation's website for grant opportunity announcements and application guidelines. Subscribe to their RSS feed. To find community foundations in your state, visit www.cof.org/whoweserve/community/resources/index.cfm?navItem Number=15626#locator.

Local Clubs, Agencies, and Organizations

Talk to friends and contacts who are associated with local agencies and organizations that may fund projects like yours. Visit with your Chamber of Commerce and local clubs to tell them about your project. Look at a local corporation or foundation website for detailed information about their community involvement. Talk to local banks and stores to find out if they have giving programs. Ask your board for help in connecting with potential funders in your community. Watch the local newspaper for articles about grants given to other non-profits in your community and follow up with the funders. Join your local chapter of the Association of Fundraising Professionals (www.afpnet.org/international.cfm?folder_ id=873).

Research your local community directory and refer to Michigan State University's list of service clubs and civic organizations that provide funding (www.lib.msu.edu/harris23/grants/servicec.htm). Your yellow pages, library board or friends, and staff may also help identify local clubs and organizations that provide funding. The best way to find out about these opportunities is through local websites or by contacting the associations directly.

Newsletters

Read newsletters from local non-profit agencies, your state library, state library association, local public library association, or special library association chapter for announcements of recently funded library projects in your area. Contact your colleagues at these libraries and ask how they found their success, ask them to tell you about their project, about the grant process, and whom they worked with at the funding source.

State Agencies and Departments

State agencies that offer grants include:

- State Library Agency: To find out if your state library offers LSTA subgrants, state grants-in-aid, or other funding or state resources, check on their websites (www.publiclibraries.com/ state_library.htm); many provide applications online and some also offer free grant workshops.
- State Humanities Councils: www.neh.gov/whoweare/state councils.html
- State Arts Councils: www.nasaa-arts.org/aoa/saaweb.shtml
- State Departments of Education: wdcrobcolp01.ed.gov/ Programs/EROD/org_list.cfm?category_ID=SEA

Professional Associations

Check your professional associations' websites for grant funding that is available for members. Join their electronic discussion groups.

Talking with Funders

Throughout your research, as you work with your Funder Summary Worksheets, you will be contacting funders to clarify your questions, and to discuss their possible interest in your project—all the time developing working relationships with them. Remember that funders are people, too, and grant work involves building relationships with them. At this point in your research, you should feel comfortable calling any of the contacts on your "match" list should questions or concerns arise.

Now it is time to write your proposal.

Creating and Submitting the Winning Proposal

IN THIS CHAPTER:

✔ Overview

✔ Writing Tips

✔ Role of Partners and Collaborators

✔ Communicating with Funders

✔ How Grants Are Reviewed and Evaluated

✔ Specifications and Requirements

✔ Types of Applications

✔ Key Proposal Components

✔ Submitting Your Application

✔ Confirmation of Submission

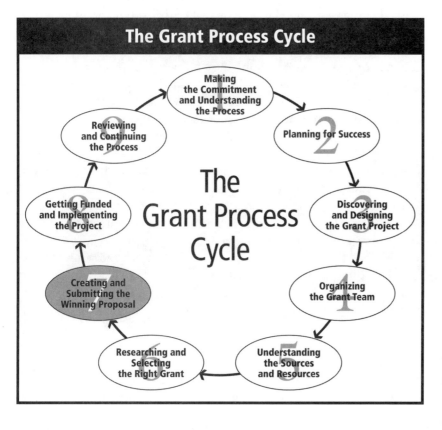

The Grant Process Cycle

Overview

Writing the winning proposal requires planning and organization. It is very important to realize the beginning of the grant process doesn't start with a grant application. Having a strategic plan as the foundation of your grant work ensures you are supporting your library's mission and goals and demonstrates to funders that the grant project is not just a haphazard idea. You also must be aware of any local procedures or requirements that would affect your library's ability to apply for a grant.

Make certain you have met any necessary stipulations dictated by your library's infrastructure whether that means your city, school, or university policies on grant work.

Putting together an effective grant proposal is more than just answering questions and filling out forms. You must examine your community, societal impacts, and the current issues affecting the people you serve. Just because you admire the library programs in a nearby town does not mean they would be a good fit for your community. You should understand the grant maker you are approaching, as your grant project should support not just your library's mission, but also your community and funder's interests, priorities, needs, and wants. All the work you've done in the previous steps will make this part of the grant process cycle flow smoothly.

Begin by reading the entire grant application carefully, especially the qualifications and the evaluation criteria. You don't want to be almost finished writing a proposal when you realize that you do not qualify, that you've missed a deadline, that you needed to partner with the local health department, or that you must provide unplanned services. Highlight all of the questions you must answer and make a list of the resources and materials you will need. Underline key words or phrases you might want to incorporate into your proposal. The Grant Submission Checklist at the end of this chapter (see p. 123) can be helpful for organizing this information. It is also on the DVD so you can adapt it to your specific needs.

Be prepared to write one or more drafts, as you want your proposal to be concise and easily understood. You certainly don't want to have a grant rejected due to typographical errors. Let others read your proposal and get their feedback. Especially helpful are those who are not connected to the library or the project. Even a family member could provide an interesting and helpful perspective. Just ask them to read your proposal for 15 minutes, and tell you what they understood. This may be more time than most preliminary reviewers will give your proposal on the first read-through. An objective reader can also catch any use of library lingo or acronyms that might be confusing to a grant reviewer. If they didn't immediately see what you want to achieve, rewrite it until it is clear. We've reviewed some grant proposals that we were unable to discern exactly what project the library was asking to fund. It should not be difficult to understand exactly how much you are requesting or for what purpose.

Writing Tips

Writing a proposal is different from other types of writing. Proposal writing is similar to sales or marketing work, or even good storytelling. You are attempting to convince the funder to sponsor and support your idea and project. Your proposal should tell the story of the people in your community, the need that they have and how your project, supported by the funder's grant, can make a positive and even life-changing impact in their lives. Creative storytelling techniques can be useful in demonstrating need, helping the funder see your community as real people with real problems. Your well-planned grant project with objectives and activities are the resolution to the need.

Making your story come alive successfully is especially important in the proposal summary or abstract, as some grant reviewers may use only this one section of your grant to judge your entire proposal. At the very least, your summary or abstract will make a first impression that will color the reviewer's approach to the rest of your proposal.

Display confidence and capability by approaching your project with the belief that it will be successful. Use language throughout your proposal that shows positive assurance. Demonstrate your ability to achieve the stated objectives. Your grant must show that you will be able to implement the project with success. Be persuasive, but reinforce your claims with plans, as bravado alone will not impress a funder. Be specific and include your goals, measurable objectives, and outcomes.

Proposals should also be concise. Elaborations should add depth and scope, insight, and interest. The proposal will be judged on content, not weight.

For a powerful and energetic proposal, avoid using passive verbs, such as *was* and *were* or static verbs such as *am, is, are, be, have, do, could, should, would*. Use active verbs instead (see sidebar).

Using the active voice demonstrates that you own the project and the work it will involve. For instance, "Library staff will develop and provide technology classes for seniors" communicates a much different sense of your relationship to the project than, "Technology classes will be provided."

ACTIVE VERBS	
achieve	identify
analyze	illuminate
assess	illustrate
assist	implement
change	indicate
conclude	inform
connect	inspire
coordinate	instruct
create	investigate
decide	involve
define	lead
demonstrate	learn
design	maintain
develop	manage
direct	motivate
educate	organize
elevate	plan
engage	prepare
ensure	promote
establish	provide
evaluate	validate

Role of Partners and Collaborators

Emphasize collaboration and partnerships throughout your proposal. Some funders are now requiring partnerships and/or collaborations. Ignoring a partnership requirement can cost you a grant win. You can often have a wider impact when more organizations are involved. You should be reaching out to other community organizations as part of your library outreach, so finding collaborations shouldn't be difficult. These relationships should be ongoing and not just limited to grant work. Your library should have representatives at community meetings, Chamber of Commerce, Lions Club, Kiwanis, planning or task force discussions, etc. Even if partners are not required, funders will admire that you are planning for sustainability and ensuring future community support.

Collaborating with other organizations is also a beneficial way to share equipment, expertise, and resources. Many small non-profits find great fulfillment in their partnerships with libraries, as often there are similar goals. Partnerships between libraries, schools, colleges, museums, religious groups, and community organizations are often successful as well. For example, if you want to assist your community with unemployment

> Be sure to develop community support for your project. Whenever possible, collaborate with another agency in planning and implementing your grant. There's a great deal more 'bang for your buck' when you work with someone else.
>
> —"A Collage of Cooperation" Clermont County Public Library Success Story (Gerding and MacKellar, 2006: 174)

issues, you might find valuable partners that provide job training, offer child care, GED preparation, or other social services that can help create a program with many ways to benefit and support job seekers.

Letters of commitment (memoranda of understanding, or MOUs) spell out the ways groups will work together and are an important way to document a partnership and designate responsibilities. A sample is included in the Toolkit (see the Grant Partnership Agreement Worksheet on p. 191), and it can be a great addition to your grant proposal.

Communicating with Funders

Don't be apprehensive about contacting the funder if you have questions that aren't answered in the RFP or application materials. Most charitable organizations have been created out of a desire to be part of the solution to societal problems. The reason they extend grants is to help fulfill their own missions. Funders give money to meet their goals, it is their job, and they are there to help. Of course, be certain you've done your research first and that you're not asking a question already answered in their documentation. You don't want to bother a funder and become a nuisance, but if you call with a realistic inquiry, it should be welcomed. An added benefit is that the funder will be familiar with your proposal before it has been submitted. This is a good way to start building a communicative partnership with the funder. Building trust and identifying mutual goals is essential to successful grant work. You may even want to set up a time to meet in person with local funders to start building good relationships.

> Work closely with staff of the granting agency. The first draft of our proposal was not fundable, but with the help of NEH staff we were able to tailor a grant that met the needs of our library and the NEH.
>
> —"Library Expansion and Renovation"
> Clear Lake Public Library
> Success Story
> (Gerding and MacKellar, 2006: 180)

DVD For reproducible and customizable versions of this checklist, see p. 208 in the Toolkit and the companion DVD.

QUESTIONS TO ASK FUNDERS CHECKLIST

- ☐ Is my library eligible for your grants?
- ☐ How are applications reviewed?
- ☐ Are there specific screening criteria or a rubric used? May we have a copy?
- ☐ May we submit a draft of the grant proposal before the final deadline for review?
- ☐ If I briefly describe the project, would you provide suggestions or advice?
- ☐ Are copies of successful grant proposals available?
- ☐ May we include our strategic plan or other supporting documentation in an appendix?
- ☐ May we include a table of contents?
- ☐ How and when are final decisions made?
- ☐ Will we be notified that our grant proposal has been received?

Applying to Multiple Funders

You may want to apply to more than one funder at a time. If you are submitting proposals to several different funders, you should indicate this in the proposal. For example, you might state, "In addition to your foundation, this proposal is being submitted to the Community Foundation and the Mr. Wealthy Benefactor Foundation" or "We have already received a grant of $30,000 from the Happy to Give Foundation, and are requesting $15,000 from your organization, which is the balance required for the project." This will not be viewed negatively, as funders often view multiple funding sources as a significant factor in the sustainability of projects. However, if you use the same grant proposal, make sure you customize it for each funder. Some funders have told us that they have received proposals with another agency's name on them. Not a very good first impression for your proposal!

How Grants Are Reviewed and Evaluated

As with any type of writing, it is important to keep your audience in mind—the individuals who will be reading, reviewing, and making a decision about your proposal. More than one person will probably be evaluating your proposal. It may be a committee that reviews your proposal, with each individual reviewer scoring your proposal on established criteria. Some funders distribute the individual sections of the proposal to different reviewers. For example, one reviewer may be focused on judging the specific project you are proposing, while a different reviewer will focus on examining the evaluation process you have specified. Some funders use external proposal reviewers on a contract basis or as volunteers. These reviewers may be subject specialists and they may be reading hundreds of grants.

Never assume any specific knowledge on the part of the reader. Do not assume that they will know that libraries are doing incredible work, or that you are informed of your community's needs or that they will know the duties of a reference librarian or the programming and supplies involved for a Summer Reading Program. Many grants are very competitive, which means that reviewers have numerous proposals to read and hard decisions to make. Ensuring that your proposal is very clear and easy to comprehend will increase your chances of success.

Being a grant reviewer is not easy work. Difficult decisions must be made. We have given grant workshops in which we use an exercise that involves our participants forming review committees. The groups are given grant proposals and must quickly decide how to distribute funding. We are always amazed at how passionate people become, defending their choices and arguing for one grant proposal over another. We remind them this is pretend money and pretend organizations, but it is an amazing demonstration of how some decisions are personally biased. You may assume that it will be clear which proposals stand out and should be funded, but some decisions are arbitrary. It isn't as easy to "give money away" as one may think and often there are heated debates and compromises made, such as giving less funding to one organization so that another grant can be funded as well. This is another reason it can be helpful to build relationships with funders and get early feedback as to what they are looking for and how your library can best present your case.

> When composing our proposal, we kept our grant reviewers in mind. To make our proposal easy to read we used bullet points and imagery so the key points could be easily found and our wording was kept succinct. Our use of images aided in conveying our intentions, adding a richer dimension to our proposal.
>
> —"We Read Together"
> Mount Laurel Library,
> Mount Laurel, NJ
> (see Library Grant Success Stories, pp. 161–163)

Specifications and Requirements

The content of the proposal should be tailored to any specifications found in the grant guidelines. This may include details such as the number of pages allowed, required forms, formatting particulars, and number of copies. Each detail is important. If a funder receives thousands of grants, it is easy to whittle the number of applicants by rejecting those who do not comply with instructions. For example, some funders specify that proposals should not be bound, as they may need to make copies for multiple reviewers. So before you spend the extra time and funds to produce a beautifully packaged manuscript, be sure you are fulfilling the funder's specified requests. We know of a case where a federal agency rejected a grant application without reading it because part of the proposal was not double-spaced, as specified in the guidelines.

Match the arrangement of the sections of the grant proposal to those in the application; don't change the order, even if it makes more sense to you to do so. Match the names of the section headings in your proposal to the section headings provided in the instructions. This will allow the reviewer to easily determine that all required information is included. Reviewers should never have to search for needed information.

The proposal should be neat, organized, and professional. Make a checklist of the specifications so that you ensure that you've met them. A sample is included at the end of this chapter.

Types of Applications

The Letter of Intent or Inquiry Letter

Funders sometimes ask for a letter of intent to be sent to them so that they can quickly decide whether it is a project that they would like to fund. If the funder accepts your letter of intent, then you will probably be asked to submit a longer, more detailed proposal. The letter of intent is usually a two- to three-page summary that gives a brief description of the project, the amount requested, the need, and a brief organizational overview. This letter should focus on how the project aligns with the funder's mission and goals. It should describe the needs and then outline the project. Write succinctly and clearly, organizing your case so that the funder can quickly make a decision.

Similarly, you might contact a funder with an inquiry letter. Using the same type of information as you would include in a letter of intent, you would send this letter if you were considering applying for a grant from a funder but were unsure if your library or project fits their scope of work.

The RFP or Grant Application

This is the typical grant proposal and is sometimes called a Request for Proposal (RFP) or a grant application. Several examples are included in the Resources section of the DVD or by following the links on our library grants blog (librarygrants.blogspot.com). Some funders will provide lengthy forms, while others will give brief guidelines or have an online application process. There will be differing priorities, deadlines, and variant approaches to the funding process. The good news is that although there are differences, most funders are essentially asking for the same information. They just may use different wording or prefer a different order. This means that once you've gone through the grant process cycle and written one quality grant proposal, the subsequent proposals will be less challenging and will not require the same intensive background work as the first. Common application forms are shared by some organizations, usually in a specific geographic area. Some grant applications only require a brief 1-page form, while others might be 30 to 40 pages, or some federal government applications may total hundreds of pages.

The Online Proposal

Many funders, especially government organizations, require proposals to be submitted online. There are usually detailed instructions with FAQs (frequently asked questions) and contact information for questions related to electronic submissions. Some sites have forms that you can download to your computer, fill out, and then upload to submit. Others only have an electronic form that must be completed while connected to the Internet. For those, we've found it best to first create the proposal in a word processor and then you can easily cut and paste into the web form. There have been proposals lost in the Ethernet, especially if uploaded on the due date when the server may be overloaded, so always make sure you have a backup copy and try to submit as early as possible.

Key Proposal Components

There are many ways to organize proposals. A Request for Proposal (RFP) will stipulate the requirements, and some are more detailed than others. Read the guidelines for specifications about required information and how it should be arranged. Most grant proposals are usually 15 pages or less. Government grants may require that you fill out lengthy forms and may be a lot longer. The Grant Proposal Template in the Toolkit section of this book (see pp. 209–219) and on the DVD contains a sample of a typical grant application that includes all the common components that you may customize to create your own application. Following are the most standard grant proposal components:

- Title Sheet
- Cover Letter
- Table of Contents
- Proposal Summary or Abstract
- Organizational Overview
- Statement of Needs

- Project Description
- Timeline
- Budget
- Evaluation Process
- Appendix

Title Sheet

This is your opportunity to display creativity and develop an ingenious title for your project or program—something that the grant reviewer will remember. However, if you are not particularly inspired, don't let this be a stumbling block. A title that is descriptive and informative is perfectly acceptable. You should also include the name of the funder you are directing the proposal to, the name and address of the submitting library, and the date.

Cover Letter

This is a basic letter outlining your proposal. This cover letter sets the tone for your proposal and should therefore be convincing. It should be easy to read, interesting, and comprehensive. Anyone reading this cover letter should be able to quickly determine exactly what your organization does, the purpose or reason for your request, and the amount of the request.

Keep it to one page and use your library's or organization's letterhead. The header should include the date, the name of the contact person at the funding organization, the name and address of the funding organization, and the title of your grant. The first paragraph should declare your pleasure in submitting the grant in order to serve your target audience.

Incorporate the following information from your Project Planning Worksheet:

- Grant Project Title
- A few sentences from your Project Description, including outcomes
- Needs Statement
- Two to three sentences from your Organizational Overview
- Names of Grant Project Partners
- Funding Requested and any in-kind, matching, or outside grant funds
- Any planning accomplished and involvement of the target audience

Conclude by offering to provide additional information, if any is needed. The library director or another authority should sign the cover letter.

Table of Contents

As in a book, a table of contents will help organize your proposal and make it easy for reviewers to locate necessary information. Different reviewers may be responsible for analyzing different parts of your proposal, so make sure each section can be comprehended independently. If it is not specified in the guidelines that you should include a table of contents, this may be one of the questions you want to ask the funder.

Proposal Summary or Abstract

Although this section appears at the beginning of the proposal, it should be written last. This ensures that it contains all the issues included in the proposal. The summary will essentially be a condensed form of your entire proposal. Nothing should be in your summary that is not in your proposal. It is your three-minute advertisement. This summary serves as the first impression and can be critical to the success of the proposal. It may be carefully scrutinized to determine if the rest of the proposal should even be considered, so it needs to be able to stand on its own.

Include the following in your summary:

- Library's exact legal name and full mailing address
- Contact information for the library director and the grant coordinator
- A few sentences summarizing the library's Organizational Overview, showing why the library is the best choice for implementing the grant project
- Project title
- Project description (from your Project Planning Worksheet), including the needs statement, as well as the target audience, and a summary of the project goals
- Partners
- Amount requested, including project funding from other sources
- Project time period
- Brief overview of the evaluation methods to be used

In the Proposal Summary, you should be succinct, sell your idea, and make your point precisely. You should present your whole case: what you want to do, why it's important, why you will succeed, and how much it will cost. It should be immediately clear why your project is unique and so compelling that the funder will want to immediately read your entire proposal. Be sure to avoid any library jargon that may be unclear or unfamiliar to the reviewer. This abstract should tie to the funder's mission and display the impact of your project and how the project will help fulfill the funder's goals.

Organizational Overview

Before funders will invest in a program, they must be certain that the funding will be managed by a capable, dependable, effective organization. The overview helps the funder judge the integrity and worthiness of your organization. This is your opportunity to sell what it is you do. Libraries have an instant reputation of credibility and trust, but remember that not everyone understands everything a library does, so don't assume that they will understand your terminology or basic processes. Libraries are the centers of communities, but to some people, they only represent books.

Detail your history, mission, who you serve, achievements, primary programs, current budget, leadership, board members, and key staff members. Brief success stories and human interest can be included, but should be relevant to the project and to the funder's interests. Answer the questions, "Who are we?" and "How are we qualified, and why should we be trusted?" A funder needs to deem your organization trustworthy and reliant for a true partnership to develop. Having a strategic plan is another way to demonstrate that your organization is well managed. If an appendix of supporting material is allowed, including the plan can be beneficial.

Granting agencies want to make the best use of their funding, and want to be assured that your project will be successful and help fulfill both your mission and theirs. If you've done your research, your organization should be a good match with the funder, so as they are reading your overview, they should immediately recognize similarities in mission, vision, and goals. A great match will mean that reviewers should think to themselves, "Hey, we want to accomplish the same things!"

Statement of Needs

In this section you will describe the current situation in your community and how your project will address it. Provide a compelling, logical reason why the proposal should be supported and is important. Start with the facts and then move on to the solution. This is not a list of wants, but the need for your project that will bring about a change in your target audience. You will include your needs assessment and show what your community really does require. Support this assessment by including qualified research and evidence to justify the need. Use both statistics and human interest stories for supporting examples. Include data that is historical, geographic, quantitative, and factual. Identify any other existing projects being implemented in your library or community that are related to the problem.

Remember that the need is never for things—not for new computers, new chairs, new books—but for solving a problem or addressing a need in your community. Focus on how the library can help improve your community. Funders want to help people, not buy things. Your proposal should tell the story of the people who will be helped.

Avoid describing the needs of your library as the problem. Not having enough computers at your library is not the problem. Rather, the problem might be the increase of deaths due to preventable illness and lack of health literacy. Providing more consumer health materials and health-related programming on free online health databases is a better solution. Explain how you will attempt to fulfill the need. Define what you intend to do.

For example, a rural librarian wanted to apply for books for the children in her community. She filled out the Project Planning Worksheet (see p. 198) and we reviewed it for her. When describing the need in her community that the project would address, she wrote, "Kids will have books." In the goals section she wrote, "Get books for kids." In the section addressing changes to the community and activities to take, she wrote, "Get books for kids." When we sat down to discuss her grant project, she said, "I can think up great ideas for grants, but when it is time to sit down and write about them, I get a mental block." So we asked her WHY she wanted the children to have books. She described her situation very enthusiastically, "Oh! We live in a very rural, very poor town. Many of the children don't own a single book of their own. I want to get a grant so we can give them a book of their own. One they can write their name in, take home with them, and read again and again. A book they can select based on their interests and that they can take pride in starting their own book collection and enjoying reading books from the library as well. I want them to not have to worry about the date it is due, and to have a brand new book of their own." Of course, this is a much more compelling need argument than just, "kids need books." We wanted to go and buy those kids some books right then! She was passionate about her project and about wanting to help the children. Her community had a real need, and many funders are interested in giving books to rural libraries. She just needed to figure out how to be as compelling in her writing as she was in person. When writing your grant proposal, don't forget that a real person with real feelings will be reviewing it. Unless you are dealing with a very bureaucratic grant maker, don't be afraid to appeal to their emotive interests.

We know a woman who was a volunteer librarian for a short time in a rural school in South Africa. She took the school's principal and librarian to a book distribution center to buy books for the school with money that she had raised. After they had selected some great purchases, and spent all the funding, the principal approached the volunteer. He said, "Will you buy a set of encyclopedias for my school? They are on sale and we do not have a set. You can buy the first set of encyclopedias ever for these students and they will have a wealth of knowledge about Africa and the world available to them." He wasn't afraid to ask, even though much had already been given, and the volunteer couldn't refuse him. Try to make your grant proposal one that can't be denied.

Sometimes it is all about the phrasing. For example, your library has budget cuts and you have had to cut staff. There are long checkout lines and your board thinks you could convert to using RFID so you can install self-checkout. Of course, this is not in your budget, so the board tells you to write a grant. When writing this proposal, it is important to think about what the real benefits are for the community. NOT: The lines are too long and we can't afford desk staff. INSTEAD: Focus on how RFID will free staff from checking out books so they can be available for community programs and one-on-one assistance, and how patrons will be able to check out books faster, with shorter lines. Explain how RFID will benefit those using your library.

Don't put the focus on the state or the country's needs, unless your project will serve those larger regions, but rather focus on the needs of your specific and unique community. The exact target population should be identified. Many funders are interested in knowing that the people who will benefit from the project are actually supportive of the grant. If the audience has had input and assisted with designing the program, make sure you include this information. Projects that are created with the involvement and input of the targeted population are more likely to be successful.

Prove why the library has the ability to respond to the need you have identified. Link the fulfillment of the need to your library's mission. Answer the questions:

- Why this issue?
- Why this target population?
- Why this funder?
- Why your library?

Project Description

This section is a more in-depth narrative than the project summary. In the previous section you discussed the needs, and now you will focus on the solutions. Acknowledge that you are aware of several solutions and that you have chosen the approach that will be most successful. State the advantages and any limitations of the solutions.

You should explain the significance of your project. Clarify how your work differs from, is related to, or extends earlier work. Back this up with research that proves it. Funders are more inclined toward a well–thought-out project that includes assurances of sustainability and that the funds will be used appropriately. Funders want to fund projects that will be successful, and these are often the indicators.

Don't assume that the reader is familiar with the subject. You could include articles in the appendix to support topics they may be unfamiliar with. For example, if requesting a computer lab, you could include studies done on public access computing, the digital divide, and the number of people that use library computers. This is an especially important part for someone outside of your organization to review for you to make sure it is easy to comprehend.

Include information on your target population, specifically, the number to be served, how you will attract them to the project, and how you will involve them. You may have more than one target population. For example, a reading program may involve children and their parents.

Sustainability of projects can be a big obstacle. Funders realize this and are more likely to favor organizations that address this issue in their proposals. Having partners and supporters and showing that you are investigating other sources of funding for the future, including matching funds, proves your project isn't short term, but a project that is worth investing in and supporting because it will make a true difference. Also include any ways that the project might leverage impact for other library goals or for other community needs.

Mention if research or planning has begun. This will enable the funder to see that you are prepared and committed to implementing the project. Some funders would rather support new activities and programs rather than existing ones. They would like to be connected to something original, exciting, groundbreaking. They want to see that their funding will make a difference that wouldn't otherwise be possible. Try to show how your project could support these desires.

Include the following topics and information:

- Project Significance and Uniqueness (include one or two sentences developed from the Needs Statement)
- Target Audience
- Project Goals
- Project Objectives
- Project Partners
- Plans for Sustainability and Leveraging Impact

Timeline

This section can require a lot of detail. In Chapter 3, you identified project activities from your goals and objectives. These activities will define how you are going to accomplish your project goals. In your timeline, you will estimate the duration of each major activity of your project; from the moment you get the grant check until the conclusion of your grant project when you are evaluating its success. This may be portrayed through a calendar format with start and end dates, project activities, and outcomes listed. If you are unsure of specific dates, you can instead break the timeline into months, for example: Months 1–2 Recruit and hire temporary employees; Months 3–4 Form advisory committees; Publish website. See Chapter 3 and the DVD for a sample timeline.

Budget

Budgets are cost projections and should be very detailed and well researched. Some funders will provide budget forms that must be submitted with the proposal, while others are less specific. The application may include a budget request section that covers the grant project specifically and another area to include the entire organizational budget. Costs should be reasonable with thorough explanations. Although it may be difficult to calculate some of the necessities, make a good effort. Taking the time to obtain exact costs instead of estimating will not only keep your budget detailed, but will also ensure that you really have enough funds to cover what you want to do. You most likely will want to involve your fiscal office or financial administrators at this point, as they may have a better awareness of cost projections and your library budget. Incorrect budget balancing is one of the most common errors in grant proposals, and can lead the funder to conclude that your proposal contains other inaccuracies as well.

A budget may include the following areas:

- Project or program budget: Your grant project income and expenses
- Library budget: Your entire library's income and expenses, including personnel and overhead

- In-kind contribution budget: Donated goods and services from partners and contributors that will be used for the grant project

Chapter 3 contains more information on developing the project budget. Be prepared to be flexible about your project budget in case the funder chooses to negotiate costs.

Provide information on other funding sources and efforts to supplement your grant request, including any financial commitments or support that will be provided by your library (often called in-kind contributions). This can include office space, computers or equipment, and personnel salaries. Few funders want to support an entire project; however, like most non-profits, libraries never have enough funding. When a funder sees that a library is willing to dedicate a portion of its budget to a project, it demonstrates the importance and support of the initiative. This also proves your organization's commitment to the project and indications for future sustainability. Funders also value matching funds and support from other sources, so include partners' contributions as well. Other income may include individual contributions, a special fundraising event, or grants from more than one source. Each possible revenue source should be included in the budget.

If the funder gives no specifications regarding the budget, you should make sure to include all expenses including: personnel, direct project costs, and administrative expenditures.

Personnel Expenses

This area consists of the salaries or a portion of salaries for everyone at your library. If you are including just the grant project personnel expenses, you will include everyone who will have a role working on the project. Some funders will allow you to include payroll taxes and benefits, such as insurance. If you are hiring contractors, consultants, evaluators, or trainers that will be working specifically on this project, you can include either the flat fee or hourly wage you will be paying them.

Direct Project Expenses

These are expenses that occur as a result of the project. It may include project-related travel, photocopies, postage fees, supplies, materials, advertising, marketing, space rentals, equipment, fees, and books.

Administrative/Overhead

These are costs that would be part of your annual budget, regardless of whether your library implements the grant project. This includes the cost of the library building, utilities, phone and other telecommunication costs, insurance, taxes, security systems, and maintenance costs. Some funders will not cover overhead costs, while others will specify a flat percentage acceptable for inclusion. Depending on the funder, personnel costs may be included as overhead as well. If the library is part of a larger organization, the institution may have a required/specified overhead cost already determined. For example, universities may have a set overhead percentage established for federal grant purposes.

Generally, funders expect to see a balanced budget for a project, so include both income and expenses. You may be able to include a budget narrative to explain any items that aren't immediately clear or to describe and justify specific items, relating each budget item to the grant activity it supports. See the Budget Templates on pages 201 and 202 in the Toolkit section for example budget forms. Further project budget details are included in Chapter 3 as well.

Evaluation Process

Evaluation is a method to examine, monitor, and determine the effectiveness of a project or activity. Evaluation aids in determining grant achievements, outputs, and outcomes, and communicating those results to the funders and to your community. It is important to know what the funders expect when it comes to evaluation. Most funders are very interested in ensuring that the funding and resources that they provide are used for a successful and intended purpose. Conducting a well-done evaluation can help sustain the partnership you have developed with your funder.

Funders usually specify the methods they require for evaluation. The Project Evaluation Plan introduced in Chapter 3 (see p. 60) will be helpful for this section. Make sure you review the Key Considerations on page 61. If you have questions regarding evaluation, contact the funder, as this is often an important part of the grant requirements.

Appendix

Supporting materials are often arranged in an appendix. Find out what documents and materials are desired or allowed. These materials may endorse the project and the applicant, include strategic plans, certifications, add information about project personnel, consultants, and board members, or include statistical information. Some funders will ask for financial statements, annual budgets, an IRS letter confirming that your organization is tax exempt, or additional articles or subject matter information.

Endorsements from supporting or partnering organizations may be included. Find support for your proposal from partners, other types of libraries, politicians, professionals, local government agencies, or public officials. The State Librarian or the State Library Association president may be willing to write a letter of support for a large grant. Endorsements are especially important for federal funding.

Policies about the inclusion of supporting materials differ widely among funders. Whether to allow them usually depends upon how materials contribute to a reviewer's evaluation of the proposals. Restrictions are often based on volume, bias, and relevance. Be prepared to invest the time to collect resources, document capability, update a résumé, and obtain letters or reports. Documents may include the following:

- Letters of support
- Letters of agreement
- List of board members or trustees, with titles

- Library's annual budget
- Library's mission statement
- Library's most recent accomplishments
- List of other sources of funding
- Copy of your 501(c)(3)
- Any additional information about your library that will help the funder determine your ability to succeed (press clippings, service brochures, statistics, staff awards, for example)
- CV or résumé of participating staff members, including this information:
  - Education: degrees, fields of study, institutions, locations
  - Professional work experience: positions, including institutions and locations
  - Honors and awards
  - Relevant publications
  - Qualifications and responsibilities associated with the grant

Authorized Signatures

Authorized signatures are usually required. Proposals may be rejected for lack of a specified signature. Be sure to allow the time to acquire all needed signatures. Particularly in universities or large metropolitan settings, acquiring signatures can take some time. The last thing you want to find out is that a necessary signatory is on vacation the week your proposal is due. You may have to have signatures from your board of directors or from your city fiscal office.

Submitting Your Application

Your proposal may be judged against some major criteria. Read through your proposal, and answer the questions in the Grant Proposal Checklist (see p. 220 in the Toolkit and the companion DVD).

GRANT PROPOSAL CHECKLIST

- ☐ Does the proposal address a well-formulated problem or need?
- ☐ Is it a real need of your community, or are you just trying to find a reason to justify a project you think would be fun to implement?
- ☐ Is it an important problem, whose solution will have useful effects?
- ☐ Is special funding necessary to solve the problem, or could it be solved using existing library resources?
- ☐ Does the proposal explain in sufficient detail to convince the reader that the project has significant substance, and is a justified plan to meet the need?
- ☐ Does the proposal explain clearly what work will be done?
- ☐ Does the proposal explain what results are expected, how they will be evaluated, and whether you can determine the success of the project?
- ☐ Is there evidence that the library knows about the work that others have done on the problem or issue?
- ☐ Does the library have a good track record with grants and will the library leadership be committed to implementation of this grant project?

Creating and Submitting the Winning Proposal

The first thing we recommended you should have done with your application guidelines was to highlight all the questions you needed to answer and all the materials you needed to include. Add these items to the Grant Submission Checklist (see p. 221 in the Toolkit and the companion DVD), if you haven't already. When you are ready to submit your entire application, turn to your Grant Submission Checklist and go through it carefully, item by item, to make sure that you have followed all the directions and guidelines. You want to double-check that you have included everything the funder requested.

You don't want your application disqualified on a technicality. For instance, be sure that you have not single-spaced the application when the funder specified that the application must be double-spaced; included brochures about your library programs in the appendix when they clearly stated not to include an appendix; or overlooked the lobbying form and forgot to include it in a federal application. After all this hard work, you don't want your application to be tossed into the trash for

GRANT SUBMISSION CHECKLIST

- ☐ The funder is interested in receiving my proposal.
- ☐ This proposal reflects the funder's areas of interest.
- ☐ We have followed the instructions and guidelines of the funder's specifications.
- ☐ Our proposal meets the page/word limits.
- ☐ The font type and size are correct.
- ☐ The margin size is correct.
- ☐ The line spacing is correct.
- ☐ We have used the specified type of paper, if indicated.
- ☐ We did not bind unless we were told we could.
- ☐ The correct number of copies and the original was sent; we also retained a copy for ourselves and copies were made for partners and supporters.
- ☐ We included letters of support.
- ☐ We have the required signatures.
- ☐ The proposal components are titled and compiled in the order specified.
  - ○ Title Sheet
  - ○ Cover Letter
  - ○ Table of Contents
  - ○ Proposal Summary
  - ○ Organizational Overview
  - ○ Statement of Needs
  - ○ Project Description
  - ○ Timeline
  - ○ Budget Request
  - ○ Evaluation Process
  - ○ Appendix
- ☐ The cover letter explains the project, states the total cost of the project, the amount expected from other sources, and the amount requested.

- ☐ The project description specifies the need that will be met and how people will benefit.
- ☐ The project description tells the whole story of our project in clear, understandable language.
- ☐ The objectives are measurable.
- ☐ The methodology explains how the objectives will be met.
- ☐ The timeline includes all major activities and who will do them.
- ☐ The evaluation plan measures the degree to which the objectives and outcomes are met.
- ☐ The project includes partners and reflects community involvement.
- ☐ The budget is reasonable and the calculations are correct.
- ☐ The project is sustainable.
- ☐ Adequate personnel are identified in the proposal to do the project.
- ☐ Adequate resources exist to do the project.
- ☐ Our library has the capacity to do the project.
- ☐ The proposal contains no jargon or acronyms.
- ☐ If attachments are included, we have confirmed that the funder allows them.
- ☐ The proposal has been proofread by an impartial person.
- ☐ The proposal is clear and easy to understand by someone outside the grant team.
- ☐ Letters of agreement from partners and letters of support from supporters are included, if allowed.
- ☐ We have met the deadline.
- ☐ The proposal looks professional.

reasons like these. You may think that funders should just overlook such little details. But following the guidelines can be one of the most important steps toward success.

Funders eliminate applications that don't comply with their guidelines all the time. It makes their jobs easier—they will have fewer applications to read. This practice also eliminates candidates who don't follow directions. Usually funders have many more worthy applications than they can possibly fund. They don't have the time to deal with applicants that don't comply with the instructions. Also, they don't want to give money to an organization that cannot follow directions. So, if you want the funder to read your proposal, follow the instructions and use the checklist.

Carefully go through your application with your checklist and check off every item as you make sure it is in place. Once everything is checked, you may seal the envelope and head for the post office or other delivery service. Using the options of delivery confirmation, a signature upon delivery, or some kind of tracking number can be helpful so that you know when the proposal has been delivered and it hasn't just disappeared without a trace after all your hard work.

Confirmation of Submission

Now, take a deep breath and congratulate yourselves for a job well done! Wait one week, and then contact the funding source to make sure that they received your proposal if you haven't received an e-mail confirmation or other form of communication. Validate that you are the contact person for your proposal and ensure that they have your correct phone number and e-mail. Let them know that you want to be notified about the status, evaluation, and outcome of your proposal. Keep in mind that it may be months before decisions are made, so don't expect to hear news soon. You just want to confirm receipt.

You can also request that you would like feedback about your proposal's strengths and weaknesses, although this information is sometimes unavailable, especially with a large volume of submissions. This may also be useful if you choose to approach the same funder again, or if you decide to contact another funder with the same project idea. More discussion on this topic is available in the next chapter.

Getting Funded and Implementing the Project

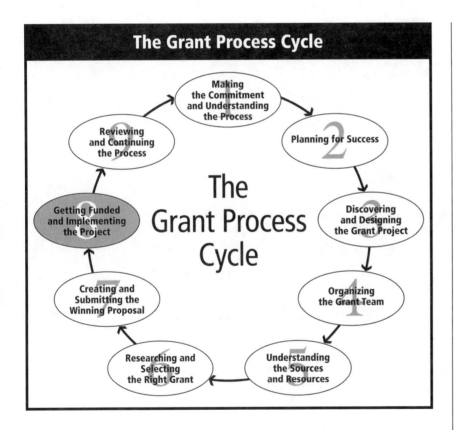

After You Submit Your Application

The processes that funders use to review and evaluate proposals vary widely. Some funders send proposals to reviewers who rate them based on a predetermined scoring system. Other systems for evaluating proposals may include review committees or panels of government officials, experts in a specific field, and community-based reviewers. Or, it might be a multiphase process where your proposal is first rated by an expert in projects like yours—such as literacy programs—and then rated by a foundation advisory board. If the funder's proposal evaluation method is not outlined in the grant guidelines, you should be able to find out this information by calling your contact at the funding agency. It sometimes helps to know their timeline, so you will have an idea about when to expect to hear from them about whether your project has been funded. You don't need to be anticipating a response right away if it will be two months before the funder makes a decision about which projects to fund.

It is not unusual for funders to contact applicants to ask questions or to clarify information in a proposal. Getting a call or e-mail from the funder during the proposal evaluation process is a good sign; it means you are still in the running and that the funder is interested enough in your proposal to request more information. Keep your project and proposal files organized and close at hand so you can answer quickly and effectively without rifling through drawers of files and piles of paper. Funders are often busy people and they want to complete the selection process in a timely and efficient manner. If you tell them you will "get back to them on that" or you don't promptly know the answers to their questions, your proposal may go to the bottom of the pile. This is not to say that your proposal will be discredited; but it may indicate to the funder that you are not very well organized, you are not very familiar with the details of your project, or that it will be difficult to work with you.

You may get a call about the budget or a specific activity or objective in your project. Or, you may receive a list of questions that the reviewers want you to answer in writing prior to making their decision. Take care of these things promptly and follow up with the funder to make sure they received your responses, and that you have answered all questions to their satisfaction. If you have been contacted with questions or a request for clarification, after you have responded, confirm that the funder has everything requested. This is your responsibility.

When Your Project Gets Funded

Funders may notify you that they have decided to fund your project by letter, an e-mail, or a phone call.

The first thing to do after you are notified that your project has been funded is to thank your funder! Write a brief letter or note on behalf of the grant team expressing thanks to the funder for supporting your project, and expressing excitement about implementing the project. Assure the funder that you are anticipating a project that will successfully meet specific needs in your community.

Inform your team about their success, congratulate them for a job well done, and honor their hard work by celebrating. Don't forget to include your partners and supporters in the celebration. It doesn't have to be a major event or cost a lot of money. It can be as simple as cake and ice cream during an afternoon break. Decorate with crepe paper streamers and play some upbeat music. The most important thing is to acknowledge the people and their hard work that made your proposal a success.

Verify with the funder that you are cleared to make an announcement, and then let the community know about your success. Send a press release to the local paper and media, and to state and regional library publications. This is a good time to call for volunteers if your project will require them. People will be excited about becoming involved in the project at this beginning stage.

You may be required to sign a contract that stipulates the conditions of the grant. Be aware that the amount you are awarded may not be the amount you requested. The scope of work the funder has agreed to fund may not exactly match the scope of work you proposed. Reporting requirements may have changed or may not be what you expected. Make sure you understand the terms of the grant contract and the work the funder expects you to do for the funds awarded to you. If you need additional funding to successfully implement your project, secure all necessary funding before you announce that your project has been funded.

Review your budget, especially if it has been a long time between submitting your proposal and the notification of your award. Check salaries and benefits costs, technology and equipment costs, rent, and other dollar amounts that may have fluctuated since you submitted your proposal. Contact the funder immediately to talk about these changes. The funder may ask you to readjust items within your budget, totaling the same dollar amount. In other words, the funder may fund your project only for the amount you requested even if actual costs have risen. Or, the funder may be in a position to fund the entire project, including higher cost adjustments. If you find the project will cost less than you proposed, get the funder's approval to use the excess funds to support your project in other ways. If you do readjust your budget, make sure this is reflected in your project activities. For instance, if personnel hours are not funded at the requested level due to higher personnel or benefits costs, this will reduce the activities they can be expected to accomplish.

Be sure you are comfortable with what is in the grant contract and that it makes sense to you, especially if it differs from your proposed project and budget. Your authorizing agent will most likely need to sign the grant contract. Then return the signed contract to the funder.

What to Do If Your Project Is Not Funded

If your project is not funded, contact the program officer and ask for feedback on your proposal. When proposal reviewers read proposals, they take notes and write comments. These comments are compiled for the final review that determines which projects are funded and which ones are denied. If available, these comments will be valuable to you as you write your next proposal. They will often tell you where you can make improvements, where you did not make yourself clear, and where you were successful.

Remember to put these comments and the denial of funding in perspective. You may have written an outstanding proposal by most standards.

If the funder had the resources to fund only a fraction of the proposals submitted, even some excellent proposals had to be denied. It is possible that the same proposal might have been funded if submitted to a funder with more resources.

Proposal reviewers are humans who come with their own biases, preferences, and opinions. Judging grant proposals is by nature a subjective activity. The same proposal read by a different team of reviewers may have been funded.

Putting things into perspective does not mean that your proposal doesn't require some work. Read the reviewers' comments and get opinions from people you know who are not involved with your library or the proposed project. Sometimes an impartial reader can see things that you cannot because you are so close to it.

Common Reasons Why Projects Are Not Funded

- **The project does not match the purpose of the grant.** Thoroughly research the purpose of the grant and the funder's priorities and interests. Make sure your project matches them before applying for funding.

- **The applicant is not located in the funder's geographic area.** Read the guidelines carefully for geographical limitations. Some funders only fund projects in their own geographic area or in areas where they have business locations.

- **The proposal does not adhere to the guidelines.** Read the application information and proposal guidelines very carefully and follow them exactly. Then read them again. Before you submit your proposal, read the instructions one last time to make sure you have followed all the requirements. Meet the deadlines.

- **The proposal is poorly written.** Get help writing the proposal if you need it. Write clearly and succinctly. Eliminate jargon and acronyms. Spell-check your proposal and use correct grammar and punctuation.

- **The budget doesn't add up.** Check and double-check your math. Don't inflate prices. Ask only for what you need to implement your project.

- **The proposal is disorganized or difficult to understand.** Take the time and effort to prepare your proposal in a professional manner. Have friends and people with experience in the field critique the proposal before you submit it. Make sure that the purpose of the project is clear and that impartial readers understand what it is you want to accomplish.

- **The grant request is not within the funding range.** Research the average size of grants the funder awards and don't request amounts significantly out of that range. Be realistic.

- **The funder doesn't know who you are or if you are credible.** If possible, set up an interview or phone call before submitting

> They don't spend the time upfront to really research and see if there's a match. I always say that the time they spend researching will be returned tenfold.
>
> —Jim Durkan, President
> Community Memorial
> Foundation, Hinsdale, IL

the proposal and have board members and other funded organizations help you establish a relationship to give you credibility. Write an Organizational Overview that clearly explains who you are. Provide documented evidence that you are up to implementing the project you are proposing. Include your long-range plan and how your project relates to it.

- **The necessity for your project and its potential impact are not clear.** Demonstrate the need for your project in the community with real information and data. Clearly identify the population that will benefit from your project and how the project will improve their quality of life. Don't base your proposal on the things you need. Your aim is to stress the importance of your project, but not to sound like you are in crisis mode.

- **The budget is unrealistic or inaccurate.** Never guess at the cost of items in your budget. Do not rely on sales or limited-time offers for an accurate price. When it comes time to purchase the equipment, that sale price may no longer be available and prices may even be higher than the regular price. Do not forget supplies like paper, pens, toner, and copying costs when preparing your budget. Be realistic about the cost of personnel benefits and taxes. Only promise what can realistically be delivered for the amount requested.

- **No partners or collaborators are indicated.** Make sure your proposal clearly shows that you have support from other organizations and that they are involved in your project. If allowed, you should include a letter of support from all partnering organizations in your proposal. It needs to be obvious to the reviewer that the partnering organizations are aware of the project, that there is partner buy-in and that they have agreed to actively participate.

- **No clear and relevant evaluation plan is evident.** Evaluation is a critical component of any proposal. Numbers and statistics alone don't effectively evaluate a project. Outcome-based evaluation will measure how your project will change the behavior, skills, attitude, knowledge, status, or life condition of the people your project serves.

- **The project isn't sustainable.** Most funders require you to show how you intend to support your project after the grant ends. Add a section to the proposal about your plans for self-sufficiency and develop a long-term strategy. Perhaps a partner organization is willing to take the lead at the conclusion of the current funding.

Don't be discouraged. It is not uncommon, especially in the federal arena, for funders to receive more money after funding the first round of applicants. This means that they must go to the next level—those applicants that just missed getting funded the first time. If this happens to you, you must be ready to think and act quickly.

After you have been turned down and you are looking for other funding, you may get a call from the funder to whom you originally submitted your proposal asking if you are still seeking funding for your project. Even if you have received other funding for your project in the meantime, surely a second phase of your project, a sustainability component, or a similar project you have planned for the future could use funding. Talk to the funder about the possibilities. Most funders who are interested in your proposal will be open to reconfiguring your project, talking about your project's current funding needs, or discussing other related projects you have planned.

Implementing the Project

Contact Your Funder

After celebrating your success, call your program officer to get reacquainted, or introduce yourself if you haven't already spoken with the program officer. Confirm that the funder has the contact person's name, correct phone, fax, and e-mail. Make yourself available. Ask any questions you may have, and begin to develop a working relationship with your program officer. Ask the program officer to call if any questions or concerns arise. The program officer can be very helpful to you as you begin project implementation and throughout the life of your project.

Establish a Baseline for Evaluation

It is important to begin implementing the evaluation process for your project as soon as you receive funding. Of course, you have already thoroughly planned your evaluation methodology as part of planning your project; however, after securing funding and before your project is implemented, you must establish a baseline or starting point against which you will measure your success. This may require conducting an assessment of current knowledge among the beneficiaries of your project or establishing the state of technology in your library prior to the start of your project. You may need to do a pre-project survey or an updated needs assessment to establish an accurate baseline. Your community needs assessment may have taken place months ago, and recent changes in your population demographics must be taken into account. Where you start depends on the nature of your project. Re-read your objectives and the evaluation methodology described in your proposal and start working on this right away. Your project cannot begin until you have established a baseline for your evaluation.

Hire Personnel

If you need to hire staff, post or advertise the positions as soon as possible. In some organizations this takes some time, so you will want to take care of this right away. If your project will employ consultants, you may want to issue a request for proposal for the scope of work you need accomplished.

If personnel changes occurred in your organization since you submitted the proposal, introduce new personnel to the project and clarify their roles. Make sure they understand your expectations and adjust their project responsibilities based on individual strengths. When you add new project responsibilities to their workloads, you must remove other responsibilities to not overburden their time commitment in your organization.

Purchase Equipment, Materials, and Supplies

After the positions are advertised, begin to purchase equipment, technology, materials, supplies, and any other items you need for your project. Since you confirmed costs in your budget right after being notified that you were funded, this is the best time to purchase—before costs fluctuate again.

Designate a Work Space

It is very important for the project to have a "home" and a physical place for project personnel to work in close proximity to one another. If you expect project personnel to find a random empty desk, counter space, or tabletop to do their work, the results will show in your project. Give your project the recognition it deserves by defining a place for it to thrive. People need to have a place to work—one that encourages them to communicate easily as they make your project come to life.

Update the Timeline

Update the project timeline to include each detailed step, specific personnel responsible for each activity, and inclusive dates for all activities. It is sometimes helpful to post the timeline in a prominent place where project personnel will see it daily.

Understand the Funder's Reporting Requirements

Familiarize yourself with your funder's reporting requirements so that you gather the right information, you are ready to prepare your reports when they are due, and you send them to the funder on time. Some funders require one final evaluation at the conclusion of the project, while others require periodical reports throughout the life of the project.

Your project evaluation should be based on the original purpose of the project and indicate the extent to which that purpose was achieved. If you didn't accomplish all the grant objectives, it does not necessarily mean the project was a failure. Valuable lessons may have been learned or the population served may have been positively affected in ways other than those planned. The evaluation should outline any unexpected results or consequences and should also specify how the grant will affect

We were lucky to have some salary savings from staff vacancies that allowed our medical librarian on staff to work at least five extra hours per week. This way, we could offer all the new services associated with our grant, and continue to offer our regular services, which is very important to the overall success.

—"Promoting Easy Access to Online Consumer Health Information for Los Alamos County Senior Citizens" Los Alamos County Public Library System, Los Alamos, NM (see Library Grant Success Stories, pp. 158–160)

We used a grid format to identify the different aspects of the project: when, what is done, by whom, and outcomes-based evaluation. This breaks down the entire grant into manageable pieces. As the grant period progresses, it is easy to see what needs to get done and by whom.

—"We Read Together" Mount Laurel Library, Mount Laurel, NJ (see Library Grant Success Stories, pp. 161–163)

future projects. Evaluation reports that are due periodically throughout the project will present opportunities for you to adjust any project components that are not working as expected.

If you based your evaluation plan on outcome-based evaluation, as discussed in Chapter 3, the outcomes should be used to evaluate the impact on the population served as indicated by change in knowledge, attitude, behavior, status, skills, or life condition. Include any relevant information gained from your evaluation, such as data collected from focus groups or surveys, and statistical data. To enhance your evaluation, include qualitative data such as stories or anecdotes, interviews and case studies that illustrate how individuals benefited from the project.

The evaluation must also report on how the grant money was used. This report should correspond with the budget agreed upon by you and the funder. This may be the original budget appearing in your proposal or an amended budget approved by your funder. Any deviations from this budget should be explained.

Here is a sample of the kinds of information funders request in a grant evaluation or progress report:

- Grantee Organization Name
- Grant Number
- Project Name
- Evaluation Due Date
- Original Project Purpose
- Population Served
- Extent Purpose Achieved
- Summary of Outcomes/Results Achieved
- Report of Expenditures
- Future Plans for the Grant Project
- Lessons Learned/Impact on Future Projects
- Telling the Story
- Publications or Presentations Connected to the Grant
- Honors or Awards Received as a Result of the Grant

Whether you are implementing a project that was funded or you are ready to research more grant opportunities for a project that still needs funding, your next step is to review the grant process cycle you have just completed. It is important to identify what you can do to improve, where you excelled, what steps in the process need more attention from you, and what you would do exactly the same way.

Reviewing and Continuing the Process

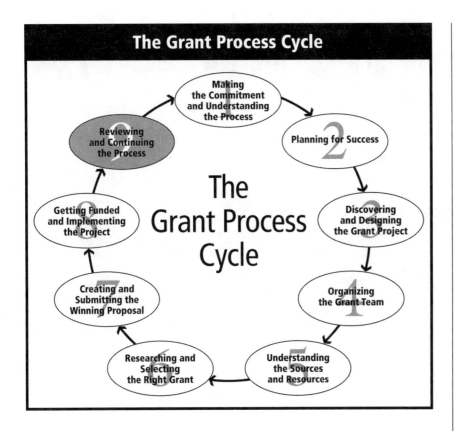

Congratulations on completing your first round of the grant process cycle!

If you have had success by winning grant funding for your project the first time around, you are now in the initial stages of project implementation. Or, if you were not successful this time, you may be ready to try again. Either way, this is the time for you to review and continue the grant process.

Debrief and Review

Take some time now to meet with your project planning team and your grant team to debrief. Often, it takes experiencing the entire process at least once before you can really understand how the process works, what the process requires of you, the value of going through each step, or what results to expect. Review the process and ask yourselves honestly, "How did it go?" Use the Debrief and Review Checklist to prompt discussion.

Reviewing your experiences at this stage in the process will give you an opportunity to learn from your successes and failures and make the necessary improvements or adjustments for your next attempt at winning a grant. Whatever you can learn at any stage in the process can only help you to do better the next time around. As you can see, this process is never done; there is no last step. However, the best time to look back on a project is after you have just completed a grant process cycle.

DEBRIEF AND REVIEW CHECKLIST

_____ Did we remain true to the strategic plan?

_____ Was our project designed to meet community needs?

_____ Did we work well as a team?

_____ Where did we excel as a team? Where could we improve?

_____ Did we delegate well?

_____ Is there anything we overlooked?

_____ What would we do differently?

_____ Did we forget to include a potential partner?

_____ Did we feel rushed getting authorizing signatures, submitting the proposal before the deadline, getting proper approvals, or gathering letters of support?

_____ Was everything completed on time?

_____ If we were successful this time, why were we successful?

_____ If we were not successful this time, why were we unsuccessful? (Review the funder's comments about the proposal and discuss how to improve it.)

For reproducible and customizable versions of this checklist, see page 222 in the Toolkit and the companion DVD.

After debriefing and reviewing, continue with the grant process. There may be some steps that you can go through quickly now that you have your strategic plan in place, your community profile and needs assessment have been updated, and you have discovered and designed several projects.

Keep Your Project Plans Up-to-Date

The grant process is always aligned with your library's strategic plan and project plans. Therefore, when you update your strategic plan or you are aware of new community needs, you must build these changes into your existing project plans or create new project plans. If you update a funded project, make sure to contact the funder about changes to the plan before you proceed. When you update and review your project plans continuously, as changes occur in your community and your strategic plan, this becomes a matter of course, a normal part of your job. When you keep your plans up-to-date, you are always ready for a new grant opportunity. Creating strategic plans, performing needs assessments, and designing project plans can be overwhelming tasks when you do this only every three to five years. Save yourself from being unprepared by updating your plans frequently.

Update Grant Proposal Components

Some grant proposal components can be updated periodically and kept in a file ready to go into a new proposal when the time is right. Doing this will save time, allowing you to concentrate on new ideas and spend less time gathering facts.

Update your Organizational Overview as you would your résumé. Add new achievements, events and programming, leadership, board members, and key staff members. If your mission or vision has changed, make these changes in your Organizational Overview. Updated budget figures can illustrate funding trends in your library, and new anecdotes, success stories, and endorsements from satisfied customers can keep this component fresh and current. As you update your strategic plan, community needs assessment, and project plans, keep current versions of these on file and also update Project Description components.

The Statement of Needs can be adjusted as your community needs assessment is updated. You may have several of these statements, depending on your particular community and various grant projects. Your Community Profile, often part of the Statement of Needs, can be updated as your municipality, college or university, school or organization changes and updates information about its residents, students, employees, or people served. When new census data is released, incorporate this information into your Community Profile. Note any current articles about your community's status such as unemployment rates, high school dropout rates, health concerns, or illiteracy that are published in your local newspaper.

Participate in Professional Development and Continuing Education

There is always more to learn about grants and proposal writing, so stay current and up-to-date by taking tutorials, classes, and webinars whenever you can.

- Attend workshops on researching grant opportunities or preparing grant proposals given by your local community foundation.
- Attend individual foundation information sessions where you will learn about their interests, priorities and preferences, their funding opportunities, and have an opportunity to ask questions and develop new relationships.
- Attend proposal writing workshops given by your local community foundation, community college, State Humanities Council, or regional library system.
- Take an online course, tutorial, webinar or attend classroom training at the Foundation Center (foundationcenter.org). You can learn about proposal writing, proposal budgeting, funding research, corporate giving, and more.
- The Grantsmanship Center (www.tgci.com) offers an intensive five-day Grantsmanship Training Program in various locations across the United States.
- Your state library may offer workshops or guidance on grant research, proposal writing, or how to apply for LSTA and other funding they offer.
- Federal agencies often offer free regional proposal writing workshops and/or informational sessions on upcoming funding opportunities. They offer tips for writing proposals and how to be more competitive. These workshops and sessions are usually held in various locations nationwide.
- Attend workshops on grants research, proposal writing, and project planning at your state library association conference, regional library association conference, or national library conferences such as ALA or PLA.

Foster Partnerships and Build Relationships

The best time to create and nurture partnerships is when you are not under pressure to write a proposal or find partners for a grant with a tight application deadline. It is best to continuously work on these relationships as a matter of course. Make a point of meeting people outside your organization, leaders in the community, and key people in agencies or businesses who are doing activities that relate to the projects you have planned. Get out of your library building and attend community meetings, join community groups, volunteer to give talks to local groups, or visit local schools. Be visible.

Tell others in the community about your new ideas and plans. Speak at civic club meetings and other community organization events about your goals, the community needs you would like to address, and prospective projects. Volunteer to help with your partner's or potential partner's fundraising events, or create an e-mail distribution list announcing your accomplishments.

Build relationships with potential funders. If you have already received a grant, recognize your funder by using the funder's name and logo on project materials, distribute press releases, spread the word in your newsletter, and make links to articles about the funder on your library's webpage. Invite the funder to special events, and recognize the funder at your annual award program. Make sure to thank your funders and keep them updated about the progress of your project, or about special accomplishments related to the project they funded. Send them publicity materials and copies of articles about your library and the funded project.

> Fortune favors the bold.
> —"New Library Signage"
> Columbia County Library,
> Magnolia, AR
> (see Library Grant Success
> Stories, pp. 148–149)

Join Fundraising Groups and Associations

Join your state or local chapter of the Association of Fundraising Professionals (www.afpnet.org). You will meet others in your community who are experienced fundraisers and proposal writers, and you will be invited to association events that may include workshops about grants and proposal writing or talks by local funders. You will have the opportunity to network and join a supportive group with others like you who are searching for grants, writing proposals, and securing the funds.

Be a Grant Reviewer

Consider volunteering to be a grant reviewer. You can learn a lot about the grant process and how to build stronger proposals while also building relationships with funders and making new connections with other non-profits.

Continue to Do the Research

In Chapter 6 we stressed the importance of staying up-to-date with new grant opportunities using blogs, current awareness services, electronic newsletters, periodicals, online discussion groups, and RSS feeds. This is the time to update your subscriptions and ensure this part of your research is in place. Refer to Chapter 6 for detailed information about these resources.

- Grants.gov Subscriptions
  www.grants.gov/applicants/email_subscription.jsp
- *RFP Bulletin*
  foundationcenter.org/newsletters
- *Philanthropy News Digest*
  foundationcenter.org/pnd
- *Primary Source*
  www.imls.gov/news/source.shtm
- TGCI Federal Register Grant Announcements
  www.tgci.com
- *Grants for Libraries E-News Alerts*
  west.thomson.com/signup/newsletters/209.aspx
- *Chronicle of Philanthropy*
  philanthropy.com
- Charity Channel Forums
  www.charitychannel.com

Library Grants Blog

librarygrants.blogspot.com

We maintain a blog that lists national grant opportunities available for libraries. We do the searching for you! Subscribe to the RSS feed and you will receive new opportunities as they are posted. The blog is updated regularly as we discover new grant announcements. We do not post local, regional, or state-specific grant announcements.

The time you take to debrief and review, keep your plans and proposal components up-to-date, participate in professional development and continuing education, foster partnerships and build relationships, become involved in fundraising groups, and learn best practices is an investment in yourself and in the library.

Top 10 Tips for Grant Success

What are our best tips for grant success? "Please" is the most important word when it comes to asking for funding, but here are ten other important elements to keep in mind.

1. People
2. Planning
3. Priorities
4. Purpose
5. Pursuit
6. Partnerships
7. Passion, Positivity, and Persuasion
8. Precision
9. Pitch
10. Perseverance

1. People

The most important thing to remember is that grants are about people. Grants are not about getting money or items on a wish list. Funders want to make a difference in the lives of people and they decide to fund your project so you can carry out their goals. Focus on how the grant project will help people and their needs, not the money or the "stuff." Involve as many community members as possible throughout the process. Always ask your target audience for feedback and don't just "listen" to them; HEAR them.

Also remember that funders are people, and not just ATMs! Talk with funders about their organization's interests and priorities, and develop good working relationships with them. Keep them up-to-date on your library, even after grant projects are completed.

2. Planning

As this book explains, the most important aspect of grant seeking is thorough development and planning before you write a proposal. Funders often attest that they receive many proposals that are full of great ideas. It's the practical implementation plan with clear goals and objectives that is often missing.

Grant work should always begin with planning, using your library's mission, strategic plan, and needs assessments as a foundation. Once you review this information, validate a real need your library can help address, and brainstorm solutions. You are then ready to determine a grant project idea. By planning and having a project in mind before you begin researching funding sources and selecting specific funders and grants, writing the grant proposal will be much easier. Funders prefer well-planned grant projects.

An effective proposal describes a program for change, not a list of wants. You must have a detailed plan that describes exactly where you are going and how you will get there. Be specific about broad goals, measurable objectives, and quantified outcomes and outputs. Otherwise you will never know if you truly made a difference. Often libraries do programming such as summer reading or computer classes, but never really know if reading skill levels are increased or if adults are promoted at their jobs due to increased technology knowledge. Wouldn't those be great things to know and share with your funders, board, community, and other stakeholders? Wouldn't you feel like your library really made a difference in people's lives if you knew these things?

Not only must your goals be achievable, they must be measurable. You'll want to report your incremental achievements as you go along. Don't wait until the end of the grant to see if you got it right. Benchmarks that are realistic, performed monthly and quarterly, and involve both quantitative and qualitative measurements are very important. Often knowing if you've been successful starts with knowing where you started. Evaluations and surveys should be conducted prior to project start dates and then repeated. Know how you are going to evaluate your grant project—throughout the grant process cycle.

3. Priorities

Verify your library's organizational capacity and support. Know what you can and can't do, based on local resources, priorities, and policies. Be certain that your library can follow through and achieve the results intended for your project; otherwise, you should not be applying for a grant. Funders need to be sure your library is competent and that the leadership can be trusted to carry out their intentions and truly deliver what has been promised.

Your library must be invested in the project. Two of the most precious resources of any library are its funds and its staff. If a library is willing to dedicate a portion of those discretionary funds and staff hours to the proposed project, this signals a legitimate priority, rather than just chasing grant dollars. Get relevant staff and administrators to agree to the project. Be certain you know who will apply for the grant, and also who will follow through with implementation and reporting. Before submitting a grant application, you should have the actual names and support of the staff members who will carry out the project, file any required reports, and ensure that the funds are spent as planned. This will not only guarantee grant compliance but also a successful project.

4. Purpose

You must clearly know how the funds will be used. Target your programs and projects so that funders will know exactly what you will be doing with their money, goods, or services.

Your project should not just be a good idea, but meet a true need in your community. This grant should make a difference and you need to demonstrate how it will do so in your proposal. What are the concrete benefits to your community? You should identify a target audience that is an appropriate population to benefit. Libraries serve diverse populations, and this is attractive to funders if it matches their purpose as well. You should include the target audience in the project planning to ensure that your library is doing the project *with* the people you will be helping, not *to* them. Funders want to know that the people who will benefit from the project have provided input and assisted with designing the project, and that they truly welcome the project.

On a large scale, your project can have the power to affect public opinion and policy and transform your community. Even if your scope is not this extensive, the project should still have outcome potential for more than a few people. For example, a reading program for toddlers that only serves a few families will not have a broad impact on your community.

5. Pursuit

Do your research and don't forget to look locally for grant funding. Be actively engaged in every aspect of grant work. The OCLC Report: *From Awareness to Funding: A Study of Library Support in America* (www.oclc.org/reports/funding/default.htm) has the following important tips for pursuing funding on page 7-5:

A successful library funding support campaign must:

- Make the library relevant for the 21st century.
- Instill a sense of urgency by putting the library in a competitive context for funding, alongside the public schools, fire department and police department.
- Activate conversations about the library's importance in community infrastructure and its role in the community's future.

Get out of the library. It is important that you give the library's name, work, and achievements a voice within the community. Network, consider potential co-collaborators or partners in your work, provide potential donors with information and answer their questions, find out what other non-profits are doing (for example, to survive this economy), and make sure that you hand out your business card at every opportunity.

Share your library's work and recent achievements and successes every chance that you have the floor in front of anyone outside the library. Make sure that your staff, board, and other representatives know their personal elevator speeches about your library and use them often and regularly (see p. 71 in Chapter 4 for details). It's the best free PR and marketing that exists. Contact your community's press and media every time your library meets a benchmark, achieves programmatic successes, or raises unprecedented support. Tooting your horn when your library succeeds engenders confidence in the library's leadership, confidence that the library is succeeding at its work and meeting needs in the community, and that the library isn't failing or closing any time soon. No one wants to donate to a library that has operations, fundraising, or programming problems. Communities support success.

6. Partnerships

Collaborations and partnerships are a great way to leverage resources, share expertise, and apportion costs to tackle complex challenges. Whether you have a small or large staff, partners can also help increase your library's organizational capacity. Determine whether other groups in your community share your vision and goals. Begin collaborating with those individuals or groups before you apply for grants. Community partners, such as public agencies, businesses, or service groups, can help add validity to your proposal. Programs that are designed in isolation from the community they serve and devoid of partners are inclined to fail. Think carefully about other organizations that could be partners on your grant project.

Your relationships with funders are also a type of partnership. When you research potential funders and find that perfect fit, your goals and theirs should match like pieces of a puzzle. You should be clear about what the funder is trying to achieve, what the funder expects of your library, and what will be required throughout the grant cycle. But to truly build effective partnerships that endure, libraries need to cultivate strong relationships with funders. This means working together on an ongoing basis to share ideas and approaches to problems. The relationship requires mutual trust, honesty, and clarity, which takes time and effort to achieve.

Frequent communications, establishing personal connections, and finding creative ways to reach out to donors are all ways to build real relationships. You need to have more contact with funders than just sending the proposal and final report. Send them newsletters, periodic updates, and invitations to events, so that you aren't only contacting them when you need funds. If your library gets an award, or your grant project has produced something noteworthy, send them a clipping or reprint with a handwritten note. Build relationships with both current and potential donors.

7. Passion, Positivity, and Persuasion

Keep in mind: attitude, perception, and public opinion make a difference. Decisions to give (like most human decisions) are emotional. Facts by themselves are not persuasive, and do not motivate people to give. Provide fact-based, verifiable statements, but include the passion you feel for the people you serve. It is an art, and there is no single way to do it. But don't be afraid to include emotion with your facts and data. After all, you are communicating with people you share values with and you want to persuade them to champion your project while fulfilling their cause.

A good attitude will go a long way. Some libraries get so mired down by budget, staff, and/or space shortages that their grant applications seem like an airing of grievances rather than evidence of needs with plans for creative solutions. Although you need to demonstrate the reasons your library requires the funding, make sure that the application's overall message is encouraging and perhaps even inspirational. Funders have a vision of how they can help make the world a better place, and your library has the means to assist in fulfilling this exceptional goal. Remember to be grateful to the funder, and to all the staff that support the grant. Celebrate any success and always give recognition where it is due.

8. Precision

When completing grant proposals or award applications, follow the guidelines explicitly and answer all the questions. Make it easy for the grant reviewer to find the information requested by following the same format and headings as the application, and your proposal will be easier to read. The reviewer may have hundreds of applications to read, so don't let yours be disqualified due to a technicality. Make it a goal to rid your proposal and documentation of typos or inaccuracies that could indicate carelessness or lack of dedication.

Meet all deadlines on time or ahead of schedule. Also, be precise in the ways you implement the project, carry out the evaluation, and submit your reports.

9. Pitch

Let everyone know that you are looking for funding and pitch them your grant projects. Tell staff, boards, members, students, governmental offices, family and friends, local business leaders, teachers and academics, volunteers, anyone involved in the library or interested in library-related topics. You never know where a great contact might come from or who might be on a foundation board or know of just the right funding opportunity. Contact other libraries in your area that have received grants and ask them for advice or brainstorm on shared needs.

Make sure to ask for what you need. Everything your project will require should be listed in your budget. It is better to ask for more and be able to adjust if your proposal is only partially funded than to ask for only a portion of your needs and risk not being able to match the difference. We once reviewed grant proposals for computer laptop labs. One library asked for every part of their lab, including funding to pay for instructors for computer classes, marketing expenses, and computer tables. Another library only asked for the technology. While both libraries were fully funded, the one that asked for more got more.

Know definitely what you want and what you want to do. And then ASK, believe, and work at it. Libraries do change lives, and we need to make sure that funders and supporters know that we are not just informational, but transformational.

10. Perseverance

Try, try again. One of our favorite examples of grant success comes from a library volunteer who wrote ten grants her first year. She had never written a grant before, yet she received seven of the ten. A great achievement, but what if she had only written one that wasn't funded and then gave up? Keep trying; it is all a learning process. No one is ever 100 percent successful, but libraries have a lot of advantages in the grant world, so keep writing!

Good Luck

Best of luck in your grant-writing endeavors! There is a saying that luck—and success—is what occurs when preparation meets opportunity. Plan, prepare, and then go after those grant opportunities. Just remember that grant writing is really about four things for which librarians are best known: conducting research, answering questions, building relationships, and serving the community.

Library Grant Success Stories

Introduction

There is nothing like a "real life story" to give you inspiration, spark some grant project ideas, illustrate successful partnerships, demonstrate innovative programs, provide best practices, and teach you about what pitfalls to avoid. In response to a call for library grant success stories, we received many excellent submissions from librarians who have been through the grant process and are willing to share what they have learned. We selected stories from many types of libraries that serve various populations in diverse communities. Government, foundation, and corporate funding sources are represented here as well as grant projects that serve children, seniors, children with autism spectrum diagnoses and their families, the transgender community, and more. You will find best practices in these stories as well as solid advice from those who have experience with the grant process. Use these stories to help you in the grant process before you embark on the journey yourself.

Our sincerest thanks go to the librarians who so generously shared their stories so you can learn from their experiences.

A Few Good Women (AFGW): Advancing the Cause of Women in Government, 1969–1974

Project Description

The grant was awarded to the Education and Behavioral Sciences Library and the Pennsylvania Center for the Book through the Aetna Foundation to develop curriculum for grades 6–12 using the A Few Good Women: Advancing the Cause of Women in Government, 1969–1974 (AFGW) special collection as the core component. The AFGW collection is an oral history project at Penn State that highlights the achievement of women recruited to government positions during this period.

Library

Pennsylvania State University Libraries
University Park, PA 16802-1812

Contact

Karla M. Schmit, Education and Behavioral Sciences Librarian and Assistant Director, Pennsylvania Center for the Book

Collection Size

5 million

Population Served

42,000 students at University Park

Grant Amount

$25,000

Funder

Aetna Foundation, Inc.

Number of People Who Worked on Grant Application

Two library staff members

Partnerships and Collaborations

With the grant we were able to hire an intern who is a graduate student in social studies to help write the curriculum. We were also able to hire a web designer to develop the online curriculum website. We worked with special collections archivists/librarians to better understand the special oral history collection and to develop lesson activities that highlight the work of librarians who work with special collections and are archivists.

Diverse Audiences Reached

The impact of the curriculum is immeasurable. Young people, especially young women, will have an opportunity to explore possibilities that grew from a period of history that changed forever the role of women in government and in a greater context, society. The study of a historical time period such as this one helps young people to become literate and knowledgeable about the ways in which events of the past impact the present and continue to shape the future. Since 1969, women have achieved many milestones in government service, but the work of recruiting women into careers and service in government continues to be of high importance today. Although the copyright of materials will be held by the Penn State University Libraries, the use of these materials will be free of charge to educators and others interested in the collection. It will be widely disseminated to public and private schools, home schools, and civic and social organizations such as boys' and girls' clubs. The online curriculum was launched in fall 2009.

Innovative Programming Implemented

The curriculum is flexible for use as a whole unit of study or as sections used to enhance a school's existing curriculum. It aligns with the Standards of the National Council of Social Studies. The plan calls for the AFGW curriculum to be available as an online resource and also to have all lesson plans and activities downloadable and printable as pdf documents. Highlights of the curriculum are the WebQuests that explore the AFGW Collection. Student-centered and inquiry-based, a WebQuest challenges students to explore the web for information. WebQuests include the links needed for students to complete a unit of study, as well as provide suggestions for further research.

Key to Project/Proposal Success

Teamwork and a commitment to keep working on the grant even when there were little setbacks.

Most Difficult Part of Grant Process

The paperwork and understanding the process. It's extremely important to have good communication with all involved—from an institution's financial officers to the idea people to the entity giving the grant.

Advice for Other Grant Seekers

If you have an idea for a grant, pursue the idea, do your research, and look for funding sources. Sometimes it is through the process that unexpected sources for money or even other ideas are discovered.

Most Important Element of Your Success

The people who are involved in the grant project from beginning to end. It takes a huge commitment to see a grant project to fruition.

Credit

Karla M. Schmit

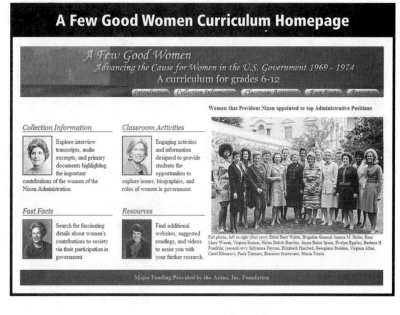

A Few Good Women Curriculum Homepage

See the actual "New Library Signage" proposal prepared by Laura J. Cleveland for this successful grant on the companion DVD for this book.

New Library Signage

Project Description

Columbia County (Arkansas) purchased a spacious new building in a well-populated area of Magnolia, Arkansas, and began building renovation. Our intent was to provide patrons with a user-friendly library. To this end, we requested a grant for directional signage, placed at prominent decision points, to assist library users with locating books and other materials.

Library

Columbia County Library
2057 N. Jackson, Magnolia, AR 71753

Contact

Laura J. Cleveland, MLIS, Director

Collection Size

160,000 in two libraries (County Library & Library for the Blind and Physically Handicapped)

Population Served

30,000

Grant Amount

$3,300

Funder

Columbia County Community Foundation (CCCF)

Grant Name

CCCF Asset Building Award

Number of People Who Worked on Grant Application

One library staff member

Diverse Audiences Reached

Our building houses two libraries. One is the Columbia County Library and the other is the Library for the Blind and Physically Handicapped, a branch of the Arkansas State Library. Because many people who use our facilities are sight-limited or otherwise handicapped, our signage needed to be exceptionally large, clear, and legible. The company who made our signs said that these were the largest signs they had ever been asked to create.

Key to Project/Proposal Success

Today we have 16 directional signs, each five feet long, which direct patrons to desired areas of the library. The signs are bright blue with white lettering and now all our library users are able to locate information independently. As we are a non-profit organization, funding for additional staff in our new building was scarce. Now our employees are largely freed from answering directional questions and, more important, our customers are happy because they can find things themselves!

Most Difficult Part of Grant Process

Estimating how much money to request for signage. In addition, it was necessary to anticipate every single kind of sign we would need in an eight-sided library lobby.

Advice for Other Grant Seekers

Apply! Apply! "Fortune favors the bold."

Most Important Element of Your Success

Since many grants target non-profit entities, success might measure the number of persons impacted by the grant implementation. Should you ask "did your grant improve quality of life for your community and especially assist handicapped patrons?" we are able to respond with a resounding "YES!"

Credit

Laura J. Cleveland, MLIS

New Library Signage at Columbia County (Arkansas) Library

Neighbors Connecting

Project Description

The Ocean County Library has a rich history of hosting cultural programs. In 2009–2010 the tradition will continue with the new lineup, Neighbors Connecting, a series of programs and events to celebrate the many rich communities of Ocean County.

Library

Ocean County Library
101 Washington St., Toms River, NJ 08753

Contact

Susan Quinn, Library Director

Collection Size

1.2 million

Population Served

560,000 residents and 100,000 additional in summer

Grant Amount

$30,000 over two years

Funder

OceanFirst

Grant Name

OceanFirst Foundation Arts and Cultural Grant

Number of People Who Worked on Grant Application

Six library staff members

Partnerships and Collaborations

We partnered with: the Library Foundation, Friends of the Library; Children's Specialized Hospital, Toms River; HealthSouth Rehabilitation Hospital, Toms River; Mental Health Awareness Committee of Ocean County; The Kiwanis Clubs of Ocean County; The Aktion Clubs of New Jersey; NAACP, Toms River Branch; Ocean County College, Office of Multicultural Services; Toms River Businesses; Ocean County Community Development; Puerto Rican Action Board of Lakewood.

Diverse Audiences Reached

Our Neighbors Connecting series was designed to reach traditional underserved populations of Ocean County, specifically the African-American population, Hispanic population, and those with disabilities.

Innovative Programming Implemented

The 2009 portion of our series featured ten programs. Our first program, titled "Through Our Eyes," was a musical of special-needs individuals telling their stories. This program was very emotional and well received in the community. We also included programs for all age groups in this series and selected programs that would appeal to a larger audience.

Key to Project/Proposal Success

The planning process was a time for open-minded discussion. We incorporated all four stages of teamwork: forming, norming, storming, and performing. Also, PR and marketing were included in all aspects of the planning and implementing processes. This allowed us to have a cohesive marketing and communication plan from the beginning. Finally, we used outcome-based evaluation (OBE) to determine how to measure our success. OBE helped us focus our program goals and marketing strategies.

What You Would Do Differently

Our community partners were involved via e-mail and phone calls. If time had permitted, this would have been a great opportunity to bring all community partners to the table for joint planning/networking sessions. Ocean County Library believes involving the community partners in the beginning planning stages allows for innovative ideas and community ownership of the programs.

Most Difficult Part of Grant Process

Planning programs is easy for librarians. Evaluating programs in a meaningful way was much harder. Outcome-based evaluation helped us focus on the long-term measurements and success of our series.

Advice for Other Grant Seekers

Be open-minded. Do your research. Know your community. When you write the grant, less is more. Give enough detail to get your "ask"; however, follow the instructions and don't write just to write.

Most Important Element of Your Success

Having the right team and being prepared to move fast so you don't miss opportunities. Partnerships are crucial; have them ready to sign onto your programs and have them be willing to promote the programs as well.

Credit

Susan Quinn

Neighbors Connecting Soul Street Poster

See the actual "Get Graphic: Building Literacy and Community with Graphic Novels" proposal prepared by the Buffalo & Erie County Public Library for this successful grant on the companion DVD for this book.

Get Graphic: Building Literacy and Community with Graphic Novels

Project Description

Get Graphic: Building Literacy and Community with Graphic Novels engaged and excited adolescents ages 14 to 18 and their caregivers with educational and creative activities designed to increase literacy and lifelong learning in two neighboring public library systems using graphic novels. We presented innovative, creative programs, author visits, workshops, and enhanced library collections to teenagers, their caregivers, and educators. Graphic novels with different themes and issues were used in collection development, curricular support, and teen and caregiver programming in order to stimulate teen reading and library use and to encourage adult support of those activities. Resource kits were developed to provide curricular support and improved library collections.

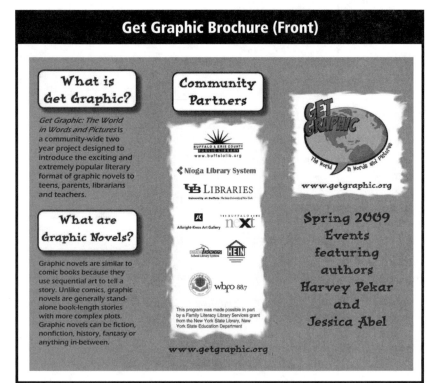

Library

Buffalo & Erie County Public Library
1 Lafayette Square, Buffalo, NY 14203

Contact

Britt White, Young Adult Librarian

Collection Size

3,683,970

Population Served

950,265

Grant Amount

$91,027

Funder

New York State Library, New York State Education Department

Grant Name

Family Literacy Library Services

Number of People Who Worked on Grant Application

Three library staff members

Partnerships and Collaborations

The Nioga (Niagara, Orleans, and Genesee Counties) Library System, Albright-Knox Art Gallery, William S. Hein & Co., Erie 1 BOCES (Board of Cooperative Educational Services), State University of New York at Buffalo Libraries, City of Buffalo Schools, and *The Buffalo News*.

Diverse Audiences Reached

Get Graphic materials were developed and provided to teachers in all kinds of schools who work with teens that function at a variety of reading levels and abilities. Get Graphic workshops were presented to middle and high school students; elementary, middle, and high school teachers; school, public, and special librarians; as well as library school and school of education students throughout the western New York area. The Get Graphic website (www.getgraphic.org) has reached a large and diverse audience across the United States. The site offers information about the graphic novel and details of Get Graphic projects, events, workshops, and kits, a "Graphic Novel of the Month," a featured author, a Get Graphic blog, and links to useful comics-related websites.

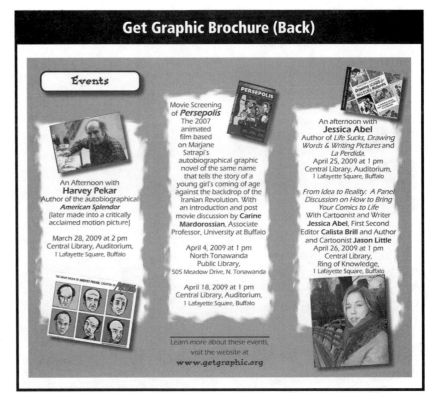

Get Graphic Brochure (Back)

Events

An Afternoon with **Harvey Pekar** Author of the autobiographical *American Splendor* (later made into a critically acclaimed motion picture)

March 28, 2009 at 2 pm Central Library, Auditorium, 1 Lafayette Square, Buffalo

THE MANY FACES OF HARVEY PEKAR, CREATOR OF

Movie Screening of *Persepolis* The 2007 animated film based on Marjane Satrapi's autobiographical graphic novel of the same name that tells the story of a young girl's coming of age against the backdrop of the Iranian Revolution. With an introduction and post movie discussion by **Carine Mardorossian**, Associate Professor, University at Buffalo

April 4, 2009 at 1 pm North Tonawanda Public Library, 505 Meadow Drive, N. Tonawanda

April 18, 2009 at 1 pm Central Library, Auditorium, 1 Lafayette Square, Buffalo

An afternoon with **Jessica Abel** Author of *Life Sucks, Drawing Words & Writing Pictures* and *La Perdida*. April 25, 2009 at 1 pm Central Library, Auditorium, 1 Lafayette Square, Buffalo

From Idea to Reality: A Panel Discussion on How to Bring Your Comics to Life With Cartoonist and Writer **Jessica Abel**, First Second Editor **Calista Brill** and Author and Cartoonist **Jason Little** April 26, 2009 at 1 pm Central Library, Ring of Knowledge, 1 Lafayette Square, Buffalo

Learn more about these events, visit the website at **www.getgraphic.org**

Innovative Programming Implemented

A summer program series helped teens from across western New York learn how to create a story and translate it into a comics format. A highlight of the series was an author talk and hands-on workshop led by Gene Yang, the award-winning author of *American Born Chinese*. Teens developed their own stories and cover art to be included in a collection titled *Get Graphic: The World in Words & Pictures* and published by William S. Hein & Co. We created kits that were used to bring graphic novels into middle and high school classrooms. Each kit contained 30 copies of a specific title, lesson plans, and support materials including A/V materials, resource lists, and study guides. Kits have been created using *Maus I, Maus II, Persepolis I, The Arrival, American Born Chinese*, and *Levitation*; and are presently being developed around *Journey into Mohawk Country* and *Satchel Paige: Striking Out Jim Crow*.

Key to Project/Proposal Success

Graphic novels are new and exciting and easily lend themselves to creative interpretation. They have become hugely popular, especially among the teen audience who are increasingly attracted to visual imagery and media with complex story lines. Graphic novels create their own buzz. Enthusiasm for the program was a direct result of this cutting-edge format itself. The educational community was excited to learn new methods to reach students, librarians were eager to learn more about graphic novels and how to include them in their collections, and teens were thrilled that graphic novels were finally being recognized. Our

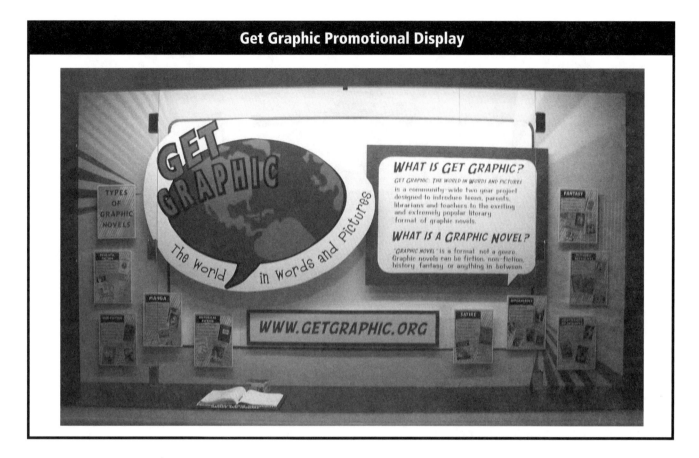

Get Graphic Promotional Display

partners were extraordinarily valuable and brought a unique element of creativity to the project. With many people focused on one objective, outstanding projects, programs, and events were conceived and multiple avenues to reach the intended audience were created.

What You Would Do Differently

During the first year of the grant project, learning and planning were first and foremost. This caused a lag in publicity that was remedied in the second grant year. We learned valuable lessons about developing relationships with people in the community who can help us reach our intended audience. In the future we will use this knowledge and these relationships to better publicize library programs and events.

Most Difficult Part of Grant Process

It was challenging to execute long-term planning while simultaneously focusing on day-to-day issues related to the project and our duties as librarians. The good news is that we were compelled to learn new time management and delegation strategies.

Advice for Other Grant Seekers

Remember that the sky is the limit! Be creative in your concepts and planning and partner with other community organizations to take advantage of the creativity of those around you.

Most Important Element of Your Success

If grant funds meet goals by ensuring that people have creative, interesting, and educational interactions with the library then the grant can be considered a success. The varied and strong partnerships of Get Graphic were a key element in achieving our success. Each partner used their own unique skills and services to create Get Graphic events and activities and market the program.

Credit

Buffalo & Erie County Public Library, Britt White, Marguerite Cheman, and Peggy Skotnicki

Step to the Library

Project Description

In 2006, the Abbeville County Library System, a rural library system, partnered with another local agency in a collaborative effort to provide increased access to its resources for children by combining virtual access with more traditional library services. These activities are coordinated with the Learning Bus, a new mobile preschool classroom developed by Abbeville County First Steps.

Learning Bus Activity

Library

Abbeville County Library System
201 S. Main Street, Abbeville, SC 29620

Contact

Mary Elizabeth Land, Director

Collection Size

53,000

Population Served

26,167

Grant Amount

$25,000

Funder

Library Services and Technology Act

Number of People Who Worked on Grant Application

Two, not all library staff members

Partnerships and Collaborations

Partnered with First Steps, a South Carolina agency whose mission is to help children enter kindergarten ready to succeed both academically and socially. Abbeville County First Steps Executive Director Angela Pruitt and I worked on the grant application together and when we received the grant, staff from both First Steps and the library system worked together. Collaboration was most definitely the name of the game!

Diverse Audiences Reached

Abbeville County has a total population of 26,167 and 2,105 are children under age six. Of these, 37.2 percent come from single-parent households, 18 percent live below the poverty line, and Medicaid serves 47 percent. The number of five-year-olds attending kindergarten who receive free or reduced-price lunch is more than 67 percent. We focused on serving these children and their families and caregivers.

Innovative Programming Implemented

The project provides computer access on the First Steps Learning Bus so that children and parents can access the Abbeville County Library System website and other resources from remote areas. This allows access to these resources by those who have no connectivity and who live in geographic areas not easily served by our brick-and-mortar libraries. Users have the ability to place holds on materials, pick them up, and return them all from the Learning Bus. In this way, the project helps alleviate some of the difficulties patrons in rural parts of the county encounter since the county has no bookmobile. High-quality children's materials are available at both the Abbeville County Libraries and on the Learning Bus, increasing motivation for children and parents who visit the bus also to become library users. The project provides opportunities for underserved preschool children to attend story hours on the Learning Bus at low-income housing developments, childcare centers, and community events. Special Library Card Sign-Up programs are held on the Learning Bus in remote, often underserved areas of the county. The First Steps Learning Bus provides additional opportunities for learning by going to the libraries before regularly scheduled storytimes and before special programs at the libraries.

Key to Project/Proposal Success

One thing that helped tremendously was extensive media coverage by local media. There were several articles about the grant itself, highlighting the collaboration of the Abbeville County Library System and Abbeville County First Steps. In addition, there were notices in the local newspaper and on the library blog whenever programs occurred. Photos of the event were highlighted in the news and on the blog. All this coverage was one way that people in the community were introduced to the many resources of the library system and of First Steps. By improving the accessibility of our offerings, we were able to raise the quality of life for our patrons. Especially in a rural county like Abbeville, which has no bookstore, no movie theater, and limited cultural offerings, the library plays a major role in providing quality materials and programming for education and enjoyment.

Children and Parents Enjoying the Step to the Library Program

What You Would Do Differently

The technology has improved so much now, that some of the hardware we purchased has been replaced. This, however, is surely going to be true of most technology programs. It seems that as soon as you get things up and running, they build a better mousetrap.

Most Difficult Part of Grant Process

Our biggest challenge was the carburetor. Due to carburetor problems, the Learning Bus was not operational for several months during the grant period and this meant that we had to do more of the programming at the libraries and less on and with the bus. Furthermore, the ability of those in rural areas to use the bus to borrow and return circulating items was badly hindered by the bus's technical difficulties.

Advice for Other Grant Seekers

Any collaboration depends on the personalities and motivation of the two groups. Before beginning such a collaborative grant effort, I would strongly caution libraries to remember that scheduling and unexpected difficulties (like carburetor problems!) do occur. Collaborating with a group that shares your mission is vital. Choose people who have a common perspective and motivation to make necessary changes along the way.

Most Important Element of Your Success

Keeping good records, keeping a good attitude, keeping the goals in mind—and, sometimes, just trying to keep up!

Credit

Mary Elizabeth Land and Angela S. Pruitt

Promoting Easy Access to Online Consumer Health Information for Los Alamos County Senior Citizens

See the actual "Promoting Easy Access to Online Consumer Health Information for Los Alamos County Senior Citizens" proposal for this successful grant and other successful grant proposals prepared by Bernadine Goldman and Lizzie Eastwood on the companion DVD for this book.

Project Description

The project goal is to educate seniors residing in Los Alamos County about how to evaluate consumer health information and provide an introduction to the National Library of Medicine online consumer health information websites, MedlinePlus and NIHSeniorHealth, at library branches and at senior residential facilities.

Library

Los Alamos County Public Library System
2400 Central Avenue, Los Alamos, NM 87544

Contact

Bernadine Goldman, Assistant Library Manager

Collection Size

173,000 holdings

Population Served

18,000

Grant Amount

$4,765

Funder

National Network of Libraries of Medicine, South Central Region (NN/LM SCR)

Grant Name

Express Consumer Health Outreach Award (2005–2006)

Number of People Who Worked on Grant Application

Five, not all library staff members

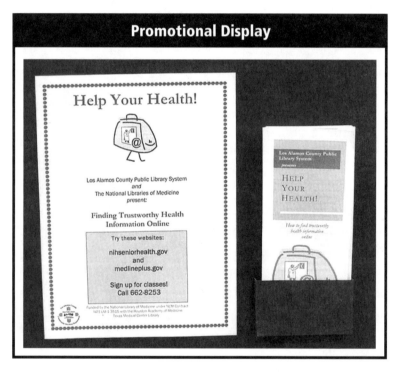

Promotional Display

Partnerships and Collaborations

We established partnerships with more than a dozen local agencies. We met with representatives of these agencies before applying for the grant, when they offered to help us get the word out; and then midway through our programming, when they gave us valuable feedback. Some of the agencies that we formed partnerships with, such as the Heart Council, the Council on Cancer, and the Senior Center, have continued to be partners for us in all our health-related outreach and collections. We also have a partnership with the

University of New Mexico (UNM) Health Sciences Center Library, an affiliate of the National Network of Libraries of Medicine.

Diverse Audiences Reached

Senior citizens were specifically targeted; however, the classes and information were available to all library patrons and community members. In addition, our project reached senior citizens from the surrounding Indian pueblos, the Jemez Mountain area, and Santa Fe, many of whom come to Los Alamos to use the Senior Center and the Library.

Innovative Programming Implemented

We offered classes off site, at the senior centers in Los Alamos and White Rock, as well as at the Sombrillo Nursing and Rehabilitation Center and at the Aspen Ridge Lodge assisted-living facility in Los Alamos. We offered classes to our own staff so they could better help patrons with their health-related questions.

We staffed booths to advertise our classes and to distribute health information and answer questions at the community health fair, the County employees' health fair, the Heart Council seminar, the Council on Cancer seminar, Senior Services days, the low vision fair, and the Harvest Festival. At these events, we gave out promotional items such as jar openers imprinted with the URLs of reliable medical websites.

Health Fair Booth

Key to Project/Proposal Success

In applying for the grant, we did a lot of demographic research and planning ahead. We were able to discover and address a genuine need in the community, as there is no other medical library in town. During the time of the grant, we did a lot of marketing, such as including a flyer advertising our health information services into everyone's utility bills. We made a special effort to meet people where they tend to go, not to require that they come into the library. In applying for and implementing the grant, we had a lot to offer because we have on staff a former medical librarian, who had expertise in the subject matter and in the sensitivity required for success in helping to change people's health habits. We were willing to prioritize this grant and to give it our all during the time it was active; and then, we couldn't just stop, so the provision of reliable and up-to-date health information has remained a priority for us.

What You Would Do Differently

We probably wouldn't do anything differently in planning, creating, and executing the program. We were able to modify the plan as we went along;

for instance, the original length of classes was proving to be too long, so we modified that to fit our patrons' needs. These types of changes we were able to tackle during the program.

Most Difficult Part of Grant Process

The paperwork was the most difficult part. This includes filling in the application, keeping statistics on everything, and sending in reports on time to the granting agency. Budgeting was difficult, too, as we had to submit a line-item budget with our application, and then ask for permission to change anything. If something cost less than we anticipated, for instance, we needed to ask for permission to spend the remaining money in that line on another item. This was very cumbersome.

Jar Opener Apple Design

Los Alamos County
Public Library System
and NLM *present*

HELP YOUR HEALTH!
library@lac-nm.us

nihseniorhealth.gov
medlineplus.gov

Advice for Other Grant Seekers

Go for it! Even though it is difficult and time-consuming to fill out a good application, winning a grant can take your library into new territory, and make exciting ventures possible. Winning a grant is definitely a commitment, however, so you do need to make sure that you have some staff time to devote to its implementation.

Most Important Element of Your Success

Staff motivation, enthusiasm, and time are most important. Some grants allow some of the money to be spent on staff salaries, but ours didn't. We were lucky to have some salary savings from staff vacancies that allowed our medical librarian on staff to work at least five extra hours per week. This way, we could offer all the new services associated with our grant, and continue to offer our regular services, which is very important to the overall success.

Credit

Bernadine Goldman and Lizzie Eastwood

We Read Together

Project Description

We Read Together is a family literacy program designed to encourage development of Early Literacy Skills in children from birth to five years old. The Six Basic Early Literacy Skills are: Phonological Awareness, Letter Knowledge, Print Awareness, Vocabulary, Print Motivation, and Narrative Skills. This program is based on the American Library Association's Every Child Ready to Read campaign. We Read Together is composed of literacy workshops, programs for children, special collections, outreach materials, computer equipment, and devoted library space.

Library

Mount Laurel Library
100 Walt Whitman Ave., Mount Laurel, NJ 08054

Contact

Laura Butler, Youth Services Librarian

Collection Size

140,815

Population Served

41,000

Grant Amount

$20,000

Funder

New Jersey State Library

Grant Name

Public Library Literacy Programs, FY 2009

Number of People Who Worked on Grant Application

Three library staff members

Partnerships and Collaborations

Partners and collaborators were the Ethel Lawrence Education Center, an educational and recreational facility for children in grades K–8 who reside at the Ethel Lawrence Homes, an affordable housing development in Mount Laurel and the YMCA of Burlington County, which offers child care and preschool programs for children from eight weeks to six years of age. Through this grant, the Library has placed deposit collections of reading and educational materials at both

Mom and Her Child Participating in a We Read Together Activity

We Read Together Library Area

Ethel Lawrence Education Center and YMCA of Burlington County. The Friends of the Mount Laurel Library pledged $3,000 toward early literacy projects.

Diverse Audiences Reached

Since the grant focused on family literacy, we were able to touch a wide audience of many different ages. In addition, by placing deposit collections outside of the library's walls, we are able to reach individuals who may not otherwise be library users.

Innovative Programming Implemented

With the funds from this grant, we were able to implement a Summer Reading Club for pre-readers and their families. This proved to be highly successful and easily repeated. We now have summer-long programs for every age. In an effort to educate parents on issues of literacy, the Library contracted with Cooper Learning Center, a local affiliate of Cooper University Hospital. Experienced educators from the Center presented a series of workshops to support parents and caregivers.

Key to Project/Proposal Success

Positive feedback received from our satellite collections and library users has indicated success. Perhaps most important, we have plans to continue working on the project into the foreseeable future, beyond the grant year. When composing our proposal, we kept our grant reviewers in mind. To make our proposal easy to read we used bullet points and imagery so the key points could be easily found and our wording was kept succinct. Our use of images aided in conveying our intentions, adding a richer dimension to our proposal.

What You Would Do Differently

Purchase collection materials earlier. This ensures that all funds are spent and received before the grant's conclusion. Due to variations in the costs of items and discounts, it took us longer than anticipated to purchase all the books for our grant. Since booksellers often don't charge until an item is shipped, we were left anxiously hoping that items would ship before the conclusion of the grant year. It would be easier to gather thorough circulation data for reporting at the conclusion of a grant year if these items had been in the collection longer.

Most Difficult Part of Grant Process

Finding the balance you need to stick to your timeline. It's easy to have grandiose plans for your grant and abilities. It's challenging to do it all. When working on a grant our everyday activities do not cease. When creating your grant proposal, it is extremely important to be realistic about what your time and capabilities can truly allow. With teamwork and patience, it's possible to maintain a balance of grant and day-to-day duties while adhering to the timeline.

Advice for Other Grant Seekers

Build your grant around an activity plan. We used a grid format to identify the different aspects of the project: when; what is done; by whom; and outcomes-based evaluation. This breaks down the entire grant into manageable pieces. As the grant period progresses, it is easy to see what needs to get done and by whom. Build in sustainability for the project after the grant ends. We came out of the grant year with a well-defined service program, a logo for that program to use in marketing, and an area in the library that is clearly defined to encourage reading among young children and their caregivers.

Most Important Element of Your Success

The objectives of a grant should be maintained after the grant has completed. Ideally, a grant jumpstarts a project. This momentum should be maintained beyond the funding cycle. This not only will indicate how successful a grant has been but also how easily another library would be able to emulate the project.

Credit

Laura Butler

We Read Together Logo

Fall into the Library

Project Description

Aided by a grant awarded by the National Network of Libraries of Medicine (NN/LM) and the Public Broadcasting System (PBS), we hosted a large open house that enabled us to bring staff and veterans into the library. We had giveaways such as rubber apples with our library contact information on them, real apples and mini pumpkins, and hot apple cider. The grant money was used for these items, decorations, and for four $100 gift certificates to our Veterans Administration (VA) canteen. Participants were eligible to win a certificate if they visited the library and signed up for remote access or participated in a PubMed learning session. Our VA provided food, flyers, and table advertisements. In a coordinated grant, the American Library Association along with PBS sent us a DVD with film shorts on social justice topics such as country doctors. We expanded the celebration to include weekly "lunch and learns" where we discussed the film shorts. NLM sent us a huge colorful six-panel display on world health issues, which we were able to display in our newly designed library for several months. It was a great success.

Front Desk at the Fall into the Library Open House

Library

Department of Veterans Affairs
79 Middleville Road, Northport, NY 11768

Contact

Mary Lou Glazer, MLS, AHIP, Department of Veterans Affairs Library

Collection Size

5,000

Population Served

3,000

Grant Amount

$1,000 plus display from PBS

Funder

NN/LM and PBS/ALA

Grant Name

Mini grant from NN/NLM and Social Justice Grant from ALA/PBS

Number of People Who Worked on Grant Application

Two library staff members

Diverse Audiences Reached

We reached clinical staff, administrative staff, and veterans.

Key to Project/Proposal Success

The coordination of library staff and carefully reading the requirements of the grants were instrumental in our success. Also, we kept detailed records and a log of the process leading up to the events.

Most Difficult Part of Grant Process

The most difficult parts were coordinating everything for that day and balancing grant and day-to-day duties while adhering to the timeline.

Advice for Other Grant Seekers

Try writing a small grant. It's a great way to obtain services and awareness of your library when funds are tight from the usual sources.

Most Important Element of Your Success

Bringing staff into the library. They continue to be surprised at the variety of resources we have.

Credit

Mary Lou Glazer

Fall into the Library Open House

Listening to the Prairie: Farming in Nature's Image

Project Description

A 1,200-square-foot panel traveling exhibit from the American Library Association (ALA) examined the transformation of the grassland prairies of central North America into cropland and grazing pastures. The exhibit featured several interactive and three-dimensional components including a giant shopping cart with touch screen and a mural. We added to the exhibit through displays on local prairies and related materials, and developed a large number of programs on campus and in the community, including a Prairie Day.

Library

Ohio State University at Marion/Marion Technical College Library
1469 Mt. Vernon Ave., Marion, OH 43302

Contact

Betsy Blankenship, Director/Head Librarian

Collection Size

52,000

Population Served

70,717

Grant Amount

ALA Traveling Exhibit

Funder

American Library Association and the Smithsonian

Number of People Who Worked on Grant Application

Two, not all library staff members

Partnerships and Collaborations

We partnered with the Marion Public Library, the local Palace Theatre, Ohio State University at Marion (OSUM) Outreach Committee, OSUM Prairie and Nature Center, OSUM Development Office and Public Relations, an OSUM Biology Professor, the Ohio State University Libraries Friends of the Libraries, Five Nights on Campus cultural programming committee, and Buckeye Backers, a group on campus that helped give tours and monitor the exhibit.

Diverse Audiences Reached

More than 2,000 schoolchildren and adults visited, including 84 classes from Pre-K through eighth grade. Visitors came from more than 30 Ohio cities and 6 states, totaling more than 2,538 visitors to the exhibit and campus prairie total. Of the 11 programs that eventually went forth, we had more than 1,131 in attendance. We extended hours to keep the exhibit open to the public on weekends. We saw Scouts, senior groups, Sunday families, and retired teachers visit in addition to the school groups.

Innovative Programming Implemented

We offered a Prairie Day, a prairie dinner and lecture on Ohio prairies, and a prairie watercolor exhibit. We brought in one of the exhibit-featured farmers from South Dakota for a program, hosted a musical performance by the duo Prairie Orchid, held an opening reception, had a quilt art show, and provided tours of the local prairies. The staff even dressed in prairie costumes for one program. We planted prairie plants around the library and had pots placed around the library and building. We hosted several speakers and created special marketing items such as brochures, teacher packets, and pencils.

Key to Project/Proposal Success

The collaboration between our library and the public library, the campus Prairie and Nature Center, the OSUM Development and PR departments helped make our project a success. Most of all, what made the difference was the dedication and commitment of the small staff of two and about six student assistants. They helped put the exhibit up, led tours, helped get the teaching materials out, attended the reception and many of the related programs, and did everything they could to promote the exhibit's success.

What You Would Do Differently

We received the grant in February 2001 to be held in September–October 2001, so we had to scramble to get information out to the schools before they closed for the year. I would push for better local PR coverage (we hosted a media day and no one showed) and try to get more of the campus folks to visit (I'm not sure many came over). I'd maybe offer fewer programs overall. We had planned 17; but 9-11 happened on the day of one of our programs, and another was canceled due to not securing a key player. We were exhausted trying to get in all the programs in six weeks AND hosting the tour groups.

Most Difficult Part of Grant Process

The amount of paperwork we had to fill out and all the supporting materials we sent. Our application went through a very competitive process and we were only one of 20 libraries nationwide that received it.

Advice for Other Grant Seekers

Don't be afraid to apply; you never know what might happen. Look for partners on campus as well as in the community. And make sure your library staff is on board with helping you. I could never have accomplished what we did without my assistant and student employees.

Most Important Element of Your Success

Our willingness to put forth the time and commitment to host related displays and programs was instrumental to our success. Also our commitment to gather the needed community support to send with the application was essential. We displayed relevance of our location to the exhibit; we had a campus prairie, which tied in very well.

Credit

Betsy Blankenship

A Reflection on Life in Georgia and the Murphy Legacy (1961–2003)

Project Description

This project has three goals: (1) to document the life and legacy of the Honorable Thomas B. Murphy, Speaker of the Georgia House of Representatives for 28 years and the longest-serving State House Speaker in the United States; (2) reflect on life and events in Georgia that occurred during his years of service (1961–2003); and (3) interpret this history to the broader public. In 2002, Ingram Library received the contents of Thomas B. Murphy's State Capitol office, promising to re-create the office on the university campus. Grant program goals will include the development of a panel exhibit highlighting Murphy's contributions in Georgia; to organize a series of exhibits and public programs in the five counties served by the West Georgia Regional Library System and the University of West Georgia's Ingram Library; and to create a website that documents the program presentations and showcases the Speaker's contributions through the decades.

Library

Irvine Sullivan Ingram Library
University of West Georgia
1601 Maple Street, Carrollton, GA 30118

Contact

Lorene Flanders, Director of University Libraries

Collection Size

450,000 volumes; 50,000 serials

Population Served

11,252 students (2008)

Grant Amount

$6,000

Funder

Georgia Humanities Council

Grant Name

Public Program Grant, secured in 2007

Number of People Who Worked on Grant Application

Eight, not all library staff

Partnerships and Collaborations

Faculty and staff from across the University of West Georgia collaborated on writing the grant proposal. The local public library system provided venues in each of the five counties served, thereby allowing the

Banner Announcing the Exhibit, Speaker Tom Murphy: Steady Leadership in Changing Times on the University of West Georgia Campus

university to reach citizens throughout the region. Collaborating partners included: Ingram Library, University of West Georgia; Annie Belle Weaver Special Collections, Ingram Library, University of West Georgia; Georgia's Political Heritage Program, University of West Georgia; Thomas B. Murphy Center for Public Service, Department of Political Science and Planning, University of West Georgia; The Center for Public History and the Department of History, University of West Georgia; The University of West Georgia Foundation, Inc.; and West Georgia Regional Library System.

Diverse Audiences Reached

West Georgia Regional Library System serves a five-county region with a total population of 415,000 in 2008. Counties include areas that are rural (Heard County has a population of just over 11,000, of which 16 percent live below the poverty level), as well as suburban communities of more

Carol Murphy, Daughter-in-Law of the Late Georgia House Speaker Tom Murphy, and His Daughter Mary Murphy Oxendine Viewing the Panel Exhibit, Speaker Tom Murphy: Steady Leadership in Changing Times

than 100,000 within a short distance of Atlanta, a major metropolitan center. The University population includes more than 11,000 students, of which 96 percent are from Georgia, 61 percent Caucasian, 25 percent African American, with smaller percentages of Hispanic and other ethnicities represented. Many students are first-generation university students.

Innovative Programming Implemented

Grant funds provided for the fabrication of a 12-panel exhibit titled "Speaker Tom Murphy: Steady Leadership in Changing Times," brochures, posters, and other promotional materials. Friends of the Library groups hosted opening receptions locally, with speakers donating their services. We were able to secure the current Speaker of the Georgia General Assembly, as well as retired politicians who had known the subject of our exhibit.

Key to Project/Proposal Success

Georgia Humanities Council indicated that the library's collaboration with other campus departments was important to their support for our grant proposal.

What You Would Do Differently

In the future, we will secure more careful cost estimates for items in our proposal prior to submitting to a funding agency. We failed to secure the services of an exhibit fabricator as we planned the grant budget. We were fortunate to find a local company to work on the project, but had to locate this company after receiving funding.

Most Difficult Part of Grant Process

It was difficult to find the time to focus on the grant-writing process amid the pressures of our "day jobs." This was our first effort, though we had a partner who had completed successful grants through the Georgia Humanities Council. The university conducts an annual grant-writing course, and we have subsequently sent three library staff through the class.

Advice for Other Grant Seekers

Since it can be difficult to find time to work on the grant-writing process, it is important to calendar a schedule. Good partners are essential. In a university setting, plan to secure a graduate assistant with research skills to support the faculty/staff team. Keep your supervisor and other administrators informed of your progress. They generally must sign off on grant paperwork, so it helps to have them informed and enthusiastic as you meet various deadlines. Public officials, school officials, and notable individuals who are interested in or associated with the topic should be informed of the grant-writing process in advance. Provide a sample of a letter of support to assist them in quickly completing letters to accompany your proposal.

Most Important Element of Your Success

The institution or organization seeking grant funding must have a strong connection to the subject to be explored. The people who contribute to the preparation process must also have or develop a passion for telling the story. Grants provide a wonderful opportunity to illuminate topics of local interest, and to build a sense of community through a series of programs. This becomes a shared community experience, and enriches lives of those involved, and of those who take advantage of program opportunities.

Credit

Lorene Flanders

EZ Strengthening Public and Academic Library Collections Grant

Project Description

This grant program grew from a pilot program funded in 2003–2004 and is designed to help North Carolina public and academic libraries develop or strengthen subject areas in their print collections to meet user needs. Libraries serving low-wealth communities and institutions are given priority for this grant program, assuming their application is eligible and meets the criteria. University of North Carolina (UNC) Charlotte has selected the B.S. program in Respiratory Therapy in the College of Health and Human Services as the target user population. The two grant writers, Lisa Nickel and Lois Stickell, selected this program for three reasons: (1) This college is the fastest-growing college at UNC Charlotte and Respiratory Therapy is a new program; (2) The library has not yet built up a collection to serve these students; and (3) When these students graduate they will be going out to serve the population of North Carolina.

Library

J. Murrey Atkins Library
University of North Carolina at Charlotte
9201 University City Blvd., Charlotte, NC 28223

Contact

Lisa Nickel, Distance Education Librarian

Collection Size

More than 1,046,000 volumes

Population Served

23,000 students plus community users

Grant Amount

$10,000 (plus $2,500 match)

Funder

LSTA (Library Services and Technology Act)

Grant Name

Strengthening Public and Academic Library Collections Grant

Number of People Who Worked on Grant Application

Two library staff members

Partnerships and Collaborations

We collaborated with the Department of Respiratory Therapy in the College of Health and Human Services at UNC Charlotte to determine appropriate resources needed to support the respiratory therapy curriculum. In addition, we consulted the Department of Distance Education because this new BA degree is offered via Distance Education.

Diverse Audiences Reached

The respiratory therapy students are distance learners who are currently working as respiratory therapists with associate degrees. This program allows them to earn a bachelor of science degree online and continue working full-time. So, they are full-time workers in the health care industry who are earning an additional degree via distance education.

Innovative Programming Implemented

We were restricted to spending grant funds on book purchases; however, we are marketing the materials purchased by the grant as well as our book delivery services for distance learners in this program.

Key to Project/Proposal Success

We were able to tie in the community need for graduates in this area by using census and other demographic data for the region and we were able to make a solid argument for why we were not able to purchase these books with our current funding.

What You Would Do Differently

We would learn more about how grant funds are administered on campus and learn more about the many departments involved in the process.

Most Difficult Part of Grant Process

The most difficult part of the process was getting access to money to purchase the materials. This was a grant program that reimbursed us for purchases, so working with campus departments to get money added to the correct purchasing funds was a bit confusing.

Advice for Other Grant Seekers

Learn about your institution's guidelines and workflow on campus so that you can access the funds soon after you are awarded the grant.

Most Important Element of Your Success

Making a good argument and showing how the grant funds will help your institution to be more successful. Don't use being poor as your argument for the money; instead, show your current successes and then explain how the grant will help you to become even more successful.

Credit

Lisa Nickel and Lois Stickell

From Anne Frank's Story to Your Story: Creating History One Person at a Time

Project Description

The purpose of our project was to host "Anne Frank: A Private Photo Album," an exhibit of 70 photographs taken by Otto Frank of his family before they went into hiding. These photos elicited a tender rendition of family life—a world that should not have been destroyed by the effects of war, intolerance, and prejudice. Our hope was to introduce Anne Frank to the public, and especially to children, in a gradual, engaging, and personal way. In addition to hosting the exhibit and celebrating *The Diary of a Young Girl*, the library offered programs for all ages on creating personal and family memoirs through writing and photography.

Library

Ela Area Public Library District
275 Mohawk Trail, Lake Zurich, IL 60047

Contact

Natalie Ziarnik, Head, Children's Department

Collection Size

250,000

Population Served

35,000

Grant Amount

$25,000

Funder

Illinois State Library

Grant Name

LSTA

Number of People Who Worked on Grant Application

One library staff member with assistance from others

Partnerships and Collaborations

We worked with the local school district to offer tours of the exhibits for classes. The Friends of the Library and the Illinois Arts Council provided funding for the exhibit opening, including a performance by the Maxwell Street Klezmer Band. The Rotary Club gave funding for the equipment

Anne Frank Brochure Cover

ANNE
Frank

Exhibit & Special Events
Ela Area Public Library

needed to hang the exhibit. The Lake County Discovery Museum provided copies of postcards from World War II and gave us advice on hosting an exhibit.

Diverse Audiences Reached

We discovered that we had been unaware of a fairly large Jewish population in our area.

Innovative Programming Implemented

For the opening day, we prepared an afternoon of festivities: the Maxwell Street Klezmer Band performed in the main meeting room; the film *The Short Life of Anne Frank* was shown continuously in the Children's Programming Room as well as in the Children's Study Room; the Teen Study room was converted into Anne Frank's room in the Secret Annex; Mediterranean and Jewish food, including Hamantaschen cookies, were available in Popular Materials; the main exhibit was upstairs in the Quiet Reading Room; and pink tulips decorated the library in honor of Anne Frank's hometown, Amsterdam. Many other related programs were offered throughout the month, including films, lectures, book discussions, and memory box classes.

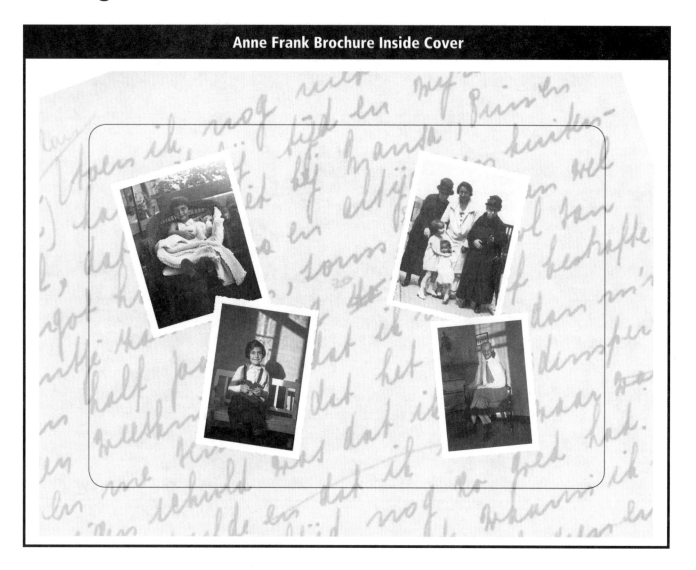

Anne Frank Brochure Inside Cover

Key to Project/Proposal Success

The publicity for the exhibit and programming was extremely appealing and stayed true to the spirit of the exhibit and Anne Frank's diary. As a result, we had thousands of visitors from a wide geographic area. The response of these visitors, written in several comments books, was moving and inspirational. There was a real outpouring of emotion, which helped strengthen community ties. The exhibit was thought-provoking, connecting to people's memories and hearts, and brought people together from different backgrounds, promoting tolerance and understanding.

What You Would Do Differently

I would have blocked out two months of my life to dedicate to this project and delegated all the "normal" aspects of my job to others.

Most Difficult Part of Grant Process

Writing up reports and responding to media questions.

Advice for Other Grant Seekers

Find a project that many of your staff members are excited about and that will be deeply moving to your public, encouraging reflection and the desire for lifelong education.

Most Important Element of Your Success

The staff must be passionate about the topic and willing to work collaboratively during the entire time of the project from the first ideas through the implementation of details. A tolerance for moments of chaos is also helpful.

Credit

Natalie Ziarnik
Anne Frank: A Private Photo Album was developed by the Anne Frank House and is sponsored in North America by the Anne Frank Center USA.

Public Library Resources for Children with Autism and Their Families

Project Description

This grant benefited low-literacy children with autism, their parents, caregivers, and educators, as well as other children with disabilities or special needs. Through this grant Kenosha Public Library (KPL) added developmental resources, print, and non-print materials about and for use by children and adults on the autism spectrum, their caregivers and educators. KPL staff worked closely with parents from the Kenosha Autism Support Group in providing workshops for the parents. Staff training was also an integral part of the grant. A representative from the Autism Society of Southeastern Wisconsin presented workshops on the characteristics and behaviors of people diagnosed on the autism spectrum to library staff.

A Sampling of Books and DVDs about Autism Purchased for Children and the Handout "Understanding Autism: Resources for Children and Young Adults"

Library

Kenosha Public Library
PO Box 1414, 812 56th St., Kenosha, WI 53141-1414

Contact

Roxane Bartelt, Head of Children's Services

Collection Size

407,000

Population Served

90,000

Grant Amount

$14,093

Funder

LSTA/IMLS

Grant Name

LSTA Literacy Grant

Number of People Who Worked on Grant Application

Three library staff members

Partnerships and Collaborations

KPL partnered with the Kenosha Autism Support Group and the Kenosha Achievement Center by meeting with staff from these agencies and groups to determine what services would be most useful to the parents of children on the autism spectrum. It was determined to plan and present five workshops for parents to include homemade toys, sensory toys, flannel boards and stories, social stories, and music play. We also worked closely with day care providers and early educators in the community to educate them on the resources we purchased and to include them in the music play workshop.

Diverse Audiences Reached

Families of all ethnic and socioeconomic backgrounds with a family member diagnosed somewhere on the autism spectrum are reached. Any child or family with special-needs children have access to all of the materials purchased through the grant including developmental resources that circulate through our developmental toy resource collection.

Innovative Programming Implemented

We implemented workshops for parents of children with autism. We scheduled three workshops at the public library and two workshops at the Kenosha Achievement Center. Due to the financial hardships an autism diagnosis can have on a family, we developed and provided workshops on making toys and sensory items that otherwise would be expensive for families to purchase. We provided a workshop where participants made their own flannel board and stories, which could be used with idea sheets we provided. Another workshop dealt with how to make social stories for their children. Resources by Carol Gray were made available and participants created their own social stories to use with their children. The final workshop was led by musician and early childhood educator Jim Gill on the topic of music play. Attendees at this workshop included parents of children with autism, early educators, librarians, and anyone working with young children.

Musician/Educator Jim Gill Performing with His List of "Silly Dances," Which Is Incorporated in His Music and Work with Children

Key to Project/Proposal Success

The keys to our success included having a children's services library staff member who is also a parent of a child with autism share her expertise on services and materials; developing a collaboration with the Kenosha Autism Support Group and realizing the challenges these families face was instrumental; continuing a collaboration with the Kenosha Achievement Center, a community organization that is committed to the growth and success of persons with special needs; and the support of

Workshop about Making Flannel Graphs

Participants copy the patterns, cut out the shapes, decorate the pieces, and take them home with handouts giving ideas for how to use the shapes.

library management in continuing our outreach activities in the community and supporting the grant project administrator in speaking at conferences and workshops around the state about KPL's autism resources and services.

What You Would Do Differently

We also hired Jim Gill to provide music/education programs for the general public and invited all families with children who have autism. We had large crowds, which proved to be too much sensory overload for the children with autism. If we could do it over again we would have had Mr. Gill present to the families of the Autism Support Group only and not the general public.

Advice for Other Grant Seekers

Develop collaborations within your community. Give yourself plenty of time to develop your grant project and be realistic about what you can accomplish.

Most Important Element of Your Success

Collaborating with other community agencies that are working toward the same goal as the public library and agencies that deal with community members that are in need of specific services and materials that the public library can provide.

Credit

Roxane Bartelt

See the actual "Crossing Barriers: Serving the Transgender Community" proposal prepared by Bleue J. Benton for this successful grant on the companion DVD for this book.

Crossing Barriers: Serving the Transgender Community

Project Description

Oak Park Public Library (OPPL) has created a groundbreaking transgender resource collection. "Transgender" is an umbrella term that applies to people whose identity or behavior falls outside stereotypical gender expectations. We purchased non-fiction books and audiovisual materials that serve, reflect, and welcome transgender people. A unique part of this grant project was an exhaustive self-study for barriers to serving or employing transgender people. We also provided mandatory staff awareness workshops that were followed up with department meetings, using scenarios to encourage deeper conversation about potential interactions in the library setting. OPPL has created a website (www.oppl.org/media/trc.htm) with a tremendous amount of information about the transgender resource collection. Included are a link to materials in the library catalog, reading lists for adults and children, and local and national resources. In addition, we have created a library toolkit that includes the full text of the self-study report, staff discussion scenarios, publicity samples, and "The $200 Transgender Bookshelf" of recommended titles for public libraries. We believe that this holistic approach is an excellent model for collection development in other libraries.

Library

Oak Park Public Library
834 Lake Street, Oak Park, IL 60301

Contact

Bleue J. Benton, Collection Manager

Collection Size

250,000

Population Served

52,000

Grant Amount

$3,000

Funder

LSTA—Illinois State Library

Number of People Who Worked on Grant Application

Two library staff members

Partnerships and Collaborations

We worked with the Chicago Gender Society, enlisting their help in publicizing this project in untraditional places such as bars, nightclubs, and electrolysis offices.

Diverse Audiences Reached

We reached transgender people locally and regionally. Transgender people are a marginalized group, often facing widespread and even socially condoned discrimination, harassment, and violence.

Key to Project/Proposal Success

Our project was successful because we targeted an unserved group and really focused the collection. Also, going beyond the bookshelves and looking for barriers to service was groundbreaking, we believe.

What You Would Do Differently

We would have implemented innovative programming.

Most Difficult Part of Grant Process

Estimating publicity costs.

Advice for Other Grant Seekers

It's so hard to see what you're missing in terms of service or collections. Self-reflection is crucial.

Most Important Element of Your Success

Looking at the big picture.

Credit

Bleue J. Benton and Sharon Grimm

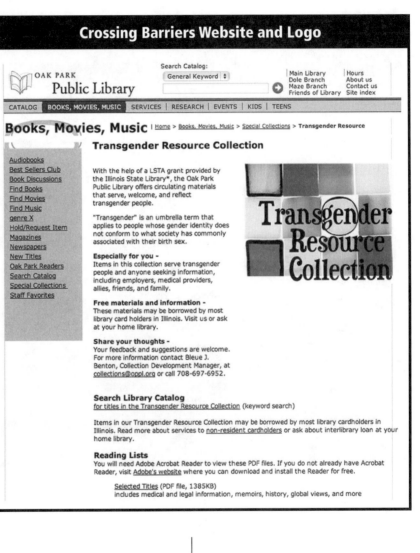

Crossing Barriers Website and Logo

See an actual proposal, "Read to Me Mini-Grant," prepared by Karen Yother for a successful grant on the companion DVD for this book.

From Your Library

Project Description

From Your Library's (FYL) mission is to provide library service to people who do not have access to walk-in libraries. The bookmobile, children's services, and branch libraries have identified potential customers through years of exploring better ways to reach underserved patron groups. We recognize that people don't have access to libraries for many reasons: they may live too far from the local library, they may be financially struggling and lack transportation, they may be confined to a treatment facility, in day care or Head Start programs, or reluctant to use services due to past negative experiences with libraries.

Library

Kootenai-Shoshone Area Libraries
8385 N. Government Way, Hayden, ID 83835

Contact

Karen Yother, Youth Service Coordinator

Collection Size

163,354

Population Served

31,523 children birth to 18 years old (2006 Census)

Grant Amount

$83,385 grant funds plus $40,263 local match

Funder

Library Services and Technology Act

Number of People Who Worked on Grant Application

Three library staff members

Partnerships and Collaborations

The FYL program reached children and families throughout our communities through partnering with area food banks, Head Start programs, and park departments. This program worked because of the partnership between the library, the City Parks Department, and Food Service at the School District.

Diverse Audiences Reached

Our target group was at-risk and underserved children from birth to age 18 who would not have access to traditional library services. Within this group we had children with special needs, minority children, and teen parents.

Innovative Programming Implemented

We purchased a Sprinter van to take library services to the community. Patrons were able to check out materials and receive library services. Deposit collections of new books were created and delivered to the partner sites. The 25-book collections included a variety of titles and genres based on the children at each site. These collections changed monthly and provided staff and children an opportunity to read great books all year long. We offered weekly summer storytime in the park near the library. Children participated in storytime and crafts, as well as received a free book, and were able to check out books from the Bookmobile or Sprinter service. Plus the local school district provided free lunch to all children from birth to age 18. Nearly 300 children and parents came each week. Unique, innovative programming included art, photography, scrapbooking, and book talks.

Key to Project/Proposal Success

Over the course of the year we strengthened our partnerships with sites that served our target population. Most important, we were able to reach an audience who had not received library service due to various circumstances. Having the opportunity to distribute nearly 30,000 books to children in our communities, thus allowing them to build a home library, is invaluable. Staff were very enthusiastic about this project and it showed in the programming and when they talked about it to partner sites.

What You Would Do Differently

I would ask for more staff. We hit the ground running and could have used at least two more staff to run this program. There is always a need for outreach, and focusing our resources in this area is vital to the success of our libraries.

Most Difficult Part of Grant Process

Managing staff time. Once the word got out that we were offering free programs, library services, deposit collections, and books for kids to take home, we had a waiting list of potential sites. We had a hard time saying no to a site that served homeless children or a special-needs child who loved the personal storytime each month. At the end of the grant year it was hard to tell sites that we did not have the funding level to provide the free books to children at each visit.

Advice for Other Grant Seekers

Think big! Look to your community and listen to their needs, then work together to see how the library can fit in and fill the gap. Also, strong programs take time to grow. Building relationships with patrons who have limited exposure to library services took time. We never placed the expectation on the families that they needed to come to our physical branch libraries. They were always encouraged and welcomed, but it was extremely difficult for families who do not have transportation or for a single parent working two jobs to come to the library.

Most Important Element of Your Success

For us the most important elements of a successful grant are strong partnerships and community support. Because we have strong partnerships we have strong programs; because we have strong programs we have strong partnerships.

Credit

Karen Yother

ELL (English Language Learner) Storytime Project

Project Description

Boise Public Library offered storytimes to preschoolers and parents for whom English is a second language. The storytimes were designed specifically to meet the needs of this growing population and provided participants with opportunities to begin to develop and to improve English-language skills, to improve and promote literacy within the target population, and to provide opportunities for participants to interact with others using English. Boise Public Library worked with a contractor to develop three to four thematically linked programs that ran in six-week blocks. Each individual storytime program ran for approximately 30 minutes and focused on concepts in simple English, utilizing storybooks, music, images, and other materials. These program blocks were designed to be repeatable and related to specific materials to provide portability. These features ensured that the programs can be provided with consistency at alternate locations and times by trained staff and/or volunteers.

Library

Boise Public Library
715 S. Capitol Blvd., Boise, ID 83702

Contact

Tobie Garrick, Librarian

Collection Size

366,000 over three branches (fourth branch opening with approx 36,000)

Population Served

Approximately 198,000

Grant Amount

$10,000

Funder

Wal-Mart Foundation (administered through the Idaho Commission for Libraries)

Grant Name

Wal-Mart "Strengthening Library Services for Youth"

Number of People Who Worked on Grant Application

Eight, not all library staff

Unusual Funding Source

When first thinking about applying for a grant, we spoke with Idaho Commission for Libraries about grants that may be available to us.

There were several traditional grants including Read to Me and LSTA; however, the timing and purpose of the new Wal-Mart Mini Grants were perfect for our project.

Partnerships and Collaborations

Boise Public Library partnered with community organizations including local schools, preschools, refugee resettlement agencies, and other community groups serving the target population, ensuring that the program was promoted appropriately and effectively and to recruit volunteers. Boise Public Library offered the programs on-site at its four branches. It also worked with partners to identify off-site locations for the program that were most convenient to attendees in an effort to enhance delivery. Three elementary schools, one preschool (Head Start), and several resettlement agencies were recruited as partners.

Diverse Audiences Reached

Children and adults for whom English is a second language and professionals in several fields who work with the target audience.

Innovative Programming Implemented

Currently in the state of Idaho, there is no such service, although several libraries across the United States have developed programs such as this one. We looked at several as models and decided that we wanted to contract a professional who works with early literacy and English acquisition to help us incorporate these important components into our storytimes and enhance the programs we can offer.

Key to Project/Proposal Success

Our grant proposal was successful for several reasons:

1. Need: Boise has a rapidly growing population of people for whom English is a second language.
2. Documentation and evidence of research
3. Partnerships sought DURING the grant-writing period
4. Buy-in: Boise Public Library has incorporated services for the target population of this grant as part of its strategic plan. Also, there is a groundswell of community services focusing on this population from education to health and welfare to legal services to local business and amazing partnerships are currently being formed to support this.
5. Communication between Boise Public Library staff, partners, community members, and the staff of the administering agency (Idaho Commission for Libraries)

What You Would Do Differently

Perhaps gotten more of the partnerships off the ground prior to submitting the application. This is difficult to navigate, however, because you must balance the excitement over the new program with the reality that it may not be funded.

Most Difficult Part of Grant Process

Moving from ideas and concepts to the writing phase. We initially pulled together a small group of staff to brainstorm ideas, look at existing models, and gather information. Two individuals from this initial group then took the work of the group to date and wrote the application, and the shift to this phase was challenging. An amazing team with a willingness to release the responsibility of writing the grant and get reinvolved when it was time to review the application removed much of the difficulty.

Advice for Other Grant Seekers

Do your due diligence: Research your project, your community needs, and evidence these. Partner: Find people who are enthusiastic about your project and who can really make significant contributions to it. Make sure that you can give something back to these partners through your project. Communicate with the granting agency. Any information that they can share with you will be vital. Some organizations review drafts of grant applications prior to the deadline and their feedback is invaluable.

Most Important Element of Your Success

An outcome that serves an unserved or underserved need in the library's community.

Credit

Tobie Garrick, Tamra Hawley-House, Diane Broom, Kathleen Callahan, Melody Eisler, Joanne Hinkel, Elizabeth Prusha-Parlor, Becca Stroebel, and Cheryl Zobel

The Winning Grants Multimedia Toolkit and DVD

Winning Grants Tools

This section consists of 19 tools corresponding to the following chapters:

Tools for Chapter 1, "Making the Commitment and Understanding the Grant Process"

Tool 1.1: Grant Partnership Agreement Worksheet

Tool 1.2: Making the Commitment: A Checklist for Committing to Library Grant Work

Tools for Chapter 2, "Planning for Success"

Tool 2.1: Library Planning Checklist

Tool 2.2: Links to Example Library Strategic Plans

Tools for Chapter 3, "Discovering and Designing the Grant Project"

Tool 3.1: Strategic Plan Goals, Objectives, and Activities Template

Tool 3.2: Project Planning Worksheet

Tool 3.3: Project Action Steps Template

Tool 3.4: Project Timeline Template

Tool 3.5: Personnel Budget Template

Tool 3.6: Non-personnel Budget Template

Tool 3.7: Evaluation Plan Template

Tools for Chapter 6, "Researching and Selecting the Right Grant"

Tool 6.1: Keyword Selection Worksheet

Tool 6.2: Funder Summary Worksheet

All of the tools in this section are duplicated on this book's companion DVD.

Tool 1.1: Grant Partnership Agreement Worksheet

To be completed by the library and each individual partner.

Library Name and Contact Information:

Partner(s) Name and Contact Information:

Project Name:

Overview of Project: (project description, goals, objectives, activities, and project outcomes)

Goals of This Partnership:

Resources to Be Provided: (staff, funding, equipment, facilities, and which partner will provide)

Services to Be Provided: (include programs, services and activities, and party responsible)

Project Timeline: (include period of partnership, progress review dates, activities, etc.)

Implementation Plan: (outline all roles and responsibilities regarding this partnership)

Impact of Partnership on Each Partner: (gains and losses, including any products to be created or resources purchased with grant funds or shared funds)

Sustainability Plans:

Evaluation Process: (include required reports along with due dates and party responsible)

We agree to the validity of all of the above statements, and agree to fulfill the obligations specified. We further agree to each of the following:
- To implement the project as presented in the grant application
- To use funds or services received in accordance with the grant application and any applicable laws and regulations
- To maintain honest communications with the partnering agency

Signatures:

Today's Date:

Tool 1.2: Making the Commitment: A Checklist for Committing to Library Grant Work

The following questions will help you determine if your library can really make the commitment to apply for a grant.

Commit to Accountability

☐ Will the grant project definitely support your library's vision and mission?

☐ Will your library leadership support the project?

☐ Will the library director commit the necessary resources to the project/grant?

☐ Will the library staff have the time needed to complete the application process and to implement the project?

☐ Will the grant team have the necessary supplies, equipment, services, and space?

☐ Can the library follow through on the agreements made in the grant proposal?

☐ Will the library spend the funds as specified and keep accurate accounts?

☐ Will you make sure there are no other organizations in your community already doing your project and filling the need?

☐ Can all deadlines be met and grant reports be filed on time?

Commit to Effective Communication

☐ Will your proposal be as clear, concise, and honest as possible?

☐ Will your goals, objectives, and activities be clearly identified and understandable?

☐ Will you be able to convey that your library and the project are important?

☐ Will you ask the funder for what you really need?

☐ Will all the library staff, board members, leadership, partners, and volunteers be continually informed about the grant?

☐ Will you ask the funder if the library's grant project clearly fits funder interests?

☐ Will you communicate with all your contacts?

Commit to Meeting Community Needs

☐ Will your library identify the needs of your community?

☐ Will your analysis include enough information to educate and inspire the funder?

☐ Can statistics be used to quantify the problems identified?

☐ Can stories and cases be used regarding specific patrons or programs that illustrate the needs?

☐ Will your grant project focus on solutions to meeting community needs?

☐ Will you identify a target audience for your grant project and involve representatives in the planning process?

Commit to Planning

☐ Does your library have a strategic plan? Will you review it before writing your grant?

☐ Will you have a project plan that includes goals, objectives, and activities and is based on your strategic plan?

☐ Will you set deadlines?

☐ Will you organize your materials (research, grant materials, etc.)?

☐ Will you have a budgetary goal?

☐ Will you have a method to track tasks and contacts?

Winning Grants, Pamela H. MacKellar and Stephanie K. Gerding.
© 2010 Neal-Schuman Publishers, Inc.

(Continued)

Tool 1.2: Making the Commitment: A Checklist for Committing to Library Grant Work *(Continued)*

Commit to Partnerships

☐ Will you cultivate a strong relationship with your grant funder?

☐ Will you develop the appropriate collaborations to leverage resources, share expertise, and support the project?

☐ Will you determine which groups in your community share your library's vision and goals and approach them as partners?

☐ Will you invite community members to focus groups and planning sessions?

☐ Will you complete a partnership agreement outlining goals, responsibilities, and benefits?

Commit to Evaluation

☐ Can your library clearly identify success in respect to the grant project?

☐ Will you have an evaluation plan and/or logic model to determine if your project has met its goals?

☐ Will you be able to identify what impact your project achieves? What difference the project makes?

☐ Will you identify outcomes for the project? Will your project have meaningful results that cause a change in people's behavior, attitudes, skills, condition, or knowledge?

☐ Will you have a benchmark plan designed to measure each outcome?

Commit to Sustainability

☐ Will your project be completed?

☐ Will your project be supported by leadership after grant funds are depleted?

☐ Will you plan a funding strategy to continue your project after grant funds are depleted?

☐ Does your project involve more than just one person?

☐ If your project involves hiring new staff members, will their positions be maintained after the grant period ends?

Commit to Following the Grant Guidelines

☐ Will you check and double-check all instructions?

☐ Will you answer all questions and complete any required narrative sections?

☐ Will you compile all allowable attachments including letters of support?

☐ Will you obtain all the required signatures?

☐ Will you submit the grant on time?

Tools for Chapter 2

Tool 2.1: Library Planning Checklist

In order to seriously compete for a grant, review your library's organizational attributes periodically by considering each of the following:

☐ Does your library have a clearly defined mission statement that is the foremost consideration in all decision making?

☐ Are your goals obtainable and supportive of your library's mission?

☐ Are your objectives clear, measurable, and tied to goal achievement?

☐ Do you periodically evaluate your objectives to be certain progress is being made?

☐ Have you selected a strategy for collecting data on your community and library?

☐ Are statistics aggregated to allow easy retrieval of necessary information?

☐ Are you recording all participants' attendance in all of your programs and projects, their feedback after their participation, and the participants' demographics?

☐ Are all statistics that are collected actually used?

☐ Are you involving library staff and community members in the planning process?

☐ Did you communicate the final plan to staff, leadership, and community members?

☐ Do you have an accurate timetable for implementation of your library's plan and designated specific dates for assessing progress toward goals?

☐ Are the library's programs, services, and projects current?

☐ Have you reviewed the latest needs among the population or community that your library serves?

☐ Are all programs, services, and operations conducted in a lean but sustainable fashion?

☐ Are all unnecessary expenses cut, savings implemented, and fundraising for each program and project stepped up?

☐ Are you reporting all bookkeeping and accounting thoroughly and honestly, and does your library complete grant reports and donor requests on time and honestly?

☐ Does your library use public relations and marketing opportunities to share successes, achievements, and thank the community for its support, or does the community only hear about budget cuts and closings?

☐ Are your leadership, beneficiaries, staff, and volunteers sharing information about their work with the library, and why they've chosen to become involved, with their friends, colleagues, and family?

Tool 2.2: Links to Example Library Strategic Plans

DeKalb County Public Library
Decatur, GA
DeKalb County Public Library's Strategic Plan
www.dekalblibrary.org/newsflashes/dekalb-county-public-library-s-strategic-plan.html

Las Vegas–Clark County Library District
Las Vegas, NV
The Three Year Plan 2008–2011
www.lvccld.org/about/plan.html

Montgomery Middle School
San Diego, CA
Montgomery Middle School Library Plan for 2009/2010
www.suhsd.k12.ca.us/mom/Library/LIBplan2009.htm

Shaker Library
Shaker Heights, OH
Library Strategic Plan 2009–2011
www.shakerlibrary.org/Library%20Guide/Administration/?Library+Strategic+Plan+2009+-+2011

Yale University Library
New Haven, CT
Library Strategic Planning
www.library.yale.edu/strategicplanning

Winning Grants, Pamela H. MacKellar and Stephanie K. Gerding.
© 2010 Neal-Schuman Publishers, Inc.

Tools for Chapter 3

Goals from Strategic Plan	Objectives from Strategic Plan	Activities from Strategic Plan
Tool 3.1: Strategic Plan Goals, Objectives, and Activities Template		
Goal 1	**Objective 1.1**	1. 2. 3. 4. 5.
	Objective 1.2	1. 2. 3. 4. 5.
	Objective 1.3	1. 2. 3. 4. 5.
Goal 2	**Objective 2.1**	1. 2. 3. 4. 5.
	Objective 2.2	1. 2. 3. 4. 5.
	Objective 2.3	1. 2. 3. 4. 5. 6.

Winning Grants, Pamela H. MacKellar and Stephanie K. Gerding.
© 2010 Neal-Schuman Publishers, Inc.

(Continued)

Tool 3.1: Strategic Plan Goals, Objectives, and Activities Template *(Continued)*		
Goals from Strategic Plan	**Objectives from Strategic Plan**	**Activities from Strategic Plan**
Goal 3	**Objective 3.1**	1. 2. 3. 4. 5.
	Objective 3.2	1. 2. 3. 4. 5.
	Objective 3.3	1. 2. 3. 4. 5. 6.
Goal 4	**Objective 4.1**	1. 2. 3. 4. 5.
	Objective 4.2	1. 2. 3. 4. 5.
	Objective 4.3	1. 2. 3. 4. 5. 6.

Winning Grants

Tool 3.2: Project Planning Worksheet	
1. Describe your project in one sentence. Include what you will do, where, why, and with whom.	
2. List keywords that describe your project.	
3. Describe the need in your community or the problem your project will address.	
4. Identify target audience for the project.	
5. What are the goals of the project?	
6. What are the specific changes you expect to make in your community or among the beneficiaries of your project? Articulate objectives for the project.	
7. List the steps required to make the changes listed above. Develop activities or strategies required to reach an objective. How are you going to solve this problem?	
8. List the resources you will need to accomplish the steps. What resources do you already have?	
9. Cost	
10. List your partners on this project. Who else is addressing this problem in our community? Who is likely to partner with us on this project?	
11. Describe how you will measure your success. How will things be different or what will the improvement be?	

Adapted from Project Profile/Planning Worksheet, JUST GRANTS! Arizona.
Winning Grants, Pamela H. MacKellar and Stephanie K. Gerding.
© 2010 Neal-Schuman Publishers, Inc.

Tool 3.3: Project Action Steps Template

Project Objectives	Action Steps	Personnel
1.		
2.		
3.		

Tool 3.4: Project Timeline Template

Activity	Month											
	1	2	3	4	5	6	7	8	9	10	11	12

Winning Grants, Pamela H. MacKellar and Stephanie K. Gerding.
© 2010 Neal-Schuman Publishers, Inc.

Tool 3.5: Personnel Budget Template			
Position	**Salary**	**Benefits (_____%)**	**Total**
TOTAL PERSONNEL COSTS			

Tool 3.6: Non-personnel Budget Template		
ITEM	**DESCRIPTION**	**COST**
Marketing		
Equipment		
Copying Costs		
Supplies		
Space Rental		
Travel		
Other		
TOTAL NON-PERSONNEL COSTS		

Winning Grants, Pamela H. MacKellar and Stephanie K. Gerding.
© 2010 Neal-Schuman Publishers, Inc.

Tool 3.7: Evaluation Plan Template				
Goal	**Outcome**	**Objective**	**Evaluation Method**	**Timeline**

Tools for Chapter 6

Tool 6.1: Keyword Selection Worksheet	
Project Plan	**Keywords**
Goals 1. 2. 3.	
Objectives 1. 2. 3.	
Outcomes 1. 2. 3.	
Activities and Action Steps 1. 2. 3. 4. 5. 6. 7. 8. 9. 10.	

Tool 6.2: Funder Summary Worksheet

Funder Name	
Address	
Contact	

Funder's Financial Information

Amount given last year	
Number of grants given	
Average amount awarded	

Funder's Interests and Criteria

Purpose	
Fields of interest	
Type of support	
Eligibility	
Geographic area	
Limitations	

Application Information

Approach	
Application form	Y N Where found/format
Deadline	

Sources Used

Directories/indexes and page/entry numbers	
Websites	
990 PF	
Annual report	
Personal contact	
Notes	

Winning Grants, Pamela H. MacKellar and Stephanie K. Gerding.
© 2010 Neal-Schuman Publishers, Inc.

Tool 6.3: Links to Funding Sources and Resources for Libraries

FEDERAL GOVERNMENT SOURCES

U.S. Department of Agriculture

Cooperative State, Research, Education, and Extension Service
www.csrees.usda.gov/fo/funding.cfm

Rural Development Community Connect Grant Program
www.usda.gov/rus/telecom/commconnect.htm

U.S. Department of Education Grants and Contracts
www.ed.gov/fund/landing.jhtml?src=rt

Institute of Education Sciences (IES)
www.ed.gov/about/offices/list/ies/index.html

Office of Innovation and Improvement Funding Opportunities
www.ed.gov/about/offices/list/oii/funding.html

Office of Elementary and Secondary Education
www.ed.gov/about/offices/list/oese/index.html

Office of English Language Acquisition, Language Enhancement, and Academic Achievement for Limited English Proficient Students
www.ed.gov/about/offices/list/oela/index.html?src=oc

Office of Postsecondary Education
www.ed.gov/about/offices/list/ope/index.html?src=oc

Office of Special Education and Rehabilitative Services
www.ed.gov/about/offices/list/osers/index.html?src=oc

Office of Vocational and Adult Education
www.ed.gov/about/offices/list/ovae/index.html?src=oc

Department of Health and Human Services

Administration for Children and Families
www.acf.hhs.gov/grants/index.html

Health Resources and Services Administration
www.hrsa.gov/grants/default.htm

National Library of Medicine
www.nlm.nih.gov/grants.html

National Network of Libraries of Medicine Regional Awards
nnlm.gov/funding/

Department of Justice

Office of Juvenile Justice and Delinquency
ojjdp.ncjrs.org/funding/FundingList.asp

Institute of Museum and Library Services
www.imls.gov/applicants/name.shtm

National Endowment for the Arts
www.nea.gov/

National Endowment for the Humanities
www.neh.gov/grants

National Historical Publications and Records Commission (NHPRC)
www.archives.gov/grants/index.html

National Institute for Literacy
www.archives.gov/nhprc/announcement/

FEDERAL GOVERNMENT RESOURCES

Catalog of Federal Domestic Assistance
www.cfda.gov

Federal Register
www.gpoaccess.gov/fr/index.html

Grants.gov
www.grants.gov

Primary Source
www.imls.gov/news/source.shtm

TGCI Federal Register Grant Announcements
www.tgci.com

STATE AND LOCAL GOVERNMENT SOURCES AND RESOURCES

State Libraries
www.imls.gov/programs/libraries.shtm

State Humanities Councils
www.neh.gov/whoweare/statecouncils.html

State Arts Councils and Agencies
www.nasaa-arts.org/aoa/saaweb.shtml

State Departments of Education
wdcrobcolp01.ed.gov/Programs/EROD/org_list.cfm?category_ID=SEA

Winning Grants, Pamela H. MacKellar and Stephanie K. Gerding.
© 2010 Neal-Schuman Publishers, Inc.

(Continued)

Tool 6.3: Links to Funding Sources and Resources for Libraries *(Continued)*

PRIVATE FUNDING SOURCES AND RESOURCES

Foundation

Council on Foundations' Community Foundation Locator
www.cof.org/Locator/index.cfm?menuContainerID=34&crumb=2

The Foundation Center
www.foundationcenter.org

Foundation Center Cooperating Collections
foundationcenter.org/collections

Foundation Center's Foundation Finder
www.foundationcenter.org/findfunders/foundfinder/

Foundation Directory Online
www.fconline.fdncenter.org/

Foundation Grants for Preservation in Libraries, Archives, and Museums
www.loc.gov/preserv/foundtn-grants.pdf

Philanthropy News Digest (PND) and RFP Bulletin
foundationcenter.org/pnd/info/about.jhtml

Corporate

Corporate Giving Online
foundationcenter.org/getstarted/tutorials/corporate/

Clubs and Organizations

Michigan State University's List of Service Clubs and Civic Organizations
www.lib.msu.edu/harris23/grants/servicec.htm

Professional Associations

ALA Awards and Grants
www.ala.org/ala/awardsgrants/index.cfm

American Association of School Librarians Awards and Grants
www.ala.org/ala/mgrps/divs/aasl/aaslawards/aaslawards.cfm

Association for Library Service to Children
www.ala.org/ala/mgrps/divs/alsc/awardsgrants/index.cfm

Association for Library Collections and Technical Services
www.ala.org/ala/mgrps/divs/alcts/awards/index.cfm

Association of College and Research Libraries
www.ala.org/ala/mgrps/divs/acrl/awards/index.cfm

Association of Specialized and Cooperative Library Agencies
www.ala.org/ala/mgrps/divs/ascla/asclaawards/index.cfm

Library Leadership and Management Association
www.ala.org/ala/mgrps/divs/llama/llamaawards/default.cfm

Public Library Association Awards and Grants
www.ala.org/ala/mgrps/divs/pla/plaawards/index.cfm

Reference and User Services Association
www.ala.org/ala/mgrps/divs/rusa/awards/index.cfm

Special Library Association Scholarships and Grants
www.sla.org/content/learn/scholarship/index.cfm

Young Adult Library Services Association
www.ala.org/ala/mgrps/divs/yalsa/awardsandgrants/yalsaawardsgrants.cfm

OTHER RESOURCES

Grants for Libraries E-News Alerts
west.thomson.com/signup/newsletters/209.aspx

Grants for Libraries Hotline
west.thomson.com/productdetail/139015/40560036/productdetail.aspx

Library Grants Blog
librarygrants.blogspot.com

Private Grants Alert
www.cdpublications.com

State and Local Funding Directories: A Bibliography
foundationcenter.org/getstarted/topical/sl_dir.html

The Grantsmanship Center
www.tgci.com/funding/states.asp

Tools for Chapter 7

Tool 7.1: Questions for Funders Checklist

☐ Is my library eligible for your grants?

☐ How are applications reviewed?

☐ Are specific screening criteria or a rubric used? May we have a copy?

☐ May we submit a draft of the grant proposal before the final deadline for review?

☐ If I briefly describe the project, would you provide suggestions or advice?

☐ Are copies of successful grant proposals available?

☐ May we include our strategic plan or other supporting documentation in an appendix?

☐ May we include a table of contents?

☐ How and when are final decisions made?

☐ Will we be notified that our grant proposal has been received?

Tool 7.2: Grant Proposal Template

Library Name

Library Address

Library Address2

Library Telephone Number

Date

Grant Proposal submitted to:

Name of Prospective Funder

Grant Project Title

(Continued)

Tool 7.2: Grant Proposal Template *(Continued)*

Date

Name, Title (Funder Contact Person)
Funder Name (Foundation, Government Agency, etc.)
Funder Address
Funder Address2

RE: Title of Grant

Dear: Insert Name of Funder Contact

Name of Library is pleased to submit this proposal for your review. We look forward to your partnership in our efforts to serve *Name of Your Community*.

Our much needed project, *Title of Project*, is a partnership among *Insert name of Library and project partners. Insert the one-sentence Project Description from your Project Planning Worksheet.*

Insert the Needs Statement from your Project Planning Worksheet. Insert the Project Goals from your Project Planning Worksheet.

The *Name of Library* is committed to the success of this project. *Insert a statement of any outside funding that will be used toward the project.* Our request to *Name of Funder* is for *Total Amount of Funding Requested. Insert a statement regarding planning accomplished and/or involvement of target audience.*

Insert your Library Mission and a sentence or two from your Organizational Overview. Particularly demonstrate why the library is a viable grant candidate.

Thank you for your time and attention. We look forward to working together to build a better community. Please do not hesitate to contact us with any questions or requests for additional information.

Sincerely,

Name of Library Director, or other Authority
Title of Library Director or other Authority

Winning Grants, Pamela H. MacKellar and Stephanie K. Gerding.
© 2010 Neal-Schuman Publishers, Inc.

(Continued)

Tool 7.2: Grant Proposal Template *(Continued)*

TABLE OF CONTENTS

Winning Grants, Pamela H. MacKellar and Stephanie K. Gerding.
© 2010 Neal-Schuman Publishers, Inc.

(Continued)

Tool 7.2: Grant Proposal Template *(Continued)*

PROPOSAL SUMMARY

Date of Application:

Name of Library (exact legal name)
Library's Full Mailing Address

Library Director: *Library Director's Full Name*
Library Director's Contact Information

Grant Coordinator: *Grant Coordinator's name, if not Director; include title*
Grant Coordinator's Contact Information

Project Title: *Project Title*

Project Description: *One-sentence Project Description from Project Planning Worksheet*

Amount Requested: *$$*

Project Funding from Other Sources: *$$ Include in-kind contributions from library, other grant funds*

Total Project Budget: *$$*

Project Budget Time Period: *Dates covered by project budget (June 1, 20xx – May 31, 20xx)*

Grant Abstract: *In 500 words or less condense the major points of each of the grant proposal components. You will want to write this section last, and definitely review it as the last step in editing your proposal.*

Include:
- A few sentences summarizing the library's Organizational Overview, which will show why the library is the best choice for implementing the grant project
- Any partners, and how they are contributing
- The Need Statement, as well as the target audience
- A few sentences from the Project Description detailing what the project entails and how it fulfills the needs
- The project goals, objectives, and/or outcomes
- A brief overview of the evaluation methods to be used
- How the funder's mission aligns with your grant project

(Continued)

ORGANIZATIONAL OVERVIEW

Include a brief overview of the library's history, mission, qualifications, trustworthiness, community served, achievements and impact in community, primary programs, and current budget. Provide a sentence or two detailing the qualifications of key staff and library leadership/board. Include brief success stories if relevant to the project and funder.

(Continued)

Tool 7.2: Grant Proposal Template *(Continued)*

STATEMENT OF NEEDS

Establish the existence and importance of the problem. This is a critical part of your proposal. A compelling need statement will motivate the funder to assist in the solution. Prove that the need is relevant to the funder. Why should they fund this project; why now and how will it benefit the library community?

The need should focus on those your library serves, not just the library. Support the need with evidence (research from statistics, experts, or census data; or information from the library's long-range plan such as the community analysis or needs assessments). You may even include anecdotal substantiation such as a personal story of someone who needs this project, or input from focus groups.

Then prove why the library has the ability to respond to the need you have identified. Link the fulfillment of the need to your library's mission.

Answer the questions:

  Why this issue?

  Why this target population?

  Why this funder?

  Why your library?

Winning Grants, Pamela H. MacKellar and Stephanie K. Gerding.
© 2010 Neal-Schuman Publishers, Inc.

(Continued)

Tool 7.2: Grant Proposal Template *(Continued)*

PROJECT DESCRIPTION

This section includes an overview of your project. It is a more in-depth narrative than the project abstract. In the previous section you discussed the needs; now you will focus on the solutions. Briefly summarize the project and how it will be of benefit to the target population. Include the Project Goals, Project Objectives, and Project Partners. You may also include information on how the project will be sustained after the initial funding.

Include:
  Project Significance (include one or two sentences developed from the
    Need Statement)
  Target Audience
  Project Goals
  Project Objectives
  Project Partners
  Plans for Sustainability and Leveraging Impact

Winning Grants, Pamela H. MacKellar and Stephanie K. Gerding.
© 2010 Neal-Schuman Publishers, Inc.

(Continued)

Tool 7.2: Grant Proposal Template *(Continued)*

APPROACH/METHODOLOGY

How and when will the project be implemented? Describe the strategies and methods to be used and why they are the most effective solution to the need. Include Project Action Steps, and emphasize Project Partners and Collaborators. Include a timeline (example follows). Mention how the donor will be recognized.

Activity	Jan	Feb	Mar	Apr	May	June	July	Aug	Sept	Oct	Nov	Dec
List each grant activity in this column.												

(Continued)

Tool 7.2: Grant Proposal Template *(Continued)*

BUDGET REQUEST

PERSONNEL

Position	Salary	Benefits (%)	Total
Example: .20 FTE Library Assistant	$	$	$
Example: .15 FTE Reference Librarian	$	$	$
Complete according to Budget Template	$	$	$
	$	$	$
TOTAL PERSONNEL COSTS	$	$	$

NON-PERSONNEL

CATEGORIES	TOTAL AMOUNT	AMOUNT FUNDED	AMOUNT REQUESTED
Marketing			
Insert any Subcategories (Brochures, ads, etc.)	$$	$$	$$
Equipment			
Technology			
Supplies			
Postage Delivery			
Printing and Copying			
TOTAL NON-PERSONNEL COSTS:	$	$	$
TOTAL PERSONNEL COSTS:	$	$	$
TOTAL PROJECT BUDGET:	$	$	$

(Continued)

Winning Grants

	Tool 7.2: Grant Proposal Template *(Continued)*

EVALUATION PROCESS

Provide a brief description of the evaluation plan for judging the success of the project. How will you measure success? How will you use the results? What reports will the donor receive and when?

Goal	Outcome	Objective	Evaluation Method	Time Period
1. Complete According to Project Evaluation Plan Template	Complete According to Project Evaluation Template	Complete According to Project Evaluation Template	Complete According to Project Evaluation Template	Complete According to Project Evaluation Template
2.				
3.				
4.				

Winning Grants, Pamela H. MacKellar and Stephanie K. Gerding.
© 2010 Neal-Schuman Publishers, Inc.   *(Continued)*

Tool 7.2: Grant Proposal Template *(Continued)*

APPENDIX

Some funders specify what should and should not be included in the appendices. If this is not specified in the grant guidelines, contact the funder to verify anything you wish to include that is not approved. Some examples of Appendix materials include: strategic plans, résumés or job descriptions of key personnel, organizational charts, letters of support, financial reports, the budget for the current year, lengthy charts and tables, IRS 501(c)(3) non-profit determination letter, a recent library newsletter, or relevant newspaper clippings that demonstrate the library's applicable work.

Tool 7.3: Grant Proposal Checklist

Here are some major criteria against which your proposal may be judged. Read through your application repeatedly, and ask whether the answers to the questions below are clear, even to a non-librarian.

☐ Does the proposal address a well-formulated problem or need?

☐ Is it a real need of your community, or are you just trying to find a reason to justify a project you think would be fun to implement?

☐ Is it an important problem, whose solution will have useful effects?

☐ Is special funding necessary to solve the problem, or could it be solved using existing library resources?

☐ Does the proposal explain in sufficient detail to convince the reader that the project has significant substance and is a justified plan to meet the need?

☐ Does the proposal explain clearly what work will be done?

☐ Does the proposal explain what results are expected, how they will be evaluated, and whether you can determine the success of the project?

☐ Is there evidence that the library knows about the work that others have done on the problem or issue?

☐ Does the library have a good track record with grants and will the library leadership be committed to implementation of this grant project?

Tool 7.4: Grant Submission Checklist

□ The funder is interested in receiving my proposal.

□ This proposal reflects the funder's areas of interest.

□ We have followed the instructions and guidelines of the funder's specifications.

□ Our proposal meets the page/word limits.

□ The font type and size are correct.

□ The margin size is correct.

□ The line spacing is correct.

□ We have used the specified type of paper, if indicated.

□ We did not bind unless we were told we could.

□ The correct number of copies and the original was sent; we also retained a copy for ourselves and copies were made for partners and supporters.

□ We included letters of support.

□ We have the required signatures.

□ The proposal components are titled and compiled in the order specified.

    □ Title sheet

    □ Cover letter

    □ Table of Contents

    □ Proposal Summary

    □ Organizational Overview

    □ Statement of Needs

    □ Project Description

    □ Timeline

    □ Budget Request

    □ Evaluation Process

    □ Appendix

□ The cover letter explains the project, states the total cost of the project, the amount expected from other sources, and the amount requested.

□ The project description specifies the need that will be met and how people will benefit.

□ The project description tells the whole story of the project in clear, understandable language.

□ The objectives are measurable.

□ The methodology explains how the objectives will be met.

□ The timeline includes all major activities and who will do them.

□ The evaluation plan measures the degree to which the objectives and outcomes are met.

□ The project includes partners and reflects community involvement.

□ The budget is reasonable and the calculations are correct.

□ The project is sustainable.

□ Adequate personnel are identified in the proposal to do the project.

□ Adequate resources are available to do the project.

□ Your organization has the capacity to do the project.

□ The proposal contains no jargon or acronyms.

□ If attachments are included, you have confirmed that the funder allows them.

□ The proposal has been proofread by an impartial person.

□ The proposal is clear and easy to understand by someone outside the grant team.

□ Letters of agreement from partners and letters of support from supporters are included, if allowed.

□ We have met the deadline.

□ The proposal looks professional.

Now, carefully go through your application with your checklist and check off every item as you make sure it is in place. Once everything is checked, you may seal the envelope and head for the post office.

    □ The proposal was submitted on _____.

    □ We have a dated receipt or confirmation that the proposal was submitted.

Tool for Chapter 9

Tool 9.1: Debrief and Review Checklist

Did we remain true to the strategic plan?

Was our project designed to meet community needs?

Did we work well as a team?

Where did we excel as a team? Where could we improve?

Did we delegate well?

Did we overlook anything?

What would we do differently?

Did we forget to include a potential partner?

Did we feel rushed getting authorizing signatures, submitting the proposal before the deadline, getting proper approvals, or gathering letters of support?

Was everything completed on time?

If you were successful this time, why were you successful?

If you were not successful this time, why were you unsuccessful? (Review the funder's comments about your proposal and discuss how you can improve.)

Winning Grants Multimedia Tutorials on DVD

The ten multimedia tutorials are available only on the companion DVD. The videos correspond with the ten book chapters and the Grant Cycle Process:

- Video 1: Grant Process Cycle Overview
- Video 2: Planning for Success
- Video 3: Discovering and Designing the Grant Project
- Video 4: Organizing the Grant Team
- Video 5: Understanding the Sources and Resources
- Video 6: Researching and Selecting the Right Grant
- Video 7: Creating and Submitting the Winning Grant Proposal
- Video 8: Getting Funded and Implementing the Project
- Video 9: Reviewing and Continuing the Process
- Video 10: Top 10 Tips for Grant Success

Sample RFPs and Grant Announcements on DVD

This section includes links to actual Requests for Proposals (RFPs) from a variety of funders. More links are available at librarygrants.blogspot .com.

Example Winning Grant Proposals on DVD

This section includes several successfully funded grant projects that will prove invaluable for modeling, evaluating, and improving your own submissions.

Assimilating America, Los Alamos County Public Library System, Los Alamos, NM

Breast Cancer Library Materials, Los Alamos County Public Library System, Los Alamos, NM

Crossing Barriers, Oak Park Public Library, Oak Park, IL

Get Graphic, Buffalo & Erie County Public Library, Buffalo, NY

Harry Potter's World, Los Alamos County Public Library System, Los Alamos, NM

New Library Signage, Columbia County Library, Magnolia, AR

Promoting Easy Access, Los Alamos County Public Library System, Los Alamos, NM

Read to Me, Kootenai-Shoshone Area Libraries, Hayden Library, Hayden, Idaho

Library Grants Blog: Grant Opportunities on DVD (and online at librarygrants.blogspot.com)

A shortcut to finding library grants is available on our free blog. There are new grants posted every month. We include the deadline, a brief description, and a link to more information. To save you time in grant seeking, we verify with every grant opportunity that libraries of some type are eligible to apply, we include only national or large regional grants, and we remove the listings once the deadlines have passed. All types of grants are posted. Visit us at librarygrants.blogspot.com and subscribe to the RSS feed.

Glossary

501(c)(3): A provision of the United States federal tax code that designates a non-profit organization be exempt from some federal income taxes. Organizations described in 501(c)(3) are commonly referred to as charitable organizations or public charities, and may have goals that are literary, religious, educational, or scientific. Some funders may require proof of this type of non-profit status with an application.

990-PF: The federal reporting form that private grant-making foundations are required to submit every year to the Internal Revenue Service (IRS). 990-PFs document the foundation's financial activities during the year. These are public documents and the information in them may be used to learn about a foundation, their trustees, where their funds originate, their grant-making contributions, and to whom they previously awarded grants.

abstract: Usually a one-page summary of a grant project including all pertinent activities, a summary of the objectives, and the expected results.

action steps: The specific steps taken to accomplish a grant project.

activities: The specific actions or strategies that will accomplish the long-range or strategic plan.

annual report: A report published yearly by a foundation or corporation describing its activities, including grants awarded. Annual reports may be simple or very elaborate. Annual reports may be used as a way to inform the community about contributions, programs, and activities. Annual reports may also serve as marketing tools.

appendixes/attachments: Supporting documentation that is submitted with a proposal. Requirements vary, so be sure to check the application guidelines carefully for what the funder will accept. See pages 121–122 in Chapter 7 for more details.

application: The formal documents that are submitted to a potential funder when seeking funds.

audit, financial: An examination of an organization's financial documents by an outside expert. Financial audits are usually conducted at the end of the fiscal year. The funder may require an audit of grant funds at the end of a project.

audit, program: A review of the activities and results of a funded program by the funding agency. A program audit may be mandatory or random, at the end of a project, or midstream. Also known as monitoring.

authorized signature: The official signature of the person who is responsible for an organization by law.

beneficiary: A member of the target population that the grant benefits. For example, a community member attending a library program is the beneficiary of a grant received by the library.

bricks and mortar: generally refers to capital funds used for building renovation or construction.

budget: An annual fiscal plan for an organization that contains an itemized list of revenues and expenses. The library's annual budget may be included in the grant proposal appendix. A project budget is often included in a grant proposal and covers estimated funds needed for the entire grant project.

capital/building grant: Funds that are used to purchase land and construct, renovate, or expand buildings and facilities. May also refer to major equipment purchases such as computer networks.

challenge grant: A grant that requires the grantee to generate additional funds from other sources, usually within a specified period.

community committee: A committee whose members include those served by the library and often serve as advisors to strategic or project planning. These members may include representatives from local leadership, business, government, parents, students, and all parts of the library community.

community foundation: A tax-exempt, non-profit philanthropic organization comprised of funds established by many donors for the charitable benefit of the residents in a defined geographic area or community.

cooperating collection library: A member of the Foundation Center's network of libraries, community foundations, and other non-profit agencies that provide a core collection of Center publications in addition to a variety of additional materials and services in areas useful to grant seekers.

corporate foundation: A private foundation that amasses its grant funds from the contributions of a profit-making corporation. The corporate foundation is a legally separate organization from the parent corporation. Corporate foundations are subject to the rules and regulations that oversee all private foundations.

corporate giving program: A grant-making program established and administered within a for-profit corporation. Some companies make grants through both a corporate giving program and a corporate foundation.

DUNS number: A unique 9-digit number issued by Dun and Bradstreet that is used to keep track of more than 70 million businesses worldwide. The federal government requires organizations to provide a DUNS number in federal grant applications and proposals.

demonstration grant: A grant made to implement an innovative project or program. If successful, this kind of grant may serve as a model, to be duplicated by others.

discretionary grant: The category of federal or state grants for which individual libraries, community organizations, schools, and local governments are eligible to apply. Unlike the federal grant funds that are distributed through a pass-through agent such as the state.

donated products: Any goods, products, equipment, or other tangible property that is donated to a library for its use and ownership. These may include food, paper goods, or office supplies, as well as furnishings, computer equipment, and vehicles, etc. Donated products may be considered part of "in-kind" support and can be included in a budget, at fair-market value.

drawdown: The method by which a grantee requests payment from the funding agency. Frequency of drawdowns (or draws) may be weekly, quarterly, or it may be a single lump sum payment at the end of the project.

EIN: Employer Identification Number. This number is issued by the Internal Revenue Service and must be included in all government and some foundation grant applications.

evaluation plan: An evaluation plan includes the methods used to examine, monitor, and determine the effectiveness and results of a project or activity. Evaluation aids in determining grant achievements, outputs, and outcomes, and communicating those results to the funders and to the community. Different types of evaluation plans include outcome-based evaluation, quantitative evaluation, formative evaluation, and summative evaluation.

fiscal year (FY): A 12-month accounting period that includes the period covered by an annual budget. It does not necessarily coincide with the calendar year; some fiscal years begin on July 1, others on October 1.

focus group: A group of individuals gathered together to discuss an issue or give feedback. Focus groups may be used to determine the library community's needs or to plan or evaluate a grant project.

formula grants: Grants from the federal or state government to a lower level of government where a specific monetary amount is determined based on a formula, usually derived from socioeconomic data and usually non-competitive.

foundation: A non-profit organization with its own funds/endowments that is managed by its own trustees/directors and usually benefits educational, charitable, social, religious, or other activities. Types of foundations include community foundations, corporate foundations, family foundations, and private foundations.

funder: The agency, organization, foundation, association, or governmental unit that awards grants. Also known as a funding agency, grant maker, grantor, or donor.

funding cycle: The schedule of events that starts with the announcement of the availability of funds followed by the deadline for submission of applications, submission of applications, review of applications, grant awards, contract documents, and release of funds.

goal: The broad purpose of a project or program; the result being attempted to achieve.

grant: The sum of money given to support the project or program of an agency, organization, or individual. This is usually the result of a formal proposal submission and review process. Grants are given with no conditions for repayment.

grant agreement: A contract entered into by the recipient of a grant and a funder. Based on the application submitted, the agreement commits the recipient to implement a specific project, within a certain time frame, for a specific amount of money.

grant coordinator: The individual responsible for all activities involved in the grant, including the planning, submission, evaluation, implementation, and follow-up.

grant proposal components: The standard sections of a grant proposal. These will vary according to each funder. Typical components include: Title Sheet, Cover Letter, Table of Contents, Proposal Summary, Organizational Overview, Statement of Needs, Project Description, Approach/Methodology, Budget, Evaluation Plan, and Appendix.

grant team: This team is comprised of representatives from library leadership, community advisors, grant researchers, grant writers, subject matter experts, and staff members who will plan and implement the grant.

grantee: The recipient of grant funds. May also be referred to as fundee or donee.

guidelines: A funder's goals, priorities, criteria, and procedures for applying for a grant.

IMLS: The Institute of Museum and Library Services is a federal grant-making agency that promotes leadership, innovation, and a lifetime of learning by supporting museums and libraries in the United States. Created by the Museum and Library Services Act of 1996 (www.imls.gov).

indirect cost: This represents the cost of doing business that is not readily identified with a particular grant project, but is necessary for the general operation of the organization. This may include heat, light, rent, accounting, and other supporting administrative costs.

in-kind support: A non-cash donation of labor, facilities, or equipment to carry out a project. Examples are products or equipment, volunteer services, office space or staff time, and library materials—donated for a project. In-kind support should always be included in a budget at fair-market value.

LSTA: The Library Services and Technology Act (LSTA) of 1996, a section of the Museum and Library Services Act, provides funds to state library agencies using a population-based formula. State libraries may use the appropriation to support statewide initiatives and services; they may also distribute the funds through competitive subgrant competitions or cooperative agreements to public, academic, research, school, and special libraries in their state.

lead agency: The organization with the primary responsibility for overseeing the grant project including filing reports and fiscal management.

letter of inquiry: A brief letter to assess a potential funder's interest in considering a grant proposal. It should include background on the library; a brief description of the project; the total amount required to fund the project; the specific dollar amount requested from the funder; the amount on hand from other sources; and an explanation of why the proposal matches the funder's priorities and interests. If interested, the funder will invite submission of a full proposal.

letter of intent: A letter that the grant seeker sends before writing or submitting a grant proposal to a funder to ensure that the proposal will fit within the funder's guidelines and mission. Funders may identify possible organizations they are interested in funding and request a letter of intent.

letter of support: A simple letter of endorsement or commitment to the grant project submitted with a proposal. This letter should be from project experts, supporters, partners, or collaborators who explain why they believe the project should be funded.

Library Service Responses: Library Service Responses were created by the Public Library Association and are used in the planning process in *Strategic Planning for Results* (2008). They are used to prioritize the activities most needed by the library's community. See list on page 31.

matching funds: In some grants, the portion of the project costs that the grantee is responsible for providing. Examples of matching funds are funding from other sources, personnel, or in-kind donations.

mission: A broad statement of the role or purpose of the library, who the library serves, and justification of its existence.

narrative: The written portion of a grant. The story of the grant project's who, what, where, when, why, and how.

need statement: The part of the grant in which it is explained, using both qualitative and quantitative data, the problem or opportunity addressed by the grant project or program and why the library should be funded.

needs assessment: A method of collecting information to determine how well the library is serving its community and what other services or resources it can provide in the future.

non-profit: A group that exists for reasons such as serving a public good, rather than to make a profit, such as charitable, educational, religious, or service organizations.

objectives: The desired outcomes of activities, or success indicators. Objectives specify who, what, when, and how the criteria by which the effectiveness of a project will be measured. Objectives should be specific, measurable, achievable, realistic, and time-specific (SMART).

operating expenses: Operating expenses include all the costs of keeping a library open, including salaries, utilities, maintenance, insurance, accounting expenses, etc. These are the expenses of internal and administrative operations, rather than costs for specific programs or services.

outcome-based evaluation (OBE): Sometimes called outcomes measurement, this is a systematic way to determine if a program has achieved its goals. Many government agencies require that OBE be integrated into grant projects to measure meaningful results that change people's attitudes, skills, knowledge, behavior, or life condition.

outcomes: Expected results of a project that can be used to measure its success.

PI: Principal investigator; someone in charge of directing the grant project or activities being supported by the grant.

partner: Another organization that is sharing responsibility with a library for a grant project or specific goals. Some funders require partners to be involved in grant projects.

partnership agreement: A statement or letter from partners stating that they agree to collaborate on a particular grant project, specifying their obligations and contributions to the project. This may take the form of an MOU, or Memorandum of Understanding.

pre-award office: An office within the grants and contracts office in most university settings that searches for grant opportunities, assists with developing proposals, coordinates grant seeking across university departments, reviews proposals, coordinates required signatures, and approves proposals before submission.

program officer: A staff member of a funding agency who reviews grant proposals, processes applications, and knows the ins and outs of the funder's interests, guidelines, and application procedures.

project director: The individual responsible for activities involved in the grant project, including implementation, evaluation, and follow-up.

project grant: Funds given to support a specific, well-defined project or set of activities designed to address a specific need or achieve a specific goal.

project team: Representatives from library leadership, community advisors, grant researchers, grant writers, staff members, and subject matter experts who will plan and implement the grant project.

proposal: A written or electronic application submitted to a government agency, foundation, or corporation to request a grant. Requirements vary widely among funders regarding contents, length, format, and accompanying materials.

Request for Proposals (RFPs): The formal announcement issued by a grant maker declaring that it is seeking proposals for funding in specific topic or program areas. The RFP usually includes complete details on the kinds of services or programs the grant maker will consider; proposal guidelines; deadline; proposal review and evaluation criteria; and other information to help in preparing a proposal.

research grant: A grant made to support a specific project that has a primary purpose of inquiry or examination into facts, studies, or investigations. The result may be a detailed paper with recommendations for future plans.

seed money: Funding to support a new project in its start-up stage. Sometimes seed money will be granted to begin a new program in its infancy until a larger funding source is found. Also known as start-up money.

site visit: A visit made by the funder to the grantee at the location of the project or program. The purpose is to meet with staff and beneficiaries to observe and sometimes evaluate the project in action.

state library: The official agencies charged with statewide library development and the administration of federal funds authorized by the Library Services and Technology Act. These agencies vary greatly and are located in various departments of state government and report to different authorities depending on the state. They are involved in various ways in the leadership of enhancing library service for all the residents of the state.

Strategic Planning for Results: This is the Public Library Association's library planning model. A core principle is community involvement in the planning process. Written by Sandra Nelson, the book includes case studies, work forms, and a toolkit to provide library staff with all of the tools they need to complete a successful strategic plan.

sustainability: Refers to an organization's ability to keep a grant project going after the initial funding has been used.

target population: The people who will benefit from the project the grant is funding, such as teens, the unemployed, or computer users.

timeline: A systematic method of planning activities that will be implemented, arranged by date or time. This may be the beginning, implementation, and end of each grant activity displayed in a chart or narrative format in a month-by-month time frame.

Bibliography

"Agenda." Denver: The Denver Public Library Commission. November 20, 2008. Available: denverlibrary.org/about/commission_archive/112008 meeting_materials.pdf (accessed November 29, 2009).

Annual Register of Grant Support. Annual. New Medford, NJ: Information Today, Inc.

Bauer, David G. 2001. *How to Evaluate and Improve Your Grants Effort*. American Council on Education/Oryx Press series on higher education. Westport, CT: American Council on Education/Oryx Press.

Bauer, David G. 2003. *The "How To" Grants Manual: Successful Grantseeking Techniques for Obtaining Public and Private Grants*. American Council on Education/Praeger series on higher education. Westport, CT: Praeger.

Berry, John. 2003. "Library of the Year: Las Vegas–Clark County Library District." Available: libraryjournal.reviewsnews.com/index.asp?layout=article Print&articleID=CA302409 (accessed March 2010).

Brown, Larissa Golden, Martin John Brown, and Judith E. Nichols. 2001. *Demystifying Grant Seeking: What You Really Need to Do to Get the Grants*. New York: Wiley.

Browning, Beverly A. 2005. *Grant Writing for Dummies*. For Dummies Series. Hoboken, NJ: Wiley Publishers.

Browning, Beverly A. 2008. *Perfect Phrases for Writing Grant Proposals: Hundreds of Ready-to-Use Phrases to Present Your Organization, Explain Your Cause, and Get the Funding You Need*. New York: McGraw-Hill.

Bryson, John. 2004. *Strategic Planning for Public and Nonprofit Organizations: A Guide to Strengthening and Sustaining Organizational Achievement*. 3rd ed. San Francisco, CA: Jossey-Bass.

Burke, J. 2000. *I'll Grant You That: A Step-by-Step Guide to Finding Funds, Designing Winning Projects, and Writing Powerful Grant Proposals*. Portsmouth, NH: Heinmann.

Bushe, Gervase R. 2009. *Clear Leadership: Sustaining Real Collaboration and Partnership at Work*. Mountain View, CA: Davies-Black Publishers.

Carlson, Mim. 2002. *Winning Grants Step by Step: The Complete Workbook for Planning, Developing, Writing, Successful Proposals*. Jossey-Bass Non-profit and Public Management Series. San Francisco: Jossey-Bass.

Catalog of Federal Domestic Assistance. Available: www.cfda.gov (accessed November 30, 2009).

Chronicle of Philanthropy. Available: http://philanthropy.com/section/Home/ 172 (accessed March 11, 2010).

Clarke, Cheryl A. 2001. *Storytelling for Grantseekers: The Guide to Creative Nonprofit Fundraising*. San Francisco: Jossey-Bass.

Collins, Sarah. 2003. *The Foundation Center's Guide to Winning Proposals.* New York: Foundation Center.

Corporate Foundation Profiles. New York: Foundation Center.

Corporate Giving Directory. Annual. Rockville, MD: The Taft Group.

Corporate Philanthropy Report. San Francisco: Public Management Institute.

Directory of Grants for Native American Tribes and Organizations. 2009. Silver Spring, MD: CD Publications.

Everything Technology: Directory of Technology Grants. 2009. New York: Technology Grant News.

Falkenstein, Jeffrey, A., ed. 2001. *National Guide to Funding for Libraries and Information Services.* 6th ed. New York: Foundation Center.

FC Search. New York: Foundation Center. Available: www.fdncenter.org/ (accessed November 30, 2009).

Federal Register. Available: www.gpoaccess.gov/fr/index.html (accessed November 30, 2009).

Florida Department of State, Division of Library and Information Services. 2000. *Workbook: Outcome Measurement of Library Programs.* Available: dlis.dos.state.fl.us/bld/Research_Office/OutcomeEvalWkbk.doc (accessed November 30, 2009).

Forsberg, Kevin, Hal Mooz, and Howard Cotterman. 1996. *Visualizing Project Management.* New York: Wiley.

Foundation Center. *Proposal Writing Short Course.* 2005. Available: www.fdn center.org/learn/shortcourse/prop1.html (accessed November 30, 2009).

Foundation Center's Guide to Grant Seeking on the Web. 2000. New York: The Foundation Center.

Foundation Center's User-Friendly Guide: A Grant-seeker's Guide to Resources. 2002. New York: Foundation Center.

Foundation Directory. Annual. New York: The Foundation Center.

Foundation Directory Online. Available: foundationcenter.org/findfunders/ fundingsources/fdo.html (accessed November 30, 2009).

Foundation Grants Index. Annual. New York: The Foundation Center.

Foundation Grants Index on CD-ROM. Semi-annual. New York: The Foundation Center.

Foundation 1000. Annual. New York: The Foundation Center.

Foundation Reporter. Annual. Detroit, MI: The Taft Group.

Fundsnet. Available: www.fundsnetservices.com (accessed November 30, 2009).

Geever, Jane C. 2004. *The Foundation Center's Guide to Proposal Writing.* 4th ed. New York: The Foundation Center.

Gerding, Stephanie R. 2003. "Small Library, Big Fundraising: Community Support Is Way Above Par." *Computers in Libraries* 23, no. 2 (February):16.

Gerding, Stephanie K., and Pamela H. MacKellar. 2006. *Grants for Libraries: A How-To-Do-It Manual.* New York: Neal-Schuman Publishers.

Gerding, Stephanie K., and Pamela H. MacKellar. *Library Grants Blog.* Available: librarygrants.blogspot.com (accessed November 30, 2009).

Gitlin, Laura N., and Kevin J. Lyons. 2008. *Successful Grant Writing: Strategies for Health and Human Service Professionals.* New York: Springer Pub. Co.

Golden, S. L. 1997. *Secrets of Successful Grantsmanship: A Guerrilla Guide to Raising Money.* San Francisco, CA: Jossey-Bass.

Grants for Arts, Culture and the Humanities. 2007. New York: Foundation Center.

Grants for Libraries and Information Services. New York: Foundation Center.

Grants for Libraries Hotline. Available: west.thomson.com/productdetail/ 139015/40560036/productdetail.aspx (accessed November 30, 2009).

Grants for People with Disabilities. 2007. New York: Foundation Center.

Grants Register. Biennial. New York: Palgrave MacMillan.

Grants.gov. Available: grants.gov (accessed March 11, 2010).

Grantsmanship Center. Available: www.tgci.com (accessed November 30, 2009).

Guide to U.S. Foundations. Annual. New York: The Foundation Center.

Guidestar. Available: www.guidestar.org (accessed November 30, 2009).

Hale, P. D. 1997. *Writing Grant Proposals That Win.* Alexandria, VA: Capitol Publishing.

Hall, Joe, and Hammond, Sue. *What Is Appreciative Inquiry?* Available: www.thinbook.com/docs/doc-whatisai.pdf (accessed November 29, 2009).

Hall, Mary S., and Susan Howlett. 2003. *Getting Funded: The Complete Guide to Writing Grant Proposals.* 4th ed. Portland, OR: Portland State University.

Harris, Dianne. 2007. *The Complete Guide to Writing Effective & Award-Winning Grants: Step-by-Step Instructions.* Ocala, FL: Atlantic Publishers.

Hayes, L. C., ed. 1999. *Winning Strategies for Developing Grant Proposals.* Washington, DC: Government Information Services.

Kaplan, Robert S., and Norton, David P. 2001. *The Strategy-focused Organization: How Balanced Scorecard Companies Thrive in the New Business Environment.* Boston, MA: Harvard Business School Press.

Margolin, Judith B. 2008. *The Grantseeker's Guide to Winning Proposals.* Fundraising Guides. New York: Foundation Center.

McNamara, Carter. *Basic Guide to Program Evaluation.* Available: www.mapnp.org/library/evaluatn/fnl_eval.htm (accessed November 30, 2009).

Michigan State University Libraries Grants and Related Resources. Available: www.lib.msu.edu/harris23/grants/ (accessed November 30, 2009).

Miller, P. W. 2000. *Grant-Writing: Strategies for Developing Winning Proposals.* Munster, IN: Patrick W. Miller and Associates.

National Directory of Corporate Giving. Annual. New York: Foundation Center.

Nelson, Sandra S. 2001. *The New Planning for Results: A Streamlined Approach.* Chicago, IL: Public Library Association.

Nelson, Sandra S. 2008. *Strategic Planning for Results.* Chicago, IL: Public Library Association.

Nelson, Sandra S., Ellen Altman, and Diane Mayo. 2000. *Managing for Results: Effective Resource Allocation for Public Libraries.* Chicago, IL: Public Library Association.

New, Cheryl Carter. 1998. *Grantseeker's Toolkit: A Comprehensive Guide to Finding Funding.* New York: John Wiley.

New, Cheryl Carter, and James Aaron Quick. 2003. *How to Write a Grant Proposal.* Hoboken, NJ: John Wiley and Sons.

NOZA 990-PF Database. Available: www.noza990pf.com/ (accessed November 30, 2009).

Nugent, C. 2000. *The Grant-Writer's Start-up Kit: A Beginner's Guide to Grant Proposals.* I. Successful Images (Video).

Outcomes Toolkit 2.0. Available: ibec.ischool.washington.edu/static/ibeccat .aspx@subcat=outcome%20toolkit&cat=tools%20and%20resources.htm (accessed November 30, 2009).

Peterson, Susan Lee. 2001. *The Grantwriter's Internet Companion: A Resource for Educators and Others Seeking Grants and Funding.* San Francisco, CA: Jossey-Bass.

Philanthropy News Digest RFP Bulletin. Available: foundationcenter.org/pnd/ rfp/ (accessed March 11, 2010).

Quick, James Aaron, and Cheryl Carter. 2000. *Grant Winner's Toolkit: Project Management and Evaluation.* New York: John Wiley.

Quinlan Publishing Group, and West (Firm). 2001. *Grants for Libraries Hotline.* Boston, MA: Quinlan Pub. Group.

Reif-Lehrer, L. 2004. *Grant Application Writer's Handbook.* Boston, MA: Jones and Bartlett Publishers.

Schladweiler, Kier, ed. 2001. *The Foundation Center's Guide to Grantseeking on the Web.* New York: The Foundation Center.

Schwartz, Peter. 1996. *The Art of the Long View: Paths to Strategic Insight for Yourself and Your Company.* New York: Currency Doubleday.

Smith, Nancy Burke, and Judy Tremore. 2008. *The Everything Grant Writing Book: Create the Perfect Proposal to Raise the Funds You Need.* Avon, MA: Adams Media.

Smith, Nancy Burke, and E. Gabriel Works. 2006. *The Complete Book of Grant Writing: Learn to Write Grants Like a Professional.* Naperville, IL: Sourcebooks.

State and Local Funding Directories: A Bibliography. Available: www.foundation center.org/getstarted/topical/sl_dir.html (accessed November 30, 2009).

State Library of Florida. 1999. *The Library Services and Technology Act Outcome Evaluation Plan.* Available: dlis.dos.state.fl.us/bld/Research_Office/Outcome _EvalPlan_final.doc (accessed November 30, 2009).

Taft Group. 2007. *Big Book of Library Grant Money: Profiles of Private and Corporate Foundations and Direct Corporate Givers Receptive to Library Grant Proposals.* Chicago, IL: American Library Association.

U.S. Census Bureau. Available: www.census.gov (accessed November 30, 2009).

U.S. Census Bureau. *American Factfinder.* Available: factfinder.census.gov (accessed November 30, 2009).

U.S. Census Bureau. *State & County Quick Facts.* Available: quickfacts .census.gov (accessed November 30, 2009).

United Way of America's Outcome Measurement Resource Network. Available: www.liveunited.org/outcomes/ (accessed November 30, 2009).

Index

About the Authors

Pamela H. MacKellar (www.pamelamackellar.com) is an author, teacher, and library consultant with more than 25 years of experience in libraries, including more than 10 years of management experience. She has conceived, planned, generated funding for, and implemented new library programs including a community technology center for people with disabilities in Albuquerque, New Mexico. Pam has had success in preparing winning proposals to the U.S. Department of Education, the Institute of Museum and Library Services, the National Network of Libraries of Medicine—South Central Region, the Bill and Melinda Gates Foundation, the Beaumont Foundation, American Library Association, the Albuquerque Community Foundation, and the MacArthur Foundation. She has completed The Grantsmanship Center's Grantsmanship Training Program, and she has served as a field reviewer, reading and evaluating grant proposals from libraries seeking state and federal funding.

Pam co-authored *Grants for Libraries: A How-To-Do-It Manual for Librarians* (Neal-Schuman, 2006) and authored *The Accidental Librarian* (www.accidentallibrarian.com), from Information Today, Inc., 2008. She has co-authored articles on grants for libraries, she co-authors the Library Grants Blog (librarygrants.blogspot.com), she has designed a web tutorial on grants for librarians, and presented workshops and classes on topics including grants for libraries and non-profits, and removing obstacles and creating opportunities for librarians.

Pam holds a master's degree in Library Science from the State University of New York at Albany, a bachelor's degree in Fine Arts from the State University of New York at New Paltz, and a Certificate in Graphic Design from the University of New Mexico Department of Continuing Education. Pam lives in New Mexico with her husband and two cats.

Stephanie Gerding (www.stephaniegerding.com) is a nationally known library consultant, trainer, and author. Stephanie has written more than 20 published articles on grants, and has been on all sides of the grant process as a grant writer, reviewer, and grant project coordinator at libraries, non-profits, foundations, and government organizations. Stephanie co-authors the Library Grants Blog. She is currently working with TechSoup for Libraries (techsoupforlibraries.org) as a writer, blogger, and trainer to support technology education for libraries.

Stephanie's first co-authored book, *Grants for Libraries*, was published by Neal-Schuman and received a starred review in *Library Journal*. Her second book, *The Accidental Technology Trainer*, was published by Information Today.

She presents workshops around the country and online on grants, training, research, customer service, leadership, and technology topics for all types of libraries. She has presented at national conferences including ALA, PLA, Internet Librarian, and Computers in Libraries. In 2000, Stephanie gave workshops on library topics in rural South Africa, where she was a volunteer for the World Library Partnership. She has taught online courses for many organizations, including Northcentral University, WebJunction, TechSoup for Libraries, State Libraries, and the University of North Texas.

Stephanie worked with the Bill and Melinda Gates Foundation's U.S. Library Program conducting weeklong train-the-trainer programs. She has also managed statewide library training programs at New Mexico and Arizona State Libraries. She administered a corporate library at Federal Express, and worked for SIRSI as a customer services consultant.

Stephanie has a Bachelor of Arts degree in English, with a concentration in technical writing, and a Master of Science degree in Library and Information Science with a concentration in Corporate Information from the University of Tennessee. Stephanie lives in Phoenix, Arizona, with her husband and baby girl. She may be contacted at sgerding @mindspring.com.